AAT

INTERACTIVE TEXT

Foundation Unit 2

Making and Recording Payments

In this May 2001 edition

- Layout designed to be easier on the eye – and easy to use

- Icons to guide you through a 'fast track' approach if you wish

- Numerous activities throughout the text to reinforce learning

- Thorough reliable updating of material to 1 May 2001

FOR 2001 and 2002 DEVOLVED ASSESSMENTS

BPP Publishing
May 2001

D1324009

First edition July 2000
Second edition May 2001

ISBN 0 7517 6503 1 (previous edition 0 7517 6207 7)

British Library Cataloguing-in-Publication Data
A catalogue record for this book
is available from the British Library

Published by

BPP Publishing Limited
Aldine House, Aldine Place
London W12 8AW

www.bpp.com

Printed in Great Britain by W M Print
45-47 Frederick Street
Walsall WS2 9NE

We are also grateful to the Lead Body for Accounting for permission to reproduce
extracts from the Standards of Competence for Accounting, and to the AAT for
permission to reproduce extracts from the mapping and Guidance Notes.

Contents

		Page	Answers to activities

REVIEW FORM & FREE PRIZE DRAW

ORDER FORM

HOW TO USE THIS INTERACTIVE TEXT

Aims of this Interactive Text

> To provide the knowledge and practice to help you succeed in the devolved assessment for Foundation Unit 2 *Making and recording payments*.

To pass the devolved assessment you need a thorough understanding in all areas covered by the standards of competence.

> To tie in with the other components of the BPP Effective Study Package to ensure you have the best possible chance of success.

Interactive Text

This covers all you need to know for the devolved assessment for Unit 2 *Making and Recording Payments*. Icons clearly mark key areas of the text. Numerous activities throughout the text help you practise what you have just learnt.

Devolved Assessment Kit

When you have understood and practised the material in the Interactive Text, you will have the knowledge and experience to tackle the Devolved Assessment Kit for Unit 2 *Making and Recording Payments*. This aims to get you through the devolved assessment, whether in the form of the AAT simulation or in the workplace.

Recommended approach to this Interactive Text

(a) To achieve competence in Unit 2 (and all the other units), you need to be able to do **everything** specified by the standards. Study the Interactive Text carefully and do not skip any of it.

(b) Learning is an **active** process. Do **all** the activities as you work through the Interactive Text so you can be sure you really understand what you have read.

(c) After you have covered the material in the Interactive Text, work through the **Devolved Assessment Kit**.

(d) Before you take the devolved assessment, check that you still remember the material using the following quick revision plan for each chapter.

    (i) Read through the chapter learning objectives. Are there any gaps in your knowledge? If so, study the section again.

    (ii) Read and learn the key terms.

    (iii) Look at the devolved assessment alerts. These show the sort of things that are likely to come up.

    (iv) Read and learn the key learning points, which are a summary of the chapter.

    (v) Do the quick quiz again. If you know what you're doing, it shouldn't take long.

    This approach is only a suggestion. Your college may well adapt it to suit your needs.

Remember this is a **practical** course.

(a) Try to relate the material to your experience in the workplace or any other work experience you may have had.

(b)   Try to make as many links as you can to your study of the other Units at Foundation level.

(c)   Keep this text, (hopefully) you will find it invaluable in your everyday work too!

FOUNDATION QUALIFICATION STRUCTURE

The competence-based Education and Training Scheme of the Association of Accounting Technicians is based on an analysis of the work of accounting staff in a wide range of industries and types of organisation. The Standards of Competence for Accounting which students are expected to meet are based on this analysis.

The Standards identify the key purpose of the accounting occupation, which is to operate, maintain and improve systems to record, plan, monitor and report on the financial activities of an organisation, and a number of key roles of the occupation. Each key role is subdivided into units of competence, which are further divided into elements of competences. By successfully completing assessments in specified units of competence, students can gain qualifications at NVQ/SVQ levels 2, 3 and 4, which correspond to the AAT Foundation, Intermediate and Technician stages of competence respectively.

Whether you are competent in a Unit is demonstrated by means of:

- *Either* a Central Assessment (set and marked by AAT assessors)

- *Or* a Devolved Assessment (where competence is judged by an Approved Assessment Centre to whom responsibility for this is devolved)

- Or *both* Central *and* Devolved Assessment

Below we set out the overall structure of the Foundation (NVQ/SVQ Level 2) stage, indicating how competence in each Unit is assessed. In the next section there is more detail about the Devolved Assessment for Unit 2.

All units are assessed by Devolved Assessment, and Unit 3 is also assessed by Central Assessment.

Foundation qualification structure

NVQ/SVQ Level 2 - Foundation (All units are mandatory)

Unit of competence

Elements of competence

Unit 1	Recording income and receipts

1.1	Process documents relating to goods and services supplied
1.2	Receive and record receipts

Unit 2	Making and recording payments

2.1	Process documents relating to goods and services received
2.2	Prepare authorised payments
2.3	Make and record payments

Unit 3	Preparing ledger balances and an initial trial balance

3.1	Balance bank transactions
3.2	Prepare ledger balances and control accounts
3.3	Draft an initial trial balance

Unit 4	Supplying information for management control

4.1	Code and extract information
4.2	Provide comparisons on costs and income

Unit 20	Working with information technology

20.1	Input, store and output data
20.2	Minimise risks to data held on a computer system

Unit 22	Monitor and maintain a healthy safe and secure workplace (ASC)

22.1	Monitor and maintain health and safety within the workplace
22.2	Monitor and maintain the security of the workplace

Unit 23	Achieving personal effectiveness

23.1	Plan and organise own work
23.2	Establish and maintain working relationships
23.3	Maintain accounting files and records

UNIT 2 STANDARDS OF COMPETENCE

The structure of the Standards for Unit 2

The Unit commences with a statement of the **knowledge and understanding** which underpin competence in the Unit's elements.

The Unit of Competence is then divided into **elements of competence** describing activities which the individual should be able to perform.

Each element includes:

(a) **A** set of **performance criteria.** This defines what constitutes competent performance.

(b) A **range statement.** This defines the situations, contexts, methods etc in which competence should be displayed.

(c) **Evidence requirements.** These state that competence must be demonstrated consistently, over an appropriate time scale with evidence of performance being provided from the appropriate sources.

(d) **Sources of evidence.** These are suggestions of ways in which you can find evidence to demonstrate that competence. These fall under the headings: 'observed performance; work produced by the candidate; authenticated testimonies from relevant witnesses; personal account of competence; other sources of evidence.' They are reproduced in full in our Devolved Assessment Kit for Unit 2.

The elements of competence for Unit 2 *Making and Recording Payments* are set out below. Knowledge and understanding required for the unit as a whole are listed first, followed by the performance criteria and range statements for each element. Performance criteria are cross-referenced below to chapters in this Unit 2 *Making and Recording Payments* Interactive Text.

Unit 2: Making and Recording Payments

What is the unit about?

This unit relates to the organisation's expenditure. It includes dealing with documentation from suppliers and ordering and delivery documentation, preparing payments, recording expenditure in the appropriate records, and making payments relating to invoices, wages and salaries, and petty cash.

The first element is concerned with ensuring calculations and records of expenditure are correct and deducting available discounts. It requires the individual to enter documents as primary records and to code and record entries in the appropriate ledgers. The individual is also required to handle both verbal and written communications with suppliers in a polite and effective manner. It should be noted that the individual is not expected to deal with goods supplied under leasing or hire purchase contracts at this level.

The second element relates to preparing authorised payments, relating to creditors, payroll and petty cash. The individual is expected to prepare and analyse payments according to organisational procedures. Any queries on these payments should be referred to the appropriate person.

Maintaining security and confidentiality are key aspects of performance in this element.

The final element relates to the actual making of payments. This involves the individual selecting appropriate payment methods and ensuring that all payments are recorded and entered into the accounting records. This element also requires the individual to take responsibility for ensuring the security of relevant payment methods and to refer queries to the appropriate person.

Knowledge and understanding

The business environment

- Types of business transactions and documents involved (Element 2.1)

- Basic law relating to contract law, Sale of Goods Act and document retention policies (Elements 2.1 and 2.2)

- General principles of VAT (Element 2.1)

- Types of discounts (Element 2.1)

- Automated payments: CHAPS, BACS, direct debits, standing orders (Elements 2.1, 2.2 and 2.3)

- Credit and debit cards (Elements 2.1 and 2.3)

- Different ordering systems: Internet; fax; in writing; telephone (Element 2.1)

- Documentation for payments (Element 2.2)

- Basic law relating to data protection (Element 2.2)

- Legal requirements relating to cheques, including crossing and endorsements (Element 2.3)

Accounting methods

- Double entry bookkeeping (Elements 2.1, 2.2 and 2.3)

- Methods of coding data (Element 2.1)

- Operation of manual and computerised accounting systems (Elements 2.1, 2.2, and 2.3)

- Credit card procedures (Elements 2.1 and 2.3)

- Relationship between accounting system and ledger (Elements 2.1, 2.2 and 2.3)

- Petty cash procedures: imprest and non imprest methods; analysis of items of expenditure including VAT charges (Element 2.2)

- Payroll accounting procedures: accounting for gross pay, statutory and non-statutory deductions and payments to external agencies; security and control; cumulative calculations (Elements 2.2. and 2.3)

- Methods of handling and storing money from a security aspect (Element 2.3)

The organisation

- Relevant understanding of the organisation's accounting systems and administrative systems and procedures (Elements 2.1, 2.2 and 2.3)

- The nature of the organisation's business transactions (Elements 2.1, 2.2 and 2.3)

- Organisational procedures for authorisation and coding of purchase invoices and payments (Element 2.1)

- Organisational procedures for filing source information (Elements 2.1, 2.2 and 2.3)

Element 2.1 Process documents relating to goods and services received

	Performance criteria	Chapters in this Text
1	Suppliers' invoices and credit notes are checked against delivery notes, ordering documentation and evidence that goods or services have been received	2
2	Totals and balances are correctly calculated and checked on suppliers' invoices	2
3	Available discounts are identified and deducted	2
4	Documents are correctly entered as primary records according to organisational procedures	3
5	Entries are coded and recorded in the appropriate ledger	3, 4
6	Discrepancies are identified and either resolved or referred to the appropriate person if outside own authority	2, 5
7	Communications with suppliers regarding accounts are handled politely and effectively	5

Range statement

1	Documents: orders; suppliers' invoices; delivery notes; credit notes	2, 3
2	Discounts: trade; settlement	2, 4
3	Primary records: purchase and returns day book	3
4	Ledger: main ledger; subsidiary ledger; integrated ledger	4
5	Discrepancies: incorrect calculations; non-delivery of goods charged; duplicated invoices; incorrect VAT charges; incorrect discounts	2, 5
6	Communications: oral; written	5

Element 2.2 Prepare authorised payments

	Performance criteria	Chapters in this Text
1	Payments are correctly calculated from relevant documentation	6, 8, 9
2	Payments are scheduled and authorised by the appropriate person	6, 8, 9
3	Queries are referred to the appropriate person	6, 8
4	Security and confidentiality are maintained according to organisational requirements	6, 8, 9

Range statement

1	Payments: payroll; creditors; petty cash	6, 8, 9
2	Documentation: petty cash claims; suppliers' statements; payslips; cheque requisitions	6, 8, 9
3	Appropriate person: manager; accountant	6, 8, 9

BPP
PUBLISHING

Element 2.3 Make and record payments

		Chapters in this Text
Performance criteria		
1	The appropriate payment method is used in accordance with organisational procedures	6, 8, 9
2	Payments are made in accordance with organisational processes and timescales	6, 8
3	Payments are entered into accounting records according to organisational procedures	7, 8, 9
4	Queries are referred to the appropriate person	6, 7, 8
5	Security and confidentiality are maintained according to organisational requirements	6, 8
Range statement		
1	Payment methods: cash; cheques; automated payments	6, 8, 9
2	Payment: creditors; wages and salaries; petty cash; cheque requisition form	6, 8, 9
3	Accounting records: cash book	7, 8
4	Queries relating to: unauthorised claims for payment; insufficient supporting evidence; claims exceeding prescribed limit	6, 8

ASSESSMENT STRATEGY

This unit is assessed by **devolved assessment**.

Devolved assessment is a means of collecting evidence of your ability to carry out practical activities and to **operate effectively in the conditions of the workplace** to the standards required. Evidence may be collected at your place of work or at an Approved Assessment Centre by means of simulations of workplace activity, or by a combination of these methods.

If the Approved Assessment Centre is a **workplace** you may be observed carrying out accounting activities as part of your normal work routine. You should collect documentary evidence of the work you have done, or contributed, in an **accounting portfolio**. Evidence collected in a portfolio can be assessed in addition to observed performance or where it is not possible to assess by observation.

Where the Approved Assessment Centre is a **college or training organisation**, devolved assessment will be by means of a combination of the following.

(a)   Documentary evidence of activities carried out at the workplace, collected by you in an **accounting portfolio**

(b)   Realistic **simulations** of workplace activities; these simulations may take the form of case studies and in-tray exercises and involve the use of primary documents and reference sources

(c)   **Projects and assignments** designed to assess the Standards of Competence

If you are unable to provide workplace evidence, you will be able to complete the assessment requirements by the alternative methods listed above.

Part A
Goods and Services Received

1 Revision of bookkeeping topics

This chapter contains

1   Double entry bookkeeping

2   Capital and revenue items

3   Basic business law

Learning objectives

On completion of this chapter you will be able to:

- Understand the basics of double entry bookkeeping

- Distinguish between capital and revenue items

- Understand basic business law

Knowledge and understanding

- Basic law relating to contract law, Sale of Goods Act and document retention policies

- Double entry bookkeeping

We recommend that students complete Unit 1 before commencing Unit 2. However, if you are studying Unit 1 and Unit 2 at the same time, you should complete the basic bookkeeping and basic law sections from BPP's Interactive Text for Foundation Unit 1 **before starting** your Unit 2 studies. In order to assist students who did not use BPP's Unit 1 text, this chapter contains a summary of the knowledge brought forward from that text.

Warning!

Do not attempt to study Unit 2, if you have not studied basic bookkeeping and business law at Unit 1 level.

1   DOUBLE ENTRY BOOKKEEPING

The accounting equation

1.1   The basis of double entry bookkeeping is the accounting equation. This states that **the assets and liabilities of a business must always be equal.**

1.2   An asset is something valuable, which the business owns or has the use of, eg factory, plant and machinery, stock, debtors, bank account.

1.3   A liability is something which is owed by the business to someone else, eg bank overdraft, creditors, loans.

1.4   Capital is an investment of money (funds) by the owner of the business with the intent of earning a return (profit).

1.5   For accounting purposes, a business is treated as a separate entity to its owner(s). Since the business owes the amount of capital invested to its owners, capital is a form of liability.

1.6   Therefore, an alternative format for the accounting equation is **assets = capital + liabilities.**

1.7   Another useful term is net assets. **Net assets = Total assets – total liabilities.** So it follows that **Net assets = Capital.**

1.8   Drawings are amounts of money taken out of the business by its owners.

1.9   Profit is the excess of income over expenditure. If expenditure exceeds income the business has made a loss.

1.10   Profit, like capital, belongs to the owners of a business. However, if the business keeps (retains) the profits and does not pay anything out to its owners, the **retained profits** are accounted for as an addition to capital.

1.11   Therefore capital can be restated as

Capital = Capital introduced + retained profits – drawings.

1.12   Following on from 1.11 above, the accounting equation can be restated as

Net assets = Capital introduced + retained profits – drawings.

Activity 1.1   Level: Pre-assessment

Which of the following items are assets, which are liabilities and which are capital?

(a)   Bank overdraft
(b)   Factory
(c)   Monies introduced into the business by the owner
(d)   Bank account
(e)   Plant and machinery
(f)   Amounts due from customers
(g)   Amounts due to suppliers
(h)   Stock of goods for sale

The business equation

1.13 As the business continues to trade, there will be capital introduced brought forward from previous periods, as well as capital introduced in the current period. Similarly there are retained profits brought forward from previous periods, as well as retained profits for the current period.

1.14 This gives rise to the **business equation.**

Profit earned in current period	=	Increase/decrease in the net assets in current period	+	Drawings in current period	–	Capital introduced in the current period
P	=	I	+	D	–	C

Debtors and creditors

1.15 A business can trade for cash or on credit.

1.16 A cash transaction is a sale or purchase when cash changes hands at the same time as the goods or services concerned.

1.17 A credit transaction is a sale or purchase which occurs sometime earlier than when cash is received or paid.

1.18 In this text, we are concentrating on purchases. So the following points are important.

- **A cash purchase** occurs when the goods are paid for in cash and the goods and cash change hands at the same time.

- **A credit purchase** occurs when the business receives the goods, accompanied by an invoice from the supplier. Cash is paid at a later date.

1.19 A **creditor** is a person from whom a business has purchased items and to whom the business owes money. A creditor is a liability of the business.

1.20 A **trade creditor** is a creditor arising from trading operations eg materials, components or goods for resale.

1.21 A **debtor** is a person who has purchased items from the business and who owes the business money. A debtor is an asset of the business.

1.22 A **trade debtor** is a debtor arising from trading operations eg credit sales.

Activity 1.2   **Level: Pre-assessment**

Peter has been trading for a year. At the beginning, he introduced capital of £5,000. At the end of the year, his net assets are £36,000 and his drawings were £12,000. What was his profit for the year?

Activity 1.3   **Level: Pre-assessment**

Peter has purchased goods totalling £25,000. He paid cash of £10,000 and the rest has been bought on credit. So how much does he owe his creditors?

Double entry bookkeeping

1.23 From the accounting equation in paragraph 1.6 above, we know that total assets are always equal to total liabilities plus capital. Therefore, any transaction has a dual effect. If a transaction increases an asset, it must also increase liabilities or capital, or reduce another asset. For example, if an amount of goods for resale is purchased for £50 cash, cash has been reduced by £50 but goods for resale have been increased by £50.

1.24 From this, the idea of double entry bookkeeping arises.

> ### KEY TERM
>
> **Double entry bookkeeping** is the system of accounting which reflects the following facts.
>
> - Every financial transaction gives rise to two accountancy entries (a debit and a credit).
>
> - The total value of all debit entries is, therefore, always equal to the total value of all credit entries.

1.25

DEBIT To own/have ↓	CREDIT To owe ↓
AN ASSET INCREASES eg new office furniture	AN ASSET DECREASES eg pay out cash
CAPITAL/ A LIABILITY DECREASES eg pay a creditor	CAPITAL/A LIABILITY INCREASES eg buy goods on credit
INCOME DECREASES eg cancel a sale	INCOME INCREASES eg make a sale
AN EXPENSE INCREASES eg incur advertising costs	AN EXPENSE DECREASES eg cancel a purchase
Left hand side	**Right hand side**

Activity 1.4   **Level: Pre-assessment**

Looking at Activity 1.3, what are the double entry bookkeeping implications?

---

2 CAPITAL AND REVENUE ITEMS

2.1

> **KEY TERMS**
>
>
> - **Capital expenditure** is expenditure which results in the acquisition of fixed assets, or an improvement in their earning capacity.
>
>   ○ Capital expenditure on fixed assets results in the appearance of a fixed asset in the **balance sheet** of the business.
>
>   ○ Capital expenditure is **not** charged as an expense in the **profit and loss account**.
>
> - **Revenue expenditure** is expenditure incurred in *either* of the following ways.
>
>   ○ For the purpose of the trade of the business, including expenditure classified as selling and distribution expenses, administration expenses and finance charges.
>
>   ○ To maintain the existing earning capacity of fixed assets, eg repairs to fixed assets.
>
>   Revenue expenditure is shown in the **profit and loss account of a period**, provided that it relates to the trading activity and sales of that particular period. If it carries over into the next period, revenue expenditure would appear as a **current asset** in the balance sheet.

2.2

> **KEY TERMS**
>
> - **Capital income** is the proceeds from the sale of non-trading assets (ie proceeds from the sale of fixed assets). The profits (or losses) from the sale of fixed assets are included in the **profit and loss account** of a business, for the accounting period in which the sale takes place.
>
> - **Revenue income** is income derived from the following.
>
>   ○ The sale of trading assets, such as goods bought or made for resale.
>
>   ○ Rent, interest and dividends received from fixed assets held by the business.
>
>   Revenue income appears in the **profit and loss account**.

2.3 A balance sheet is a statement of the assets, liabilities and capital of a business at a particular point in time.

2.4 Assets in the balance sheet are divided into fixed and current assets.

2.5 Fixed assets are used within the business to generate profit eg plant and machinery, computers used by employees to provide a service.

2.6 Current assets are owned by the business with the intent of turning them into cash within one year. Cash and money at the bank are also current assets.

2.7 Liabilities are divided into long-term and current liabilities.

2.8 Current liabilities are amounts owed by the business, which are payable within one year.

2.9 Long-term liabilities are amounts owed by the business, which are payable after one year.

2.10 A profit and loss account is a statement of the revenue (income) earned in a period, matched to the costs incurred (expenditure) in earning that profit.

Activity 1.5   **Level: Pre-assessment**

Which of the following items are capital and which revenue?

(a) Expenses incurred in selling
(b) Amounts owed to creditors
(c) A factory
(d) Expenses of distribution
(e) Income from sale of goods
(f) Plant and machinery
(g) Payroll expenses

---

3 BASIC BUSINESS LAW

Contract law

> **KEY TERM**
>
> **Contract law** comprises the rules in statutes and case law governing the ways in which people contract with each other. It is **civil** law, not criminal law.

3.1 When different organisations enter into transactions, they reach an **agreement**. Contract law looks at how agreements are conducted.

> **KEY TERM**
>
> A **contract** is an agreement which legally binds the parties to it.

3.2 Examples of contracts include a contract to buy a house and a contract of employment.

3.3 A contract does **not have to be in writing**. If you buy a rubber stamp for your office, you will got to a stationery supplier and exchange money for the rubber stamp.

3.4 In the above example, there has been a mutual agreement. The stationer agreed to sell you a rubber stamp and you agreed to buy it. This is a contract.

3.5 **Elements of a contract**

- Intention to create legal relations
- Offer and acceptance
- Consideration

3.6 Both parties must intend that the agreement between them is legally binding. Family arrangements are not usually intended to be binding, but commercial arrangements usually are.

3.7 A legal offer occurs when an order is made. In the example, in paragraph 3.3, the offer occurred when you picked up the rubber stamp and took it to the cash till.

3.8 The acceptance of the offer occurred when the stationer agreed to sell you the rubber stamp.

3.9 Consideration passed when you handed over your money.

Contracts for the sale of goods

3.10 The main law is the Sale of Goods Act 1979. This also covers the supply of services, eg servicing a car, repairing a fax machine.

3.11 The Act applies only where there is **money consideration** or a **price**. Exchanges of goods are not covered by the Act. However part exchange, where some money changes hands, is a contract for the sale of goods.

3.12 A contract for the sale of goods does not have to spell out every term. The Act covers certain implied terms in any sales contract.

3.13 **Implied terms**

- The effect of delay in performance
- Title, or the seller's right to sell the goods
- Description of the goods
- Quality of the goods
- Fitness of the goods for the purpose for which they are supplied
- Sale by sample

3.14 The Act also has provisions to cover the passing of property, risk and the acceptance or rejection of goods and services.

Retention of documents

3.15 Documents containing information should be filed. This is particularly true of legal documents, eg contracts.

3.16 Retention periods vary. Some recommended retention periods relevant to Unit 2 follow.

BPP PUBLISHING

Document	Years
Agreements	12
Balance sheets	30
Bank statements	6
Cheque counterfoils	1
Correspondence files	6
Credit notes	6
Customs and Excise VAT records	6
Delivery notes	1
Expense claims	1
Purchase orders	6
Quotations sent out	6
Tax records	6

3.17 You should find out the retention policies of your own organisation.

IMPORTANT

If the topics in this revision chapter are new to you, go back to your Unit 1 Interactive Text and study the basic bookkeeping and law sections **before proceeding any further** with this Unit 2 text.

2 Processing suppliers' invoices and credit notes

This chapter contains

1   Introduction

2   Purchase orders

3   Types of business purchase

4   Documenting goods and services received

5   Discounts, rebates and allowances

6   VAT

7   Checking suppliers' invoices and credit notes

8   Action to deal with discrepancies

Learning objectives

On completion of this chapter you will be able to:

- Document goods and services received

- Understand the different types of discounts

- Understand basic VAT

- Check suppliers' invoices and credit notes

- Deal with discrepancies

BPP
PUBLISHING

Performance criteria

2.1.1 Suppliers' invoices and credit notes are checked against delivery notes, ordering documentation and evidence that goods or services have been received.

2.1.2 Totals and balances are correctly calculated and checked on suppliers' invoices

2.1.3 Available discounts are identified and deducted

2.1.6 Discrepancies are identified and either resolved or referred to the appropriate person if outside own authority.

Range statement

2.1.1 Documents: orders; supplies' invoices; delivery notes; credit notes

2.1.2 Discounts: trade; settlement

2.1.5 Discrepancies: incorrect calculations; non-delivery of goods charged; duplicate invoices; incorrect VAT charges; incorrect discounts

Knowledge and understanding

- Types of business transactions and documents involved

- General principles of VAT

- Types of discounts

- Different ordering systems: Internet; fax; in writing; telephone

- The nature of the organisation's business transactions

- Organisational procedures for authorisation and coding of purchase invoices and payments

Chapter 2 scenario - Ordram Quick Ltd. This scenario applies to the majority of activities in this chapter.

On 6 April 20X7 you are the purchasing clerk of Ordram Quick Ltd, a laboratory furniture manufacturer situated at Unit 7, Aurora Business Park, Lampley LM9 9AS. Ordram Quick Ltd is registered for VAT with registration number 727 0015 54. The company purchases certain products from Lampley Laminates of 47 Gorse Road, Lampley LM2 9PR, which allows a trade discount of 10% on the list price. An extract from Lampley Laminates' price list is shown below.

```
        LAMPLEY  LAMINATES  -  PRICE  LIST

  All  prices  are  per  square  metre

  Product                          Product  code    £   p
  Enlam  20 - polar  white            9248          5.28
  Enlam  25 - polar  white            9252          5.70
  Enlam  28 - polar  white            9256          5.88
  Enlam  30 - polar  white            9259          5.99
  Onyxel  Grade  A                    0045          3.20
  Onyxel  Grade  B                    0048          2.85
  Ply-mel  20                         1041          4.08
  Ply-mel  30                         1042          4.41
  Trilam  22                          7050          5.18
  Trilam  24                          7060          5.62
```

1 INTRODUCTION

1.1 This chapter deals with the whole purchasing process.

- Raising a purchase order
- Documenting the receipt of goods and services
- Checking suppliers' invoices
- Dealing with discrepancies

2 PURCHASE ORDERS

2.1 The steps involved in the **purchasing** process for **goods and services** are similar to those for sales.

- Generating purchase orders (Chapter 2)

- Processing invoices and credit notes received (Chapter 2)

- Entering transactions in books of prime entry (Chapter 3)

- Recording transactions in individual subsidiary (purchase ledger) accounts (Chapter 4)

- Summarising transactions and posting to the creditors control and VAT accounts (Chapter 4)

- Ensuring that suppliers are communicated with effectively (Chapter 5)

2.2 The purchaser can be a **company,** a **partnership**, or someone in business on their own ('**sole trader**').

2.3 The purchaser of goods (or services) enters into a **legally binding contract** with the supplier **when an agreement is made.**

The purchasing department

2.4 The **size** of the purchasing department and its **importance** will vary according to the size and nature of the business.

(a) A **small manufacturer** may purchase raw materials from a small number of suppliers, with negotiated terms which are only reviewed annually.

(b) A **larger business** may negotiate daily with many suppliers (eg a major supermarket chain buys from a large number of suppliers and needs to negotiate the right amount and quality of goods at the best possible price).

2.5 There may not be a **separate purchasing department** at all.

(a) In a smaller business, a **manager** may make all purchases.

(b) A medium-sized or larger business usually has a **purchasing manager or director** (heading a purchasing department).

Before placing an order

2.6 The purchasing department needs to go through a number of steps before placing an order.

Step 1	A **purchase requisition** is needed in a large business where purchasing is separate from other operations. The operating unit creates the requisition and sends it to the purchasing department.
Step 2	The business sends out a **letter of enquiry** seeking a **quotation** of price, and perhaps a full specification of the product, from the seller. A letter of enquiry will not be necessary for every purchase, eg when a business makes regular purchases from the same supplier or knows the supplier's prices in detail.
Step 3	A **quotation** is received from the supplier and is assessed as to whether it is reasonable, considering any other quotations received. For an important purchase, more than one person may be involved in making the decision.

The purchase order

2.7 A **purchase order** is issued to the chosen supplier, stating the product and quantity required. A formal purchase order is usually not required for relatively small purchases.

2.8 The purchase order has two purposes.

- To notify the supplier of **what is required**
- To allow a **check** that the goods or services received are those ordered

We shall return to this point later in the chapter.

2.9 A **signed purchase order** shows the supplier that the **order** is **valid. Suppliers should be instructed not to accept verbal or unsigned orders.**

2.10 A purchase order form can be used fraudulently. Therefore access to purchase order forms must be restricted (eg to a list of named personnel). The forms should be sequentially numbered, so that it is possible to keep track of them.

2.11 A purchase order is usually produced as a four-part set.

Purchase order	Location
1	Sent to the supplier
2	Kept by the purchasing department in case of queries
3	Sent to the warehouse for checking against the goods received
4	Sent to the purchase ledger department for agreeing with the purchase invoice

2.12 Purchase orders may be sent in any of the following ways.

- By post
- By fax
- By Internet

2.13 Orders sent by Internet must be authorised and a valid order number quoted to the supplier. A copy of the Internet order should be printed off and attached to the relevant purchase order form for control purposes.

2.14 Orders are sometimes made by telephone in small organisations. However a note must be kept of the details of the order, by completing a purchase order form.

2.15 A supplier may issue an **order acknowledgement**. A **delivery note** (to be signed and returned to the supplier) and an **advice note** left with the purchaser as evidence of delivery may also be issued. Finally, a **goods received note** may be created by the purchaser. Bear in mind that procedures do vary.

2.16 There is a summary of the documentation involved on the following page.

Activity 2.1   **Level: Assessment**

You work in the purchasing department of Ordram Quick Ltd. You need to order the following materials.

180m^2 Trilam 22
250m^2 Enlam 20 - polar white
200m^2 Enlam 25 - polar white
300m^2 Onyxel Grade B

Task

Draft on a separate sheet of paper a purchase order (no 1233), including details of the trade discount claimed and delivery details (by 1 May 20X7 at the latest).

BPP
PUBLISHING

Part A: Goods and services received

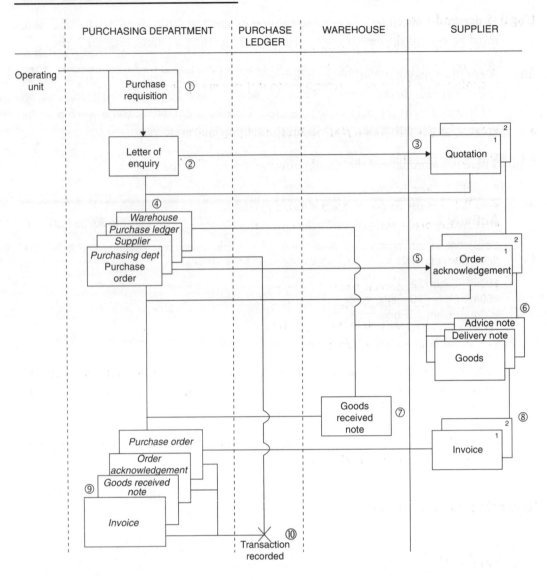

3   TYPES OF BUSINESS PURCHASE

Purchases for stock

3.1   Some purchases are **trading stock**. This includes '**raw materials**' on which the business does work to make '**finished goods**'. The following are examples of various kinds of stock.

- Goods purchased from a **wholesaler** (trading stock) and then resold at a profit to **customers**

- A steel rolling mill uses large amounts of steel (raw materials) to produce steel wire of various kinds (finished goods)

- A car manufacturer purchases many different products for **component stock** (eg vehicle components, paints and sheet metal)

Business expenses

3.2   Every business makes some purchases of goods and services which cannot be related directly to the specific production of stock which the business sells. These costs are '**business expenses**' (or '**overheads**'). Examples include electricity, stationery and cleaning services.

Capital expenditure

3.3 A purchase may be of an asset to be used continuously in the business, such as a machine or a building. The distinction between **capital** and **revenue expenditure** is explained in Chapter 1 - refer back to it if you are in any doubt.

4 DOCUMENTING GOODS AND SERVICES RECEIVED

4.1 It is important that a business only pays its suppliers for the following.

- What is **ordered**
- What is **received** (in good condition)
- At the **price agreed** (and subject to other terms agreed)

4.2 A business could end up in any of the following situations.

- Paying for goods it has not ordered
- Paying more than it should for goods or services received
- Paying for more than it has received
- Paying for substandard goods

This is a loss to the business. Overpaying can be the result of a **clerical error** or **fraud**. Fraud may involve a member of staff 'colluding' with a supplier to obtain money from the business by deception.

4.3 To avoid overpaying, a business needs to set up **controls** or **checks**. An example is to keep a record of the goods and services received.

Recording goods received

> **KEY TERM**
>
> A **goods received note** or **GRN** is a document recording what goods have been received in the purchaser's warehouse.

4.4 The details of goods received may be entered into a **book** or on **computer**, instead of a separate GRN form.

4.5 However goods received are recorded, the records will need to show the details below.

BPP PUBLISHING

```
                                                    ACCOUNTS COPY

        GOODS RECEIVED NOTE  WAREHOUSE COPY
                                                         ①
   DATE:   7 March 20X7      TIME:    2.00 pm          NO  5565
   ORDER NO:  00917   ②
   SUPPLIER'S ADVICE NOTE NO:  202/739/X   ③      WAREHOUSE A
```

QUANTITY	CAT NO	DESCRIPTION
④ 16	SR 424	Granular salt, 25kg bags

RECEIVED IN GOOD CONDITION: *G. P.*   ⑤   (INITIALS)

1   GRNs are **pre-numbered**, so checks can be made that all stock received has been invoiced.

2   This is the **purchase** order number. The warehouse staff take this from the copy purchase order held in the warehouse.

3   The supplier's advice note number allows any discrepancies to be followed up later.

4   Quantities and descriptions (including codes if known) are needed, **not** monetary values.

5   The person initialling the GRN is confirming the goods are in good condition.

4.6   One copy of the GRN is sent to the **purchasing department,** so that they can compare it with the supplier's invoice. The other copy is kept in the **warehouse,** so that a full record is available of the goods which have come into the warehouse.

4.7   **Access to blank GRN forms must be strictly controlled.** In particular, purchasing department staff should not have access to GRN forms. This stops staff from carrying out frauds involving the misuse of GRNs to validate bogus invoices.

Recording services received

4.8   A different form of recording is needed for services.

4.9   In the case of small repairs and services (eg window cleaning), the receptionist keeps a **service book** which all tradespeople sign when they begin and complete work.

4.10 EXAMPLE: RECORDING SERVICES RECEIVED

R Handy, the local plumber, is asked to carry out a small repair by K Singh, the Office Manager at Greenfields Carparks Ltd. Handy arrives at the Greenfields offices at 9 am and signs in at reception. Handy finishes the repair and signs out at 12 noon.

When the invoice arrives, it charges five hours' on-site labour. Mr Singh thinks this is excessive. A brief call to reception confirms that Handy was on site for three hours. This gives Mr Singh evidence to query the invoice with Mr Handy.

Other kinds of goods and services

4.11 Other kinds of service can be difficult to keep track of to ensure that wrong payments are not made. This also applies to some types of goods which are not received at a single location.

4.12 In a large office there may be a number of people with the authority to purchase **small items of office equipment and stationery**. An invoice arrives for some plastic wallets and office staplers. However, no-one can remember having ordered these goods. Malcolm thinks Debbie ordered them, but she is on holiday in France for three weeks. Kerry thinks Sanjit ordered them, but he has now left the company.

4.13 Can you think of some procedures which could help to avoid this situation?

- All office purchases are channelled through just **one or two people**.

- A **reference** is sent with all orders, even if it is just the name of the person placing the order.

Fraud

4.14 There have been many cases of people taking fraudulent advantage of the **lack of control over payments for services** in some businesses. Some firms were sent invoices for entry of their name in business directories, where this had not been requested by anyone in the firm. In some cases, the directory itself did not even exist. It is common for payment to be demanded immediately with serious consequences being threatened if payment is not made.

4.15 The fraudsters hope that someone receiving the invoice will make a payment, because they cannot discover whether anyone approved an order for the service. Such frauds are often tried during **holiday periods**. There is a greater chance that the usual staff will be away and the staff left in charge are less familiar with any procedures.

5 DISCOUNTS, REBATES AND ALLOWANCES

> **KEY TERM**
>
> A **discount** is a reduction in the price of goods below the amount at which those goods would normally be sold to other customers of the supplier.

Types of discount

5.1   There are two types of discount.

Type of discount	Description	Timing	Status
Trade discount	A reduction in the **cost of goods** owing to the nature of the trading transaction. It usually results from buying goods in bulk. However a regular customer may get a discount on all goods bought, because the total volume of his purchases over time is so large.	Given on supplier's invoice	Permanent
Cash or settlement discount	A reduction in the **amount payable** to the supplier, in return for immediate or early payment in cash. For example, a supplier charges £1,000 for goods, but offers a cash discount of 10% if the goods are paid for immediately, 5% if they are paid for within 7 days of the invoice date, but payment in full within 30 days.	Given for immediate or very prompt payment	Withdrawn if payment not received within time period stated

5.2   The distinction between trade and cash discounts is important as they are accounted for differently. We shall see this later in this text.

5.3   EXAMPLE: DISCOUNTS

Maurice has three suppliers.

(a)   Martin offers 5% trade discount.

(b)   Sol offers a trade discount of 7% on amounts *in excess of* £100 (ie the trade discount does not apply to the first £100).

(c)   Tony offers a 10% cash discount for immediate payment or a 5% cash discount for all items paid for within 30 days of purchase.

In January 20X7, Maurice makes purchases of goods worth the following amounts before discounts have been deducted.

(a)   From Martin: £400
(b)   From Sol: £700
(c)   From Tony: £350 cash
        £700 to be paid on 14.1.X7 for goods purchased on 3.1.X7

Calculate how much Maurice has received as discounts in January. How much were trade and cash discounts?

5.4   SOLUTION

		£	
From Martin	£400 × 5%	20	Trade
From Sol	(£700 – £100) × 7%	42	Trade
From Tony	£350 × 10%	35	Cash: immediate
	£700 × 5%	35	Cash: prompt
		132	

Trade discounts

> **KEY TERM**
>
> A **trade discount** is a reduction in the amount of money *demanded* from a customer.

5.5 If a trade discount is **received** from a supplier, the **amount of money demanded** will be **net** of discount (ie it will be the normal sales value less the discount).

Cash discounts

> **KEY TERM**
>
> A **cash discount** is an *optional* reduction in the amount of money *payable* by a customer.

5.6 Taking advantage of a cash discount is a matter of **financing policy**, not of **trading policy**. The discount is **optional**.

5.7 EXAMPLE: OPTIONAL CASH DISCOUNTS RECEIVED

A buys goods from B, on the understanding that A will be allowed a period of credit before having to pay for the goods. The terms of the transaction are as follows.

Date of sale: 1 July 20X7

Credit period allowed: 30 days

Invoice price of the goods (the invoice will be issued at this price when the goods are delivered): £2,000

Cash discount offered: 4% for immediate payment

A has the choice between:

(a) Holding on to the £2,000 for 30 days and then paying the full amount.
(b) Paying £2,000 less 4% (a total of £1,920) now.

This is a financing decision. Is it worthwhile for A to save £80 by paying her debts sooner? Or can she employ her cash more usefully for 30 days and pay the debt at the latest acceptable moment?

If A pays now, her bank account goes overdrawn for a month. The bank charges an overdraft fee of £50 together with interest of 1.6% per month (also charged on the overdraft fee). A currently has £150 in the bank (and an agreed overdraft facility). Assuming no other transactions, what should A do? Work it out before looking at the solution.

5.8 SOLUTION

A pays now, so the bank account will be as follows.

		£
Funds		150.00
Less:	payment	(1,920.00)
	overdraft fee	(50.00)
Overdraft		(1,820.00)

Interest (1.6% × £1,820) added at end of the month   29.12

The discount is worth £80, but bank charges and interest of £50 + £29.12 will be incurred. However, the amount of the discount is still worth more than the bank charges by 88p. A should therefore take advantage of the discount offered by B.

Activity 2.2   Level: Pre-assessment

Ordram Quick purchases goods with a list price of £22,000. The supplier offers a 10% trade discount, and a 2½% cash discount for payment within 20 days.

Tasks

Ignore VAT.

(a)   Calculate the amount Ordram will pay if it delays longer than 20 days before paying.
(b)   Calculate the amount the business will pay if it pays within 20 days.

5.9   Businesses may be offered other kinds of 'discounts' as incentives, to encourage them to buy in bulk or to stop them buying goods from competitors. **Rebates** and **allowances** are not as common and they are only mentioned briefly here.

(a)   An example of a **rebate** is where the gas company will lower its overall tariff for customers who use over a certain number of units per year. The rebate will be given in the form of either:

- A reduction in the bills for the following year
- A cheque for the calculated rebate amount

(b)   An example of an **allowance** is where, if a certain number of units are ordered at one time, then a few extra units are given free of charge. For instance, if a record shop orders 50 compact discs, then another five are sent **free of charge**.

6   VAT

6.1   Many business transactions involve VAT (Value Added Tax), and most invoices show any VAT charged separately.

> **KEY TERMS**
>
> - **VAT** is a tax levied on the sale of goods and services. It is administered by HM Customs & Excise, but most of the work of collecting the tax falls on VAT-registered businesses, which hand the tax they collect over to the authorities.
>
> - **Output tax**: VAT charged on goods and services sold by a business (that is, the business 'output').
>
> - **Input tax**: VAT paid on goods and services bought in by a business.

6.2 VAT is charged by all members of the European Union (EU), though at different rates. Some countries, for example, charge 5% for some kinds of product and 10% on others.

6.3 In the UK there are three rates of VAT.

(a) **Standard rate**. This is 17½% of the value of the goods. So if you buy a standard rated item, which is worth £100, you also pay £17.50 in tax, a total of £117.50. (Note that the prices you pay in shops generally **include** VAT.)

(b) **Lower rate**. This is 5% and is charged on domestic use of gas and electricity, for example.

(c) **Zero-rate**. This is 0%.

Not all goods and services have VAT on them. **Exempt items** are not part of the VAT system.

Calculating VAT

6.4 If a product has a **net price** of £120, then the VAT is 17½% of £120.

$$VAT = £120 \times 17.5/100$$
$$= £21$$

6.5 The **gross price** of the product is therefore £120 + £21 = £141. **Note that gross price = net price + VAT.**

	£
Purchaser pays gross price	141
Customs and Excise take VAT	(21)
Seller keeps net price	120

6.6 If you are given the gross price of a product (say, £282), then you can work out the VAT which it includes by multiplying by 17.5/117.5 (or 7/47).

$$£282 \times 17.5/117.5 = £42$$

Therefore the net price must be £282 – £42 = £240.

6.7 Where the calculation involves pence, then the rule (unless told otherwise in a Devolved Assessment) is to round **down to the nearest penny**. For example

	£
Net price	25.75
VAT at 17½% (£25.75 ×17½% = £4.50625)	4.50
	30.25

Activity 2.3   **Level: Pre-assessment**

The gross price of product A is £705.60 and the net price of product B is £480.95. What is the VAT charged on each product?

Input and output VAT

6.8 Usually output VAT (on sales) exceeds input VAT (on purchases). The excess is paid over to Customs & Excise. If output VAT is less than input VAT in a period, Customs & Excise will refund the difference to the business. In other words, if a business pays out more in VAT than it receives from customers it will be paid back the difference.

Output tax received	Input tax paid	Total	Treatment
£1,000	£(900)	£100 received	Pay to C&E
£900	£(1,000)	£(100) paid	Refund from C&E

6.9 EXAMPLE: INPUT AND OUTPUT TAX

A company sells goods for £35,250 including VAT in a quarter (three months of a year). It buys goods for £32,900 including VAT. What amount will it pay to or receive from HM Customs & Excise for the quarter?

6.10 SOLUTION

The **output tax** will be:

£

$$£35,250 \times \frac{17.5}{117.5} = \qquad 5,250$$

The **input tax** will be:

$$£32,900 \times \frac{17.5}{117.5} = \qquad 4,900$$

The tax **payable** is the output

tax less the input tax = 350

ASSESSMENT ALERT

Remember that, in the Devolved Assessment, if you come up with a figure which runs to more than two decimal places when you apply the VAT fraction, you should simply **round down** to the nearest penny (unless told otherwise).

Some practical aspects of VAT

Registration

6.11 It would not be easy for HM Customs & Excise to administer and collect VAT if *all* businesses had to account for it. For this reason, **only businesses with at least a certain level of sales must register**.

Administrative time

6.12 VAT affects a large number of businesses. It is something that a business spends quite a lot of time administering. There are several reasons for this.

(a) Most businesses account to HM Customs & Excise for their transactions involving VAT **every quarter**. There is a special scheme which allows accounting on an annual basis. Normally, every quarter, someone will have to work out the VAT position of the business.

(b) All transactions which are recorded involving VAT will have to show **separately** the net price, VAT and the gross price. This increases the **time taken to record** the transactions of the business.

(c) Accounting for VAT has an effect on **cash flow**, whether the business is a net payer of VAT or a net receiver.

(d) Failure to comply with all the rules relating to VAT leads to **large penalties**. HM Customs & Excise has far more wide-ranging and punishing powers than the Inland Revenue.

Discounts and VAT

6.13 If a **cash discount** is offered for prompt payment of the invoice, VAT is computed on the amount **after** deducting the discount (at the highest rate offered), **even if the discount is not taken**.

ASSESSMENT ALERT

The interaction of VAT and discounts comes up frequently in the Devolved Assessment.

Activity 2.4	**Level: Pre-assessment**

For Activity 2.2 above recalculate your answers for (a) and (b) if VAT was charged at the standard rate.

Non-deductible inputs

6.14 Sometimes traders are *not* allowed to reclaim input VAT paid on their purchases. In such cases, the trader bears the cost of VAT and accounts for it as part of the cost of the purchase. The most important example of inputs being **non-deductible** are motor cars.

Documentation and VAT

6.15 There are special rules on the content of an invoice used as proof of purchase for reclaiming VAT - a **VAT invoice**.

BANGLES LTD

Jewel House
Richmans Road
LONDON SE1N 5AB

Invoice Number: 123456
Date: 01/08/X7
Tax Point: 01/08/X7 (a)
Account Number: 3365

INVOICE

| DELIVER TO
ABC Ltd
112 Peters Square
Weyford
Kent CR2 2TA | INVOICE TO:

Same address | Telephone Number 0207 123 4567
VAT Registration Number 457 4635 19
Northern Bank plc Code 20-25-42
Account Number 957023 | (b) |

Item Code	Description	Quantity	Unit Price £	Net Amount £
Your order number: 2490				
13579A	Desks	30	250.00	7,500.00
	Delivery	1	100.00	100.00
			SALES VALUE:	7,600.00
			VAT AT 17.5%:	(c) 1,330.00
			AMOUNT PAYABLE:	8,930.00

6.16 Note the following contents which are necessary for the invoice to be a 'VAT invoice'.

(a) **Tax point**. This determines when the transaction has taken place for VAT purposes, normally the invoice date. Note that, for cash transactions, the tax point is the date the transaction took place.

(b) **VAT registration number** of the supplier. This is to prove to HM Customs & Excise that the purchase was from a real supplier of standard rated goods. It should be in the form: GB 987 6543 21, although businesses that do not export goods and services may omit the 'GB'.

(c) **VAT rate**. The correct rate must be applied to each type of goods; if the goods are zero-rated then the rate would be shown as 0%.

7   CHECKING SUPPLIERS' INVOICES AND CREDIT NOTES

> ### KEY TERMS
>
> An **invoice** is a demand for payment.
>
> A **credit note** is used by a supplier to cancel all or part of a previously issued invoice.

7.1   Suppliers often **post** invoices and credit notes. In other cases, the invoice is delivered **with the goods themselves** by the carrier.

7.2   The **invoices and credit notes** received are passed to the department which deals with suppliers (the **purchase ledger or bought ledger department**).

7.3   The purchase ledger department carries out a number of checks on the invoices and credit notes so that the business **does not pay too much.** It is equally important to make sure that goods or services **are not paid for twice**.

- Check invoices against orders (Para 7.4)
- Check calculations on invoices (Para 7.4)
- Match invoices against GRNs (Paras 7.5 and 7.6)
- Match credit notes against goods returned notes (Para 7.7)

Checks on invoices and credit notes received

7.4   The invoices and credit notes need to go through the following checks.

- Agree with **order documents**
- Agree with **goods received documents** (or other evidence)
- **Calculations** and other details are accurate

Evidence that these checks have been carried out are usually entered on the invoice itself using a **rubber stamp**.

Matching GRNs with invoices

7.5   Staple a copy of the goods received documents (eg GRNs) for the goods shown on the invoice to the invoice. Agree the details on the invoice with the GRN.

7.6   Matching GRNs with invoices helps to ensure that the same goods are not paid for **twice**. Outstanding or unmatched GRNs are kept together for matching with invoices as these are received. If a second invoice is sent by a supplier for goods already invoiced, there will be no unmatched GRN to go with the second invoice.

Matching goods returned notes with credit notes

7.7   Credit notes are matched with internally-generated **goods returned notes**. The business needs to match all its goods returned notes with credit notes within a reasonable time period. This ensures it receives the credit without too much delay.

7.8   EXAMPLE: PROCESSING INVOICES RECEIVED

Frank Okara works as a purchase ledger clerk for Ivory Carpets Ltd. The procedures of the company state that, on receipt of a supplier's invoice, a rubber stamp is entered on the front of the invoice. The stamp is set to show the date and looks like this.

```
┌─────────────────────────────────────────────────┐
│                                                   │
│  RECEIVED           17 May 20X0                   │
│                                                   │
│ ┌─────────────────────────────┬───────────────┐ │
│ │ Checked to Purchase Order No: │ ┌┬┬┬┬┬┐      │ │
│ │              Prices           │ └┴┴┴┴┴┘      │ │
│ │           Quantities          │              │ │
│ ├─────────────────────────────┼───────────────┤ │
│ │   Checked to GRN No:          │ ┌┬┬┬┬┬┐      │ │
│ │           Quantities          │ └┴┴┴┴┴┘      │ │
│ │       In good condition       │              │ │
│ ├─────────────────────────────┼───────────────┤ │
│ │ Supplier terms/discount agreed│              │ │
│ │         VAT rate agreed       │              │ │
│ ├─────────────────────────────┼───────────────┤ │
│ │ Calculations: Price extensions  ①            │ │
│ │              Additions          ②            │ │
│ │                Discount                      │ │
│ │                   VAT                        │ │
│ ├─────────────────────────────────────────────┤ │
│ │ Exceptions  _____  │ │
│ │                                               │ │
│ │ Initials  _____  Date _____  │ │
│ │                                               │ │
│ │ Payment authorised  _____  Date _____ │ │
│ └─────────────────────────────────────────────┘ │
└─────────────────────────────────────────────────┘
```

(1)   The term **price extensions** means the multiplying of prices by quantities to give a net total figure for that item (before discounts and VAT). For example:

230m^2 Twist pile carpet @ £7.42 per m^2 = £1,706.60.

(2)   **Addition** is then necessary to add up the net total figures for all the items.

7.9   Frank processes some of the invoices which Ivory Carpets receives on 17 May 20X0.

Frank processes some of the invoices which Ivory Carpets receives on 17 May 20X0.

The first invoice is a **telephone bill,** for which no purchase order or GRN applies. Frank carries out the other checks detailed on the stamp and completes it as shown below.

RECEIVED	17 May 20X0	
Checked to Purchase Order No:		N/A
Prices		
Quantities		
Checked to GRN No:		N/A
Quantities		
In good condition		
Supplier terms/discount agreed		✓
VAT rate agreed		✓
Calculations: Price extensions		✓
Additions		✓
Discount		N/A
VAT		✓

Exceptions _____

Initials _____*F.O.*_____ Date __*17/5/X0*____

Payment authorised _____ Date _____

The details on a second invoice, from Walter Wall Carpeting Supplies Ltd, agree with GRN number 240229. When he finds the purchase order (number 104299), Frank finds that the order states a price of £7.84 excluding VAT per box of brass threshold strips, while the invoice shows a price of £8.29 for these items. 200 boxes were delivered and invoiced. Frank finds no other discrepancies or errors, but he decides not to complete the calculation checks until the discrepancy has been clarified. Frank completes the invoice stamp as shown below.

RECEIVED	17 May 20X0	
Checked to Purchase Order No:	1 0 4 2 9 9	
Prices		NO
Quantities		
Checked to GRN No:	2 4 0 2 2 9	
Quantities		✓
In good condition		✓
Supplier terms/discount agreed		✓
VAT rate agreed		✓
Calculations: Price extensions		
Additions		
Discount		
VAT		

Exceptions ___*Price does not agree with order*___

Initials _____ Date _____

Payment authorised _____ Date _____

BPP PUBLISHING

When he has finished checking all the invoices, Frank sorts them into two piles. One pile contains the invoices on which some further action must be taken. Frank keeps this pile and passes the other pile to Winston Peters, the Purchasing Manager, for authorisation. Winston will authorise all purchases of stocks, but will pass other items (eg the telephone bill) to other managers as appropriate. The authorised invoices will be entered in the accounting records (see Chapters 3 and 4) and then passed to the accounts department for payment.

8 ACTION TO DEAL WITH DISCREPANCIES

8.1 As shown in the above example, processing suppliers' invoices can bring to light discrepancies and apparent errors.

- **Prices** on the invoices are not those previously agreed with the supplier
- **Calculations** on invoices are incorrect
- An invoice for goods or services for which there is **no record of receipt**
- The same goods or services **invoiced twice** in error
- **Incorrect rate of discount or VAT** shown on an invoice

8.2 Once the suppliers' invoices have been processed, and items containing discrepancies or errors identified, some action is necessary to sort out the errors. Otherwise the supplier will continue to treat the invoices as outstanding and issue reminder notices in due course.

8.3 Simple queries can be dealt with by a **telephone call** to the sales ledger department of the supplier. More complex queries, or queries involving large amounts, may need to be dealt with by **letter**.

8.4 Once an invoice has been received, it should **never be destroyed** or **forgotten** just because it contains an error. For many of the discrepancies which arise, the supplier needs to issue a **credit note** for the amount of the error.

8.5 EXAMPLE: REQUESTING A CREDIT NOTE

Frank Okara takes the following action regarding the discrepancies which he identified in example 7.8.

Ivory Carpets received an invoice showing a price which disagreed with the price shown on the purchase order. Perhaps the purchase order is wrong. It could be based on an out of date quotation or price list and does not take account of a subsequent price rise.

Frank sees that the purchase order was signed by the Purchasing Manager. He telephones him and explains the query. The manager refers him to a quotation from Walter Wall Carpeting Supplies dated 27 February 20X0. The quotation gives a price of £7.84 for the items, as shown on the purchase order. Frank notes that the quotation states that the price quoted applies for a period of three months from the date of the quotation.

Frank drafts the letter below for the Purchasing Manager to sign.

IVORY CARPETS LIMITED
24 Greensea Avenue, Brighton BN4 7ER

Walter Wall Carpeting Supplies Ltd
72 Eckersley Road
London SW19 4PN   17 May 20X0

Dear Sirs

Re your invoice number 7242

Your quotation dated 27 February 20X0 stated a price of £7.84 for boxes of brass threshold strips (your reference X18), and indicated that this price applies until 26 May 20X0. Your invoice number 7242 shows a price of £8.29 for this item.

Please would you issue a credit note to us for the amount by which we have been overcharged.

Yours faithfully,

Winston Peters

Winston Peters
Purchasing Manager

Frank files the queried invoice with a copy of the above letter, in a lever arch file marked 'invoices awaiting credit'.

8.6 Many businesses **delay payment of a supplier's invoice on which a query is outstanding** until the query has been resolved. Delaying payment is, after all, likely to help to persuade the supplier to deal with the query promptly!

Activity 2.5   **Level: Assessment**

During April 20X7, a further two purchase orders are issued by Ordram Quick Ltd to Lampley Laminates (Activity 2.1), requesting the following goods for delivery by 30 April.

Purchase order no 1241 (14 April 20X7)

100m^2 Ply-mel 30
200m^2 Trilam 24

Purchase order no 1274 (21 April 20X7)

250m^2 Enlam 20 - polar white
150m^2 Ply-mel 20
150m^2 Ply-mel 30

Goods inwards documentation up to 30 April 20X7 relating to goods received (including deliveries in response to purchase order no 1233) from Lampley Laminates is set out below.

Two invoices received from Lampley Laminates are also shown.

Tasks

Check the supplier's invoice and the goods received documentation. You should also check whether all goods which have been ordered have been delivered during April.

Indicate clearly what checks you perform. Note any discrepancies or unusual features and indicate what action is to be taken in respect of them.

Calculate the amount of any necessary adjustment arising from any pricing or calculation errors which you find on the invoices.

ORDRAM QUICK
GOODS RECEIVED NOTE

No: G924
Date: *14 April 20X7*

Item	Code	Quantity	P.O. No.
Onyxel Grade B	*0048*	*200m²*	*1233*
Trilam 22	*7050*	*180m²*	*1233*
Trilam 24	*7060*	*200m²*	*1241*

Comments
  50% of Onyxel sheets (ie 100m²) damaged and unuseable.

ORDRAM QUICK
GOODS RECEIVED NOTE

No: G977
Date: *19 April 20X7*

Item	Code	Quantity	P.O. No.
Enlam 20 - polar white	*9248*	*250m²*	*1233*
Enlam 25 - polar white	*9252*	*300m²*	*1233*

Comments
  Purchase order copy (1233) not found.

ORDRAM QUICK
GOODS RECEIVED NOTE

No: H010
Date: *April 20X7*

Item	Code	Quantity	P.O. No.
Plymel 30	*1041*	*150m²*	*1274*
Onyxel Grade B	*0048*	*200m²*	*1233*

Comments
  Onyxel - to complete PO 1233 and replace damaged goods.

 AMPLEY  AMINATES

47 GORSE ROAD, LAMPLEY LM2 9PR (Reg. office)

SALES INVOICE   No. 7221

VAT No.: 742 4424 40   Date/Taxpoint: *19 April 20X7*

Item	Your ref.	Qty	Unit price £ p	Total £ p
0048 Onyxel Grade B	1233	200m^2	2 . 85	570 . 00
9248 Enlam 20 – polar white	1233	250m^2	5 . 70	1425 . 00
7050 Trilam 22	1233	180m^2	5 . 18	932 . 40
7060 Trilam 24	1241	200m^2	5 . 62	1124 . 00

Total	4051 . 40
Discount	40 . 51
	4010 . 89
VAT @ 17.5%	701 . 90
Amount due	4712 . 79

To: Purchase Ledger Dept.
    Ordram Quick Ltd
    Unit 7, Aurora Business Park
    Lampley LM9 9AS

 **AMPLEY** 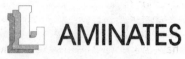 **AMINATES**

47 GORSE ROAD LAMPLEY LM2 9PR (Reg. office)

SALES INVOICE

No. 7264

VAT No: 742 4424 40

Date/Taxpoint: **30 April 20X7**

Item	Your ref.	Qty	Unit price £	p	Total £	p
0048 Onyxel Grade B	1233	$200m^2$	2	85	570	00
1041 Plymel 20	1274	$150m^2$	4	08	612	00
1042 Plymel 30	1274	$150m^2$	4	41	661	50
9248 Enlam 20 - polar white	1274	$250m^2$	5	70	1425	00
9252 Enlam 25 - polar white	1233	$300m^2$	5	70	1710	00

	£	p
Total	4978	50
Discount	49	78
	4928	72
VAT @ 17.5%	862	52
Amount due	5791	24

To: Purchase Ledger Dept.
    Ordram Quick Ltd
    Unit 7, Aurora Business Park
    Lampley LM9 9AS

Activity 2.6   Level: Assessment

Purchase order forms are produced in sequentially numbered 4-part sets. The first part (copy 1) is sent to the supplier; the second (copy 2) is retained in the purchasing department for their records; the third is sent to the goods inwards department; and the fourth is sent to the purchase ledger section of the accounts department.

Purchase invoices are checked to purchase orders and then to goods received notes. Other checks are also carried out before purchase invoices are approved.

The organisation has announced a suggestions scheme inviting employees to suggest improvements which might enhance efficiency in the organisation. A colleague of yours tells you that he is thinking of making a suggestion to the scheme about the processing of purchase invoices. He feels that four-part purchase invoices are an example of unnecessary 'red tape'. He intends to suggest that the third and fourth parts of the purchase order form be scrapped. Only copies 1 and 2 are needed, he says, as all purchase invoices are checked against goods received notes in any case.

Task

Write a memo to your colleague on this matter.

Will you support your colleague's suggestion? Are there any reasons for retaining the third and fourth parts of the purchase order form?

Activity 2.7   Level: Assessment

You receive a credit note from a supplier relating to goods worth £100, excluding VAT at 17½%.

(a)   What is the significance of a credit note?

(b)   List *three* situations which give rise to a supplier sending you a credit note.

(c)   Most of the following assist you in checking a credit note. Say which will help you, and why.

   (i)   Purchase invoice received
   (ii)   Goods received note
   (iii) Sales despatch note issued by you
   (iv)   Goods returned note (drawn up by you)
   (v)   Debit note (drawn up by you)
   (vi)   Purchase order
   (vii) Supplier's price list
   (viii) Your pocket calculator

Key learning points

*   Businesses make **purchases** of different kinds. **Raw materials** form part of the trading stock of the company. There may also be other **business expenses**. A purchase is called '**capital expenditure**' if it results in the acquisition of fixed assets or an improvement in the earning capacity of fixed assets.

*   **Quotations** or **price lists** will be obtained before a purchase order is made. A copy of the **purchase order** will be kept for checking later with the invoice.

*   **A business needs to keep track of the goods which it receives.** A warehouse will keep documents to record receipt of goods and any discrepancies or damaged goods. It may be **more difficult to keep a track of all the services** which a business receives, but this is important too for checking later with invoices.

*   There are two kinds of **discount.**

- ○ **Trade discount:** a reduction in the cost of the goods
- ○ **Cash or settlement discount:** a reduction in the amount paid to the supplier

- • VAT rules are complex. The main ones to remember here are:

  - ○ **Output VAT** is charged on sales and **input VAT** is paid on purchases

  - ○ **VAT invoices** must contain specific information to enable a purchaser to reclaim input VAT

- • **Procedures should exist to ensure that the business only pays what it should for goods and services received.** Suppliers' invoices and credit notes will be checked against order documentation and evidence that the goods or services invoiced have been received in good condition.

- • **All calculations on suppliers' invoices and credit notes need to be checked for accuracy.** The calculations to be checked will include prices, price extensions, discounts and VAT calculations.

- • Discrepancies and inaccuracies which may be found could include **incorrect calculations, goods invoiced** which have **not been received, duplicated invoices** or **incorrectly calculated VAT** or **discounts.**

Quick quiz

1   Why should a purchase order be signed?

2   What is a goods received note?

3   Why should GRNs be sequentially pre-numbered?

4   List four checks that must be carried out on invoices and credit notes.

5   What does 'price extensions' mean?

6   What might a business do to encourage a supplier to deal with its query promptly?

7   What is input tax?

Answers to quick quiz

1   So that the supplier knows that the order is valid, ie only authorised orders are made.

2   A document recording what goods have been received in the purchaser's warehouse.

3   So that they can be checked easily when a supplier's invoice is received. Also to prevent theft of GRNs to support a fraud.

4   (i)   Check invoices to orders.
    (ii)   Match invoices against GRNs.
    (iii)   Check calculations on invoices.
    (iv)   Match credit notes against goods returned.

5   Multiplying unit prices by quantities to give a net total figure.

6   Delay payment of the invoice until the query is settled.

7   Input tax is VAT paid on purchases.

3 Purchase and purchase returns day books

This chapter contains

1   Introduction

2   What is the purchase day book?

3   What is the purchase returns day book?

4   Entering purchase transactions in the day books

5   Methods of coding data

6   Posting the day book totals

7   Manual and computerised accounting systems

8   Batch processing and control totals

Learning objectives

On completion of this chapter you will be able to:

- Record suppliers' invoices in the purchase day book
- Record credit notes in the purchase returns day book
- Post the day book totals to the main ledger

Performance criteria

2.1.4 Documents are correctly entered as primary records according to organisational procedures

2.1.5 Entries are coded and recorded in the appropriate ledger

Range statement

2.1.1 Documents: suppliers' invoices, credit notes

2.1.3 Primary records: purchase and returns day book

Knowledge and understanding

- Basic law relating to data protection
- Double entry bookkeeping
- Methods of coding data
- Operation of manual and computerised accounting systems

1 INTRODUCTION

1.1 A business needs to keep track of **all of its purchases** combined, so that it knows how much it owes to particular suppliers at any one time.

(a) A business will receive a number of invoices (with perhaps some credit notes) from each of its suppliers each month. It will be simpler to administer if the business **makes a single payment** monthly rather than paying the supplier separately for each invoice.

(b) A supplier's terms of business will usually allow the business some time to pay (say 30 or 60 days). It makes sense to take advantage of these terms and **to pay close to the end of the credit period allowed**.

(c) A business needs to keep a **record of the total purchases** made in each period (eg each month, quarter or year).

1.2 Taking advantage of suppliers' allowed credit terms will help the 'cash flow' of the business, because it can keep the money due to the supplier for longer. If the business pays its suppliers earlier than it needs to, it may incur the following.

- More interest payable on a larger bank overdraft
- Lose out on interest earned on a positive bank balance

2 WHAT IS THE PURCHASE DAY BOOK?

2.1 The first step in the process is the **recording of the source documents** - the suppliers' invoices - in the **purchase day book**.

The function of the purchase day book

> **KEY TERM**
>
> The **purchase day book** is used to keep a list of all of the invoices received from suppliers of goods and services to the business. It is a 'book of prime entry' or a 'primary record' and not a ledger account.

2.2 Later in this chapter, we shall see how the information collected in the purchase day book is posted in the ledger by the double entry system of bookkeeping.

Activity 3.1   **Level: Pre-assessment**

Which one of the following would you expect to see in a purchase day book?

(a) Cash payments
(b) Invoices received from suppliers
(c) Cash purchases
(d) Personal accounts
(e) Purchase ledger control accounts

2.3 EXAMPLE: PURCHASE DAY BOOK

An extract from a purchase day book for Doppel Printers Ltd is shown below.

Date	Ref	Supplier name	Supplier a/c no	Total before VAT £	VAT £	Invoice total £
10.1.X1	1423	V Princely	4009	152.00	26.60	178.60
	1424	Grantcroft Ltd	5020	28.00	4.90	32.90
	1425	Midnorth Electric plc	4010	116.80	20.44	137.24
	1426	Hartley & Co	5008	100.00	17.50	117.50
	1427	Cardright Ltd	3972	278.00	48.65	326.65
				674.80	118.09	792.89

2.4 The purchase invoices for any one day will be from lots of different suppliers and, therefore, they are not sequentially numbered. Some organisations assign **sequential numbers to purchase invoices** (using a stamp or a sticker), as Doppel Printers Ltd has (1423 – 1427). This can help to ensure that all purchase invoices are included in the records.

3 WHAT IS THE PURCHASE RETURNS DAY BOOK?

3.1 A business may return goods to suppliers and will expect to be issued with credit notes.

> **KEY TERM**
>
> The **purchase returns day book** lists credit notes received in respect of purchase returns in chronological order.

3.2 Columns in the purchase returns day book will record similar details to those in the purchase day book illustrated in Paragraph 2.3 above.

3.3 Goods may be returned to the supplier in the following cases.

- Goods that are **faulty** or **damaged** and a credit note requested

- Goods purchased on a '**sale or return**' basis are returned if they cannot be sold

- Goods may be returned in good condition but **surplus to requirements** at the supplier's discretion

3.4 A business does not have to keep a separate purchase returns day book. Many businesses record credit notes for goods returned as a negative in the purchase day book.

Activity 3.2   **Level: Pre-assessment**

Which of the following cases would you classify as a purchase return? (*Helping hand:* there may be more than one right answer.)

(a) Goods purchased by a customer and returned to you.

(b) You have been billed twice, by accident, for a single amount of goods, and you return the superfluous purchase invoice.

(c) You have received some goods which are faulty and you send them back. You have posted the invoice received in respect of the goods.

(d) A customer sends back some sub-standard goods to you.

(e) A supplier sends back some goods to you which you have delivered there by mistake, thinking the supplier was in fact a customer.

(f) An item of stock is damaged in a fire at your warehouse and you have to go back to the original supplier to order a replacement.

(g) You question an invoice because you have been billed for items which you have not ordered, and which you have not received.

(h) You have been delivered a quantity of goods in excess of your requirements. The supplier agrees that you can return them.

4 ENTERING PURCHASE TRANSACTIONS IN THE DAY BOOKS

4.1 **Writing up the day books**

- In a **manual system,** invoice details will be entered by hand in the purchase day book and credit note details in the purchase returns day book

- In a **computerised purchase system,** purchase invoice and credit note details will be entered directly into the computer records

Analysis of purchases

4.2 Many purchase day books have further columns which split the purchases into different categories.

4.3 EXAMPLE: ANALYSING PURCHASES

We can add additional columns to the purchase day book at Paragraph 2.3.

Doppel Printers Ltd makes purchases of raw materials for stock which include paper, card and ink. The company wants to analyse its other purchases into 'electricity' and 'other' categories. The purchases made on 10 January 20X1 consisted of the following.

Ref	Supplier name	Supplier a/c no	Details
1423	V Princeley	4009	Paper
1424	Grantcroft Ltd	5020	Ink
1425	Midnorth Electric plc	4010	Electricity
1426	Hartley & Co	5008	Desk fans for administrative office
1427	Cardright Ltd	3972	Card

The invoices can be analysed in the purchase day book as follows (we have omitted the column for supplier name, which can be identified from the supplier account number).

PURCHASE DAY BOOK
Date: 10.1.X1

Ref	Supplier	Net total £	VAT £	Gross total £	Paper £	Card $_n$ £	Ink £	Electricity £	Other £
1423	4009	152.00	26.60	178.60	152.00				
1424	5020	28.00	4.90	32.90			28.00		
1425	4010	116.80	20.44	137.24				116.80	
1426	5008	100.00	17.50	117.50					100.00
1427	3972	278.00	48.65	326.65		278.00			
		674.80	118.09	792.89	152.00	278.00	28.00	116.80	100.00

Note that the analysis columns show amounts *exclusive* of VAT.

4.4 **How a purchase is analysed** will depend upon the nature of the business. In a television and hi-fi shop, purchases of paper are not purchases of stocks. It is likely that the paper is for office use and so is analysed as stationery or office expenses.

4.5 Some businesses keep separate day books for stock purchases (the purchase day book) and for expenses (the **expenses day book**).

4.6 A spreadsheet can be used to analyse the information desired in the purchase day book. Alternatively, an analysed purchase day book might be available in a computerised accounting package.

5 METHODS OF CODING DATA

5.1 Each account in an accounting system has a **unique code** used to identify the correct account for a posting (to be keyed into the computer if the system is computerised). If there are two suppliers called Jim Jones, you can only tell their accounts apart by a different code.

5.2 Coding also saves time in copying out data because **codes are shorter** than 'longhand' descriptions. For the same reason, and also to save storage space, computer systems make use of coded data.

5.3 In purchase accounting systems, the most obvious examples of codes are as follows.

- Supplier account numbers
- General ledger account numbers

- Stock item codes

These are all codes a business sets up and applies internally. External codes which affect the business include **bank account numbers** and **bank sort codes**.

5.4 Various coding systems (or combinations of them) may be used when designing codes. The systems are described below.

Sequence codes

5.5 **Sequence codes** make no attempt to classify the item to be coded. It is simply given the next available number in a rising sequence. New items can only be inserted at the end of the list and therefore the codes for similar items may be very different. For example:

1 = saucepans
2 = kettles
3 = pianos
4 = dusters

5.6 Sequence codes are rarely used when a large number of items are involved, except for document numbering (eg invoice numbers).

Block codes

5.7 **Block codes** provide a different sequence for each different group of items. For example , suppliers may be divided up according to area.

North East	code numbers 10,000-19,999
North West	code numbers 20,000-29,999
Scotland	code numbers 30,000-39,999

The coding of supplier accounts is then sequential within each block.

Significant digit codes

5.8 **Significant digit codes** use some digits which are part of the description of the item being coded. An example is:

5000	Electric light bulbs
5025	25 watt
5040	40 watt
5060	60 watt
5100	100 watt
etc	

Hierarchical codes

5.9 **Hierarchical codes** are allocated on the basis of a tree structure, where the relationship between items is of utmost importance. A well known example is the Universal Decimal Code used by most libraries. For example:

5	Business
5 2	Finance
5 2 1	Cost accounting

5 2 1.4	Standard costing
5 2 1.4 7	Variance analysis
5 2 1.4 7 3	Fixed overhead variances

Faceted codes

5.10 **Faceted codes** consist of a number of sections, each section of the code representing a different feature of the item. For example in a clothing store there might be a code based on the following facets.

Garment type	Customer type	Colour	Size	Style

If SU stood for suit, M for man and B for blue, a garment could be given the code SU M B 40 17. Similarly ND F W 14 23 could stand for a woman's white nightdress size 14, style 23. One of the great advantages of this system is that the type of item can be recognised from the code.

Faceted codes may be entirely numeric. For example, a large international company allocates code numbers for each suppliers' representative.

Digit 1	Continent (eg America - 1, Europe - 2)
Digits 2/3	Country (eg England - 06)
Digit 4	Area (eg North - 3)
Digits 5/6	Representative's name (eg Mr J Walker - 14)

The code number is then expressed as 2/06/3/14.

Coding in the general ledger

5.11 A general ledger will consist of a **large number of coded accounts**. For example, part of a general ledger might be as follows.

Account code	Account name
100200	Plant and machinery (cost)
100300	Motor vehicles (cost)
300000	Total debtors
400000	Total creditors
500130	Wages and salaries
500140	Rent and rates
500150	Advertising expenses
500160	Bank charges
500170	Motor expenses
500180	Telephone expenses
600000	Sales
700000	Cash

5.12 A business will, of course, choose its own codes for its general ledger accounts. The codes given in the above table are purely imaginary.

Activity 3.3   **Level: Pre-assessment**

State what type of code is being used in paragraph 5.11 above. Explain your answer.

---

6 POSTING THE DAY BOOK TOTALS

6.1 We have seen above how the details of purchase transactions are entered into the purchase day book.

6.2 We will now look at the recording of the information in the accounts of the business. The **posting** from the purchase day book to the purchase ledger and the main ledger is very important for you to understand.

Recording transactions in personal accounts for creditors

6.3 A business needs to keep a record of all the purchase invoices received, so that it knows **what it owes to each supplier.**

6.4 Why do the day books not meet this need? The answer is because they provide only a **chronological** listing of purchase transactions. This could involve large numbers of purchase invoices and credit notes each day or each week. It is not practical for firms to work out from the day books alone how much they owe a particular supplier.

6.5 There is a **purchase ledger** (or 'creditors ledger' or 'bought ledger') **containing personal accounts for each trade creditor or supplier of the business.**

6.6 As each invoice or credit note is recorded in the day books, it is also entered in the personal purchase ledger account of the supplier. The personal accounts in the purchase ledger are **memorandum** accounts, not part of the double entry system.

Posting totals to the general ledger: double entry recording of purchases

6.7 In the general ledger, there is a **creditors control account** (or 'purchase ledger control account'). This records **in total** the amounts which are posted individually to the personal accounts in the purchase ledger.

6.8 When a business purchases something on credit from a supplier, the double entry will be:

(a) a **credit** to the total creditors account (the 'control account')

(b) a **debit** to either:

    (i) purchases (a purchase for stock) or expenses (such as office stationery, electricity, rent)

or (ii) fixed assets (if the item is capital expenditure)

6.9 We can show the basic double entry as follows.

		£	£
DEBIT	Purchases/expenses/fixed asset account	X	
CREDIT	Total creditors account		X

6.10 There is a different expense **ledger account** for each expense shown in the profit and loss account, and also for capital expenditure on fixed assets.

Activity 3.4	**Level: Pre-assessment**

(a)   What is the double entry for posting invoices for goods received on credit?

(b)   What is a debit note?

VAT and purchases

6.11   In most businesses part of the amount due to the creditors is input VAT, which the suppliers charge to the purchasing business. The other side of the double entry for VAT is a **decrease** in the liability to HM Customs & Excise. So this is a **debit** to the VAT (control) account in the main ledger.

6.12   The double entry for **VAT and purchases** will therefore be as follows.

		£	£
DEBIT	Purchases/expenses account	X	
	VAT account	X	
CREDIT	Total creditors account		X

6.13   When we wish to record the **return** of goods, we want to 'reverse' the transaction (or the relevant part of the transaction). The double entry for **purchase returns including VAT** (credit notes received) will be as follows.

		£	£
DEBIT	Total creditors account	X	
CREDIT	VAT account		X
	Purchases/expenses account		X

6.14   **EXAMPLE: POSTING PURCHASES AND RETURNS**

Show the double entry postings for the purchases made at Paragraph 2.3 by Doppel Printers Ltd on 10 January 20X1. The following credit note (in respect of damaged paper) is shown in the purchase returns day book of Doppel Printers Ltd for 10 January 20X1.

				RDB07
Ref	*Supplier a/c no.*	*Net total*	*VAT*	*Gross total*
		£	£	£
C014	4009	30.00	5.25	35.25

6.15   **SOLUTION**

First show the posting summary for the purchases. Check that you can see how the necessary information is derived from the analysed day book shown at Paragraph 4.3.

		£	£
DEBIT	Paper account	152.00	
	Card account	278.00	
	Ink account	28.00	
	Electricity account	116.80	
	Other expenses account	100.00	
	VAT account	118.09	
CREDIT	Total creditors account		792.89
		792.89	792.89

And now the purchase return.

		£	£
DEBIT	Total creditors account	35.25	
CREDIT	VAT account		5.25
	Paper account		30.00
		35.25	35.25

Doppel Printers Ltd might use a posting summary like the one below.

DOPPEL PRINTERS LIMITED
General ledger postings sheet

Account name	Account code	General ledger Dr £	Dr p	General ledger Cr £	Cr p
Total creditors	70100	35	25	792	89
Paper	02400	152	00		
Electricity	03215	116	80		
Other expenses	03428	100	00		
Paper returns	02401			30	00
VAT	70200	118	09	5	25
Card	02500	278	00		
Ink	02600	28	00		
TOTALS		828	14	828	14

Posted by ............A.B............   Date ....10/1/X1............

6.16 What entries are to be made in the memorandum purchase ledger? Using the details from the analyses shown at Paragraph 4.3 on purchases and at Paragraph 6.14 on purchase returns, we have the following postings to make to the purchase ledger.

Ref	Account name	Account code	Debit £	Credit £
1423	V Princeley	4009		178.60
1424	Grantcroft Ltd	5020		32.90
1425	Midnorth Elec plc	4010		137.24
1426	Hartley & Co	5008		117.50
1427	Cardright Ltd	3972		326.65
C014	V Princeley	4009	35.25	
			35.25	792.89

Suppliers' accounts as part of the double entry

6.17 In some computer-based accounting systems, there will be a separate account for each supplier in the general ledger. In such an integrated system, there will be **no**

need for a creditors control account. The individual suppliers' accounts will form part of the double entry rather than being 'memorandum' accounts. This will be dealt with in more detail in Unit 3 of your course.

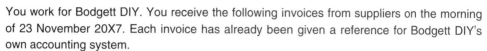

Activity 3.5   Level: Assessment

You work for Bodgett DIY. You receive the following invoices from suppliers on the morning of 23 November 20X7. Each invoice has already been given a reference for Bodgett DIY's own accounting system.

Tasks

(a)   Post the invoices to the purchase day book, using the sheet provided on Page 52.

(b)   Set out the *double entry* for these transactions, assuming that totals are posted to the general ledger at the end of each working day. Use the *account postings* form provided on Page 53.

Supplier account codes
Macin   1310
Payper, Overr, Crackes   1510
Pitiso Tools   1550
Throne Bathware   2010

Nominal ledger account codes
VAT   0694
Total creditors (purchase ledger control account)   0730
Tool purchases   4000
Painting and decorating purchases   5000
Bathroom items purchases   6000

Part A: Goods and services received

<table>
<tr><td>To: Purchase ledger
Bodgett's DIY
Broad Street
Stornaway
ORKNEY</td><td colspan="2" align="center">PITISO TOOLS

Zhivago House
Lawrence Street, Edinburgh
Phone: 01939 72101</td><td>SALES
INVOICE

No: 21379
Date: 21/11/97
Tax point: 21/11/97</td></tr>
</table>

Stock code	Item	Quantity	£ p	£ p
0105	Hammer drills	20	70.00	1,400.00
0210	Hacksaw	10	5.00	50.00
0340	Electric screwdriver	15	7.00	105.00
0560	Hammers (10 in)	7	1.50	10.50
0791	Vices - metal	4	3.95	15.80
				1,581.30
		VAT 17 ½%		276.72
		TOTAL PAYABLE		1,858.02

Delivery

- as above

Bodgett's reference number 712

Pitiso Tools Ltd Registered Office: Zhivago House, Lawrence Street, Edinburgh
Reg No: 322 1014   VAT: 875 2121 91

MACIN

Macin (UK) Ltd
Northern Region
Convention Street
GLASGOW

(Phone 01838 89414)
VAT reg 389 4121 05

To: Purchase Ledger
Bodgett's DIY Superstore
Broad Street
STORNAWAY

Invoice No: 84/Q	Customer No: BODG 1
Date/tax point: 21/11/97	Terms: 28 days

Items ordered	Quantity	Unit price £ p	Total £ p
Paint stripper PYB75	200 tins	4.00	800.00
White gloss paint DUL10	400 x 1 litre	12.00	4,800.00
Primer SX91	800 x 0.5 litre	5.00	4,000.00
Wallpaper paste 'STICKO-2000'	500 packets	3.50	1,750.00

Total			11,350.00
VAT @ 17½%			1,986.25
Total payable	*Bodgett's reference number: 713*	⟶	13,336.25

Reg office: Water Street, Rainham, Essex
Reg no: 528 1000

THRONE Bathware

Habsburg Street
Windsor
BERKS
01421 374911

VAT reg 413 9721 08

SALES INVOICE

No: 4963

Date/tax point: 21/11/X7

Purchase Ledger Bodgett's DIY Superstore Broad Street STORNAWAY	£ p	Quantity	£ p
Wash basin 12 x 15	25.90	2	51.80
Kitchen sink 'Excelsior'	31.20	3	93.60
Steel taps	7.40	7	51.80
Gold plated taps	60.50	6	363.00
Baths	200.20	4	800.80
Micro-whirlpool bath	250.10	1	250.10
'Luxor' shower units	70.30	5	351.50
'Standard' shower units	50.30	4	201.20
Total			2,163.80
VAT @ 17½%			378.66
Total including VAT			2,542.46

Bodgett's reference number: 714

Reg office: Habsburg Street, Windsor, Berks
Reg no: 7000

Bodgett DIY Broad Street Stornaway ORKNEY	Delivery if different

PAPER, OVERR, CRACKES HOME FURNISHINGS

Plastery House, Rachman Street, Inverness
Phone: (01563) 810372

SALES INVOICE: 0711	DATE/TAX POINT: 21/11/X7

Item	Code	Quantity	£ p	£ p
Towel rails for bathroom	B121	1	16.90	16.90
Wallpaper 4 x 20 metres	H272	10	8.50	85.00
Wallpaper 4 X 40 metres	H274	15	16.25	243.75
Curtain rails 'A'	H351	10	20.00	200.00
Curtain rails 'B'	H352	12	35.00	420.00
				965.65
Value Added Tax				17½ %
				168.98
Total payable				1,134.63

Bodgett's reference number: 715

VAT registration no: 434 5567 89

	A	B	C	D	E	F	G	H	I	J	K	L	M
1	Bodgett Purchase day book analysis												Page 41
2	Date	Ref	Supplier	Supplier account	Total	VAT	Purchase cost	Tools	Painting& decorating	Bathroom items			
3													
4	23/11/X7												
5													
6													
7													
8													
9													
10													
11													
12													
13													
14	Total for 23/11/X7												

ACCOUNT POSTINGS			DR	CR
Account code	Ref		£ p	£ p

DATE

Posted by ....

Activity 3.6   **Level: Assessment**

Tasks

(a) Enter the details supplied below into the *purchase returns day book* of Bodgett DIY for 23 November 20X7, using the sheet provided on page 55.

(b) Write the necessary double entry on the account postings form provided on page 56.

Items to be entered to purchase returns day book

1   A consignment of bathroom units from Dothelot DIY was found to be infested with woodworm. It was billed on invoice 7912, and the purchase day book reference is 613. The amount is valued at £176.25 inclusive of VAT.

2   Some paint stripper bought from C and R Builders Merchants Wholesalers plc had to be returned because it did not comply with the safety standards specified by Bodgett's DIY a while before. The amount was £221 excluding VAT. This was on supplier invoice 794, purchase day book reference 612.

3   Some items of bathroom equipment from The House Foundation had to be returned as they were leaking. The value of the goods returned, excluding VAT, was £959.59. This was found on supplier invoice 91113, purchase day book reference 627.

Dothelot, C and R, and The House Foundation will be sent debit notes number 64, 65 and 66 respectively dealing with these items.

 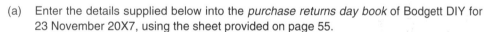

Part A: Goods and services received

Account numbers in Bodgett's accounting system are as follows.

Purchase ledger account codes

C and R	7211
Dothelot	8523
The House Foundation	6644

General ledger account codes

Purchases returns (bathware)	6050
Purchases returns (painting and decorating)	5050
Purchases returns (tools)	4050
VAT	0694
Total creditors	0730

	A	B	C	D	E	F	G	H	I	J	K	L	M
1	Bodgett Purchase returns day book												Page 5
2	Date	Debit note ref	Supplier	Supplier account	Total	VAT	Purchase return total	Tools	Painting& decorating	Bathroom items	Purchase ref		
3													
4													
5	23/11/X7												
6													
7													
8													
9													
10													
11													
12													
13													
14	Total for 23/11/X7												

BPP PUBLISHING

ACCOUNT POSTINGS			DR	CR
Account code	Ref		£ p	£ p
DATE				
Posted by				

7   MANUAL AND COMPUTERISED ACCOUNTING SYSTEMS

7.1   It is important to realise that all of the books of prime entry and the ledgers may be either hand-written books or computer records. Most businesses use computers in some way.

7.2   All computer activity can be divided into three processes.

Process	Activity
Input	Entering data from original documents
Processing	Entering up books and ledgers and generally sorting the input information
Output	Producing any report desired by the managers of the business, including financial statements

Activity 3.7   **Level: Pre-assessment**

Your friend Ivan Issue believes that computerised accounting systems are more trouble than they are worth because 'you never know what is going on inside that funny box'.

Task

Explain briefly why computers might be useful in accounting.

Computers are discussed in detail in the Unit 20 Working With Information Technology Interactive Text.

Refer back to your Unit 1 text to revise the law relating to data protection.

8   BATCH PROCESSING AND CONTROL TOTALS

KEY TERM

Batch processing is where similar transactions are gathered into batches, and then each batch is sorted and processed by the computer.

8.1   Inputting individual invoices into a computer for processing can be time consuming and expensive. Instead invoices can be gathered into a **batch** and **input and processed all together**. Batches can vary in size, depending on the type and volume of transactions, and on any limit imposed by the system on batch sizes. This type of processing is less time consuming than **transaction processing,** where transactions are processed individually as they arise.

KEY TERM

Control totals are used to make sure that there have been no errors when the batch is input. A control total is used to make sure that the total value of transactions input is the same as that previously calculated.

8.2   As an example, say a batch of 30 sales invoices has a manually calculated total value of £42,378.47. When the batch is input, the computer adds up the total value of the invoices input and produces a total of £42,378.47. The control totals agree and therefore no further action is required.

8.3   Should the control total **not agree** then checks would have to be carried out until the difference was found. It might be the case that an invoice had accidentally not been entered or the manual total had been incorrectly calculated.

Key learning points

*   The **purchase day book** lists the invoices received by a business from its credit suppliers. The **purchase returns day book** lists the credit notes received when goods are returned to suppliers. The purchase day book and the purchase returns day book are 'books of prime entry': transactions are recorded in them before being recorded elsewhere.

- An **expenses day book** may be kept to record expenses, as distinct from purchases for stock. Alternatively, all purchases of goods and services may be recorded in the same place.

- **Purchases and expenses may be analysed into different categories** in the day books. A **computer spreadsheet** might be used to produce an analysed purchase day book.

- The **day book totals** for purchases and purchase returns are **posted to the nominal (main) ledger creditors control account, the VAT control account and the relevant purchases and expense accounts.**

- Expenses accounts will include capital expenditure (fixed assets), as well as business expenses (such as administrative expenses). The **amounts owed to individual creditors** are **entered in the purchase ledger personal accounts** (where these are maintained as **memorandum accounts** separate from the nominal ledger).

Quick quiz

1 What is the purchase day book used for?

2 What does the purchase returns day book do?

3 What is the double entry for a credit purchase?

4 What is the double entry where the credit purchase includes VAT?

5 What is the double entry for purchase returns with VAT?

Answers to quick quiz

1 To keep a list of all the invoices received from suppliers of goods or services to the business.

2 It lists credit notes received in respect of purchase returns in chronological order.

3 DEBIT   Purchases
   CREDIT   Creditors

4 DEBIT   Purchases (VAT exclusive amount)
   DEBIT   VAT
   CREDIT   Creditors (VAT inclusive amount)

5 DEBIT   Creditors (VAT inclusive)
   CREDIT   Purchase returns/Purchases (VAT exclusive)
   CREDIT   VAT

4 The purchase ledger

This chapter contains

1 Introduction

2 Personal accounts for suppliers

3 Maintaining supplier records

4 Recording transactions in the purchase ledger

5 Payments to suppliers

6 The age analysis of creditors and other reports

7 Contra entries with the sales ledger

Learning objectives

On completion of this chapter you will be able to:

- Record transactions in the purchase ledger
- Produce age analysis of creditors and other reports
- Contra entries with the sales ledger

Performance criteria

2.1.5   Entries are coded and recorded in the appropriate ledger

Range statement

2.1.2   Discounts: settlement

2.1.4   Ledger: main ledger, subsidiary ledger, integrated ledger

Knowledge and understanding

- Automated payments: CHAPS, BACS, direct debits, standing orders
- Double entry bookkeeping
- Operation of manual and computerised accounting systems
- Relationship between accounting system and ledger

BPP PUBLISHING

1 INTRODUCTION

1.1 The purchase day books provide a chronological record of the invoices and credit notes received by a business from all credit suppliers. Each supplier also has a personal account in the purchase ledger.

1.2 **Reasons for separate personal accounts**

- If a supplier requests **payment of the full balance due to him**

- To check that the monthly supplier's **statement of account** is correct

- To maintain a **complete record** of the items making up the balance owed to each supplier, so that **appropriate payments** can be made

- To make **monthly payments** covering a number of invoices, rather than each invoice separately

> **KEY TERM**
>
> The personal accounts showing how much is owed to each credit supplier of the business are contained in the **purchase ledger**.

> **DEVOLVED ASSESSMENT ALERT**
>
> The AAT have indicated that they will use the following terms in assessments.
>
> - Main ledger (usually referred to as the general or nominal ledger)
>
> - Subsidiary ledger (purchase or creditors ledger for this Unit)
>
> - Integrated ledger (all accounts contained within one ledger)

The purchase ledger (subsidiary ledger)

1.3 **Summary of entries in the ledger**

- Invoices are entered on the **credit** side of the supplier account in the purchase ledger (see Chapter 3).

- Credit notes received are entered on the **debit** side of the suppliers' ledger account (see Chapter 3).

- Payments made to suppliers go on the **debit** side of the relevant supplier account (see this chapter).

- Discounts received for prompt payment (cash discounts) are entered as **debits** (see this chapter).

2 PERSONAL ACCOUNTS FOR SUPPLIERS

2.1 The entries recorded in a supplier's personal account can be represented by a 'T'-account, as follows.

SUPPLIER ACCOUNT

On the debit side		On the credit side	
Purchase returns	X	Invoices received	X
Payments made	X		
Discounts received	X		

2.2   An example of a purchase ledger account is shown below.

COOK & CO   PL32

Date 20X2	Details	£	Date 20X2	Detail	£
15 March	Purchase returns PRDB 21	50.00	15 March	Balance b/d	200.00
15 March	Cash	135.00	15 March	Invoice rec'd PDB 37	315.00
15 March	Discount rec'd	15.00			
16 March	Balance c/d	315.00			
		515.00			515.00
			16 March	Balance b/d	315.00

Debit balances in the purchase ledger

2.3   If we pay more than £315 to Cook & Co, we will be left with a net debit balance on Cook & Co's personal account. For instance, if we pay £375, there will be a net debit balance of £60. This indicates that the creditor owes us £60.

2.4   **Debit balances** in the purchase ledger are unusual, but they can sometimes arise.

- **Deposit** paid in advance of receipt of the goods
- **Overpayment** of the creditor's balance made in error
- **Credit note** received after full payment has been made of the balance

2.5   If debit balances are arising on purchase ledger accounts frequently, some **investigation** may be called for. The occurrence of debit balances could indicate that procedures in the purchase ledger department need to be improved.

Organisations not needing a purchase ledger

2.6   Maintaining a separate purchase ledger is a waste of time for businesses with very few credit purchases. Examples include small shops, clubs and associations. Any credit purchases will be posted direct to the **general ledger (main ledger) accounts**.

Trade creditors

2.7   The purchase ledger contains the personal accounts of creditors for the supply of both goods and services. It will not normally contain balances for **all** types of creditor. The purchase ledger will normally cover only the **trade creditors** of the business.

KEY TERM

Trade creditors consist of those liabilities which are related to the trade of the business.

2.8 Trade creditors include suppliers of the **trading stocks** of the business. It also includes suppliers of other goods, such as **stationery**, and services, eg telephone, electricity and the garage which repairs the business' vehicles.

Other creditors

2.9 **Other creditors** are not normally recorded in the purchase ledger and the balances owed are recorded directly in general ledger accounts for the purpose. Examples of 'other creditors' include the following.

- **Liabilities to pay wages and salaries**

- **Taxes** (eg PAYE) and other amounts (eg VAT) which are collected by the business on behalf of third parties

- Amounts payable *not* directly related to the main trade of the business, eg purchase of **fixed assets**

2.10 Some items of **overhead expenditure**, eg rent and rates, are treated as trade creditors in some businesses, while others treat them as other creditors.

Activity 4.1   **Level: Pre-assessment**

(a)   What is the status of a trade creditor in the accounts of a business?

    (i)   An asset
    (ii)   A liability
    (iii)   An expense
    (iv)   An item of revenue

(b)   Which of the following accounts are not normally found in a purchase ledger (ie which are *trade* creditors)?

    (i)   Personal accounts for suppliers of subcomponents
    (ii)   Inland Revenue
    (iii)   Customs & Excise for VAT
    (iv)   Suppliers of raw materials stocks
    (v)   Bank overdraft
    (vi)   Long-term bank loan
    (vii)   Telephone expenses
    (viii)   Drawings
    (ix)   Proprietor's capital

---

3   MAINTAINING SUPPLIER RECORDS

Opening a new ledger account for a supplier

3.1 Opening a ledger account for a new supplier must be **authorised**. The procedures of a business should specify in detail the **level of authorisation** required. One reason why this is important is that frauds sometimes involve putting transactions through a dummy supplier account.

3.2 The purchase ledger system, usually computerised, will need to be able to create, delete and amend suppliers' details on the **supplier master file**. In a menu-driven purchase ledger system, an option on the purchase ledger system might produce the following menu.

1. Update account name/address
2. Ledger postings
3. Enquiries
4. Dispute/release
5. Creditors total

Option 1 will enable the user to do the following.

- Enter new supplier details, together with discount and trading terms
- Delete supplier accounts which are no longer required
- Amend details of existing suppliers, eg change of address

3.3 Each supplier in the purchase ledger has a **unique account number** chosen by the purchasing business. The fact that the number is unique means that the business can just use the account number to identify any particular supplier.

3.4 There may be good reasons for maintaining **more than one account** for a particular supplier, eg he supplies different categories of goods and services.

(a) A printing company might order its raw materials (paper and ink) from the same company which provides office stationery.

(b) The different types of purchases are posted to different accounts in the general ledger (eg the **paper and ink** and **stationery accounts**. So operating different accounts may avoid confusion.

3.5 The purchase ledger system should have a facility for recording **suppliers' credit limits**. This is used to warn the user if the total outstanding exceeds the credit limit. Payments to the supplier are needed before more orders are placed.

Deleting and amending existing accounts

3.6 Any supplier record no longer required should be **deleted**. It may be possible to specify that a supplier account is automatically deleted if the balance falls to zero. However, there are good reasons why you should not make use of such a facility.

- Retain supplier records on the ledger for future reference

- Avoid having to create a new supplier record when you start trading again with a supplier whose balance has fallen to zero

If a business makes numerous 'one-off' purchases the facility may help reduce the size of the supplier files and to make the ledger more manageable.

3.7 **Amending the supplier record** is achieved by entering the account number and altering the particular 'fields' of data concerned. Appropriate authorisation will be necessary in order to avoid fraud.

'Open item' and 'balance forward'

3.8 In a computerised purchase ledger package, and in most manual systems, the account may be either an '**open item**' or a '**balance forward**' type account.

- By the **open item method,** cash paid is matched directly against outstanding invoices. At the end of the period (say a month), any invoices remaining unpaid are carried forward to the next period. Most purchase ledger systems are of this type.

- By the **balance forward method,** cash paid is matched against the oldest outstanding invoices. At the end of the period, a balance is carried forward to the next period. A problem of this method is that parts of invoices will be carried forward.

Dividing the ledger

3.9 The purchase ledger may be **divided up into parts,** for administrative convenience. This may reduce the risk of fraud by having different clerks post different parts of the ledger. For example, there might be three purchase ledgers.

Purchase ledger 1, for suppliers with names beginning A-J
Purchase ledger 2, for suppliers with names beginning K-O
Purchase ledger 3, for suppliers with names beginning P-Z

Alternatively, the ledger might be divided by geographical region.

Activity 4.2   **Level: Pre-assessment**

You operate a computerised purchases ledger system, and are offered the following menu.

1	Account name and address update
2	Postings
3	Enquiries
4	Dispute
5	Creditors total

(a) Briefly describe Option 1.
(b) What sort of transactions would you post in Option 2?

---

4 RECORDING TRANSACTIONS IN THE PURCHASE LEDGER

4.1 In a computer-based purchase ledger, accounts might be updated directly (**transaction processing**) or stored on a **transaction file** for a later updating run. Similarly a manual system may be posted daily, weekly or monthly.

Recording purchases and cash paid

4.2 The chart below shows how entries are made in purchase ledger accounts from the purchase day book (invoices) and the cash account (cash paid). It also shows related postings from the purchase day book and indicates how the total creditors account (or purchase ledger control account) fits in.

- **Individual invoices** are **credited** to the **individual creditors' purchase ledger accounts.**

- **Totals of batches of invoices** are **credited** to the **total creditors account,** which forms a part of the **double entry system.**

- The net amount of purchases (or expenses) **excluding VAT** are **debited** to the **purchases** (or **expenses**) account.

- The **VAT** element is **debited** to the **VAT account**, reducing the amount owed to HM Customs & Excise.

- **Cash paid to each supplier** is **debited** to the individual purchase ledger accounts.

- The **total cash paid** is posted to the general ledger, **debit total creditors account, credit cash account**.

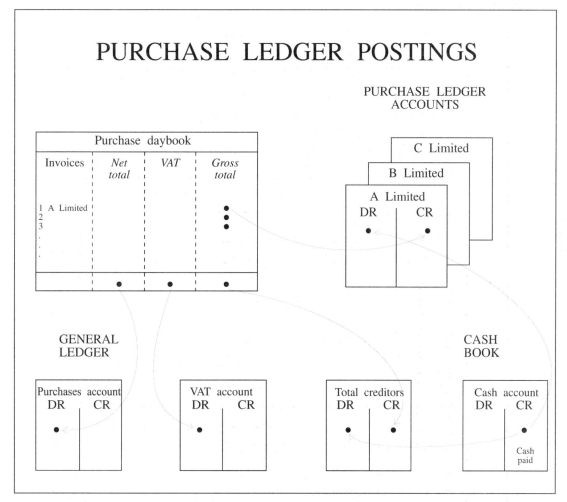

PURCHASE LEDGER POSTINGS

4.3   In some businesses, the **cash book** is a book of prime entry from which summaries are taken and recorded in a cash control account in the general ledger. In the chart above, we illustrate a business in which there is a single cash book, which forms part of the double entry.

Posting purchase returns

4.4   Postings of credit notes received are made from the purchase returns day book to the **debit** the purchase ledger accounts. In the general ledger, the postings are **debit total creditors account** and **credit purchases**.

Discounts received

4.5 Some businesses account for **cash discounts received** from suppliers by a 'memorandum' discounts received column in the cash book (see Chapter 7). This is used to **debit** the individual creditors' accounts. The appropriate general ledger entries follow.

		£	£
DEBIT	Total creditors account	X	
CREDIT	Discounts received		X

Retention of records

4.6 All purchase invoices and credit notes should be retained and filed after processing in case of query (from the supplier, the management or the auditors). Where VAT is involved, invoices and credit notes **must be retained for six years**. Filing will be dealt with in Chapter 5.

5 PAYMENTS TO SUPPLIERS

5.1 Payments to suppliers are best made on a **regular basis,** say monthly, as a matter of efficiency.

Methods of payment

5.2 Different methods of payment to suppliers are available.

Method	Comments
Cash	An unusual method, although it is used for small non-credit 'petty cash' items.
Cheque	Still the commonest method of payment.
Interbank transfer	An increasingly common means of making payments to suppliers, eg using the 'BACS' system. This can save administrative time as, instead of making out individual cheques and sending each by post, details of a full payment run to the suppliers of the business can be submitted to the bank on computer tape or disk. The funds are then transferred to suppliers' bank accounts electronically through the bank clearing system. There may also be savings in bank charges from using BACS.

Other payment methods include CHAPS, direct debit and standing orders. These are dealt with in detail in Chapter 6.

Selecting items for payment

5.3 Deciding when and who to pay is a key function of a business's management and only a senior person should decide.

All systems	Computerised purchase ledger system
The items for payment may be selected manually.	A **'suggested payments'** listing may be produced, 'suggesting' how much should be paid to which suppliers, based on settlement days and any discounts offered. A computer generated listing of this sort needs to be checked manually in case there are any reasons to make a different payment from that 'suggested'.
If **queries** on any invoices are outstanding the invoice should not be paid until the query has been settled. (The invoice should be kept in a separate 'queried invoices' file.)	There may be a facility to 'flag' items which should not be paid for the time being. For example, the invoice may be placed **'in dispute'** in the reference used for the invoice. The 'dispute' designation will need to be 'released' when the dispute is settled, so that the item can be paid in the normal way.
It may be desirable to take the full period of credit from each supplier.	The number of days before settlement can be recorded for each supplier. A computerised purchase ledger which offers the option of making automatic payments will list all items which are now due to be paid. This list will *exclude*: • Items which have not yet reached their settlement date • Items which are 'in dispute'

Computer cheques and remittance advices

5.4 A computerised purchase ledger system may offer the option of **printing cheques for payments to suppliers.** Special cheque stationery is needed. A remittance advice is normally sent with each payment to tell the supplier what the payment is for. This too may be produced by a computerised purchase ledger system.

REMITTANCE ADVICE

KT Electronics
4 Reform Road
Wokingham
Berkshire

R&B Sound Services Ltd
Belton Estate
Peterborough
PE4 4DE

Account number: 427424

30/06/X3
Your ref: RBS/2011

Date	Details	Amount/£
08/05/X3	Invoice 202481	624.60
21/05/X3	Invoice 202574	78.40
24/05/X3	Credit note C40041	(62.20)
	Payment enclosed for	640.80

Checks over payments

5.5 It is important for a business to have **procedures to ensure that only valid payments are made** - ie only the payments which *should* be made by the business.

Procedure	Effect
Authorisation of payments by an **appropriate official**, who should be a senior employee or director of the organisation.	For cheques produced by a computerised purchase ledger system, the password restrictions should limit the value of cheques which different users can authorise.
Cheques will need to be **signed** by the authorised **cheque signatories** which are recognised by the bank as authorised to sign cheques.	The bank will pay the cheque as requested.
Details and appropriate supporting documents for each payment should be presented to the person signing each cheque. '**Appropriate supporting documents**' may consist of the suppliers' invoices which are to be paid (authorised by an appropriate staff member) together with the goods received note or other document recording receipt of the goods/services invoiced.	Documents supporting payments are reviewed by people who are independent of the preparation and processing of the documents. The person carrying out this review will check for any unusual items which might need further investigation.

5.6 Automatic payment methods in a large organisation may include **mechanical signature of payments by computer**. If such a system is used, there is not the same check on individual payments as is appropriate to smaller businesses. To replace this lack of control, the organisation will need to have strong checks over whether purchase ledger balances are correct to ensure that wrong payments are not made.

5.7 If automated electronic payments methods (such as **BACS**) are used, there will need to be special procedures to ensure that all payments included on the tape submitted to BACS are properly authorised.

5.8 Sometimes, the usual payment method may need to be bypassed. For example, computer selection of payments may need to be overridden in order to make a special **manual payment** of a different amount. Proper checks will be needed in such cases and high level authorisation obtained.

6   THE AGE ANALYSIS OF CREDITORS AND OTHER REPORTS

The age analysis of creditors

6.1 An **age analysis of creditors** is produced in a similar way to the age analysis of debtors.

KEY TERM

The **age analysis of creditors** will consist of a listing of creditors' balances analysed between different 'ages' of liability represented by different items in the balance, measured in months (usually).

6.2 The age analysis of creditors serves to highlight any supplier accounts which are **long overdue,** for whatever reason. The totals of the age analysis indicate the **age 'profile'** of creditors' accounts. Information about this profile can be of use to business managers, who might ask whether the business would be better off paying creditors a little later in order to improve its cash flow position.

Other reports

6.3 Other reports which a computerised purchase ledger package is able to print out will be very similar to those produced from a sales ledger package, the more important of which were outlined in Unit 1.

6.4 Access to purchase ledger reports will normally be restricted by **password**.

Activity 4.3   Level: Pre-assessment

What, briefly, is the significance of a *creditors'* age analysis?

Activity 4.4   Level: Pre-assessment

Can you list the main types of report other than the age analysis of creditors?

---

7 CONTRA ENTRIES WITH THE SALES LEDGER

7.1 Sometimes, a business **purchases goods from** and **sells goods to** the same person on credit.

- **Purchase** invoices will be entered in the **purchase day book** on receipt and subsequently recorded in the supplier's individual account in the purchase ledger

- **Credit sales** invoices are entered in the **sales day book** and subsequently recorded in the customer's individual account in the sales ledger

7.2 Even though the supplier and the customer are the same person, he will have a **separate account in each ledger**. If A owes B £200 for purchases and B owes A £350 for credit sales, the net effect is that B owes A £150. However, in the books of A, there will be the following entries.

- A creditor in the purchase ledger - B - for £200
- A debtor in the sales ledger - B - for £350

7.3 If A and B decide to settle their accounts by **netting off** their respective debts (and getting B to write a single cheque for the balance), settlement would be made **in contra**.

KEY TERM

A **contra** entry occurs when an amount outstanding on a customer's account in the sales ledger is cancelled by a similar amount in the same entity's account in the purchase ledger, that is when the entity is both a supplier to and a customer of an organisation. The same entries also need to be made in the total debtors and total creditors accounts.

7.4 The contra entries in the accounts of A would be to set off the smaller amount (£200 owed *to* B) against the larger amount (£350 owed *by* B).

(a) In the *sales ledger* and *purchase ledger*:

DEBIT	Creditor's account (B) purchase ledger - to clear	£200	
CREDIT	Debtor's account (B) sales ledger - leaving balance of £150		£200

(b) In the *general ledger*:

DEBIT	Total creditors	£200	
CREDIT	Total debtors		£200

7.5 **The contra entries must be made in both the personal accounts of B and also in the total creditors and debtors accounts in the general ledger.**

Activity 4.5   **Level: Assessment**

The following transactions have been posted to a purchase ledger account.

Date	Narrative	Trans ref	Debit £ p	Credit £ p	Balance £ p
Balance at 31/8/X7					NIL
2/9/X7		P901		453.10	453.10
3/9/X7		P902		462.50	915.60
4/9/X7	Cash	C9901	462.50		453.10
5/9/X7		P903		705.90	1,159.00
7/9/X7		P904		25.50	1,184.50
12/9/X7	Cash	C9902	705.90		478.60
15/9/X7		P905		914.30	1,392.90
17/9/X7		P906		692.53	2,085.43
19/9/X7	Cash	C9903	692.53		1,392.90
21/9/X7		P907		805.39	2,198.29
22/9/X7		C9904	914.30		1,283.99
25/9/X7		P908		478.60	1,762.59
28/9/X7	Cash	C9905	805.39		957.20
29/9/X7	Cash	C9906	478.60		478.60
30/9/X7		P909		92.70	571.30
Balance at 30/9/X7					£571.30

Task

At close of business on 30 September 20X7, identify which invoices are outstanding, applying:

(a) the open item method
(b) the balance forward method

Activity 4.6 Level: Assessment

You are the purchase ledger clerk for a company providing financial services, and the date is 28 August 20X7. The company operates a non-integrated purchase ledger system.

The purchase ledger account for a supplier called Kernels Ltd shows the following.

		(Debit)/Credit £	Balance £
01.08.X7	Balance b/f		76.05
01.08.X7	Invoice 20624	42.84	118.89
07.08.X7	Cash	(76.05)	42.84
16.08.X7	Invoice 20642	64.17	107.01
16.08.X7	Invoice 20643	120.72	227.73
16.08.X7	Invoice 20642	64.17	291.90
21.08.X7	Cash	(400.00)	(108.10)
22.08.X7	Invoice 20798	522.18	414.08
24.08.X7	C91004	42.84	456.92
27.08.X7	Invoice 21114	144.50	601.42
27.08.X7	Invoice 21229	42.84	644.26

The following facts came to light.

(a) Kernels Ltd's invoice 21201 for £97.40, dated 23 August 20X7, was misposted to the account of MPV in the purchase ledger.

(b) The cash payment of £400.00 made on 21 August 20X7 relates to another creditor, ASR Ltd.

(c) Item C91004 dated 24 August 20X7 is in fact a credit note.

(d) Invoice 20642 has been posted to the account twice.

(e) Kernels Ltd has a balance of £37.50 in the sales ledger, which is to be set off against its balance in the purchase ledger.

Task

Draw up journal entries for the above items and write up the Kernels Ltd's account accordingly, posting the journal entries to the account.

The journal entries should distinguish between general ledger adjustments and memorandum account adjustments.

Key learning points

- The **purchase ledger contains the personal accounts of suppliers (trade creditors)** of the business. The suppliers' personal accounts provide the business with a full record of how much it owes to each supplier and of what items the debt consists.

- A **supplier's account** in the purchase ledger will **normally show a credit balance**: the supplier is owed money by the business and is therefore a creditor of the business. Other creditors which a business may have include the tax authorities, banks and employees (for any wages and salaries due).

- **Opening a new purchase ledger account or amending an existing record will require the authorisation of a senior official.** A computerised system may use a 'menu' system through which supplier records may be added, deleted or amended. Authorisation may be by way of a **password** known only to authorised employees.

- **Payments to suppliers** should be organised according to the periodic procedures of the business. **Checks and authorisation** are necessary in order to ensure that only valid payments are made. Payment methods vary, and the checks necessary will differ according to the payment methods used.

- The **age analysis of creditors** shows the age 'profile' of creditors' balances on the purchase ledger. It indicates how quickly the business is paying off its debts. A computerised purchase ledger will also allow a number of other reports to be printed out as necessary.

- **Contra entries** 'net off' amounts due to and from the same parties in the purchase ledger and sales ledger respectively.

Quick quiz

1   What does the purchase ledger contain?

2   What are trade creditors?

3   Give two examples of 'other creditors'.

4   The purchase ledger may be divided up. Suggest two ways of dividing it.

5   What does the age analysis of creditors do?

6   What does settlement 'in contra' mean?

Answers to quick quiz

1   The personal accounts showing how much is owed to each credit supplier of the business.

2   Liabilities relating to the trade of the business, eg purchases of goods for re-sale.

3   (i)   Wages and salaries
     (ii)   VAT

4   (i)   Alphabetically
     (ii)   Geographically

5   Lists creditors' balances analysed between different 'ages' of debt, eg one month old, two months old etc.

6   An amount due from a customer in the sales ledger is set off against an amount owed to the same person in the purchase ledger, and *vice versa*.

5 Communications with creditors

This chapter contains

1 Introduction

2 Suppliers' statements of account

3 Dealing with creditors' queries

4 Management of creditors

5 Retaining files

Learning objectives

On completion of this chapter you will be able to:

- Check suppliers' statements of account

- Deal with creditors' queries

- Maintain a filing system

Performance criteria

2.1.6 Discrepancies are identified and either resolved or referred to the appropriate person
       if outside own authority

2.1.7 Communication with suppliers regarding accounts are handled politely and effectively

Range statement

2.1.5 Discrepancies: incorrect calculations, non-delivery of goods charged, duplicated
       invoices, incorrect VAT charge, incorrect discounts

2.1.6 Communications: oral, written

Knowledge and understanding

- Types of business transactions and the documents involved

- Relevant understanding of the organisation's accounting systems and administrative
  systems and procedures

- The nature of the organisation's business transactions

- Organisational procedures for filing source information

1 INTRODUCTION

1.1 Maintaining good relations with suppliers are essential for the smooth running of a business.

1.2 This chapter deals with communications with suppliers (creditors) in general and dealing with queries in particular.

2 SUPPLIERS' STATEMENTS OF ACCOUNT

2.1 It is usual for a supplier to send a **monthly statement of account** to each of its credit customers. The monthly statement will show the following.

- **Any balance brought forward** from the previous month's statement

- The **business transactions** during the month

  ° The amounts of **invoices** issued
  ° Any **credit notes** issued and any **payments** received from the customer

These are often called '**supplier statements**'.

2.2 A business may not receive statements of account from all of its suppliers.

- A supplier may not send a statement for a **single purchase** or to a customer who makes **irregular purchases**. The supplier may expect the customer to pay the amount 'on invoice' rather than being sent a statement of account.

- Small suppliers (who issue few invoices) may not send out **any** statements of account.

2.3 Suppliers whose **credit terms** require payment within a certain period (commonly 30 days) of the statement date, must send statements to **all of their customers**.

2.4 Each supplier's statement should be stamped with the **date of receipt** for future reference. Some suppliers' credit terms require payment within a certain period of the **receipt** of the statement. Therefore a record of that date is needed for dealing with suppliers' queries.

Activity 5.1   **Level: Pre-assessment**

(a) What is the point of obtaining a statement from a supplier on a regular basis?

(b) If you have accounts with a hundred different creditors what would be the point of checking, say, 10% of their balances?

2.5 The supplier's statement will have been prepared from the information held on the supplier's sales ledger. A statement of account is reproduced below.

2.6 The statement is received on 1 June 20X1 and is passed to Linda Kelly who is the purchase ledger clerk at Finstar Ltd. Linda obtains a printout of the transactions with Pickett (Handling Equipment) Ltd from Finstar's purchase ledger system. (The reason why Linda has made ticks on the statement and on the printout which follows will be explained below.)

STATEMENT OF ACCOUNT

**Pickett (Handling Equipment) Limited
Unit 7, Western Industrial Estate
Dunford DN2 7RJ**

Tel: (01990) 72101   Fax: (01990) 72980   VAT Reg No 982 7213 49

Accounts Department
Finstar Ltd
67 Laker Avenue
Dunford DN4 5PS

RECEIVED
1 JUN X1

Date: 31 May 20X1

A/c No: F023

Date	Details	Debit £ p	Credit £ p	Balance £ p
30/4/X1	Balance brought forward from previous statement			492 22
3/5/X1	Invoice no. 34207	129 40 √		621 62
4/5/X1	Invoice no. 34242	22 72 √		644 34
5/5/X1	Payment received - thank you		412 17 √	232 17
17/5/X1	Invoice no. 34327	394 95 √		627 12
18/5/X1	Credit note no. 00192		64 40 √	562 72
21/5/X1	Invoice no. 34392	392 78		955 50
28/5/X1	Credit note no. 00199		107 64 √	847 86
	Amount now due		**£**	**847 86**

Terms: 30 days net, 1% discount for payment in 7 days. E & OE

Registered office: 4 Arkwright Road, London E16 4PQ   Registered in England No 2182417

FINSTAR LIMITED   **PURCHASE LEDGER**

ACCOUNT NAME: PICKETT (HANDLING EQUIPMENT) LIMITED

ACCOUNT REF: PO42

DATE OF REPORT: 1 JUNE 20X1

Date	Transaction	(Debit)/Credit £
16.03.X1	Invoice 33004	350.70
20.03.X1	Invoice 33060	61.47
06.04.X1	Invoice 34114	80.05
03.05.X1	Invoice 34207	129.40 ✓
04.05.X1	Payment	(412.17) ✓
06.05.X1	Invoice 34242	22.72 ✓
19.05.X1	Invoice 34327	394.95 ✓
19.05.X1	Credit note 00192	(64.40) ✓
28.05.X1	Payment	(117.77)
30.05.X1	Credit note 00199	(107.64) ✓
	Balance	337.31

2.7   The purchase ledger of Finstar shows a balance due to Pickett of £337.31, while Pickett's statement shows a balance due of £847.86.

Supplier statement reconciliations

2.8   Linda wants to be sure that her purchase ledger record for Pickett is correct and so she prepares a **supplier statement reconciliation**.

2.9   These are the steps she follows.

Step 1	Tick off items which appear on both the statement and the purchase ledger. This has been done on the documents illustrated above.
Step 2	Agree the opening balance on the supplier's statement. Linda notes that the balance brought forward at 30 April is made up of three invoices (33004, 33060 and 34114).
Step 3	Allocate payments. Invoices 33004 and 33060 were paid on 4 May and 34114 was part of the payment on 28 May.
Step 4	Identify differences. Pickett's statement does not show the payment made on 28 May. Also the statement shows an invoice (34392, dated 21 May) which is not shown on Finstar's purchase ledger.

It is not surprising that the payment is not shown on Pickett's statement. It was probably 'in transit' or awaiting processing when the statement was prepared.

The invoice dated 21 May seems odd. If Pickett had sent it on 21 May, it should by now (1 June) be shown on the purchase ledger. Finding the reason for this discrepancy may involve inquiries both within Finstar's offices and then, if it cannot be traced there, with the supplier.

2.10   Linda prepares the following reconciliation statement.

SUPPLIER STATEMENT RECONCILIATION
ACCOUNT: PICKETT (HANDLING EQUIPMENT) LTD (PO42)

	£
Balance per supplier's statement	847.86
Less	
Payment (28 May) not on statement	(117.77)
Invoice (supplier no 34392) on statement, not on purchase ledger	(392.78)
Balance per purchase ledger	337.31

The reasons for reconciling items

2.11   Paragraph 2.10 illustrates two examples of reconciling items.

2.12   **Reconciling items** may occur as a result of the following transactions.

Reconciling item	Effect	Status
Payments in transit	A payment will normally be shown in the purchase ledger when the cheque is issued or when a bank transfer instruction is made. There will be delay (postal, processing) before this payment is recognised in the records of the supplier. Any statement of account received by post will also be out of date by the length of time taken to deliver it.	Timing difference
Omitted invoices and credit notes	Invoices or credit notes may appear in the ledger of one business but not in that of the other due to error or omission. However, the most common reason this discrepancy will be a timing difference in recording the items in the different ledgers.	Error or omission or timing difference
Other errors	Addition errors can occur, particularly if a statement of account is prepared manually. Invoice, credit note or payment amounts can be misposted. Regular reconciliation of supplier statements will minimise the possibility of missing such errors.	Error

Frequency of reconciling supplier statements

2.13 Ideally, **all** supplier statements should be reconciled **monthly**.

2.14 In practice, many businesses cannot do this and prepare reconciliations for **major supplier's statements only**. These are not necessarily the largest credit balances in the purchase ledger. They are the accounts where it is most likely that significant errors will occur because of the volume or high value of purchases made.

2.15 Sometimes it is not possible to reconcile all suppliers' statements monthly. Then it is a good idea to cover all suppliers' accounts periodically by adopting a **rotational system of reconciliations**. Major suppliers' accounts are all reconciled monthly. Some other accounts are reconciled each month so that each is reconciled at least once every three months.

Filing and retention of suppliers' statements

2.16 Suppliers' statements should be **filed for future reference**. Each month's statements are filed by alphabetical order of supplier name. Lever arch files are commonly used for this purpose. Filing is dealt with in more detail in Section 5 of this chapter.

2.17 Suppliers' statements may need to be examined by the **external auditors** of a company during the annual audit. Reconciling suppliers' statements with the balances on the purchase ledger helps the auditors check that the accounts include all the liabilities of the business.

3   DEALING WITH CREDITORS' QUERIES

3.1   Someone working in a purchase ledger department will deal with **requests or demands for payment,** as well as discrepancies and errors. These may be dealt with by letter or telephone. It makes good business sense for all queries to be dealt with using high standards of **promptness and courtesy.**

3.2   We looked at some of the rules and principles of written communication in Unit 1. In the following paragraphs we look at a situation involving an exchange of letters between a company and its supplier.

Example of dealing with creditors' queries

3.3   Pay attention to the **style of the language** used in the examples below. Also note the **format of the letters** and the **problem which is being addressed.**

3.4   EXAMPLE: BEING CHASED FOR PAYMENT

You are Ms Mai Ling, Senior Accounts Clerk of Tradewell Office Products and Services Ltd, of Easy Street Manchester M12 7SL. It is 22 June.

Your firm has an account (No: 33521) with Britline Carriers plc, who transports many of your products for you. You have just received a statement from Britline, accompanied by the following letter.

BRITLINE CARRIERS PLC
Sutton Lane, Liverpool LW6 9BC
Telephone: 0151 - 324 7345/6

Directors: Registered office:
D Smith (Managing)   Sutton Lane Liverpool LW6 9BC
P Patel   Reg. No 34567
C Wilkes   Reg. in England

Ref: NC/nn TO 16   21 June 20X0

Accounts Department
Tradewell Office Products & Services Ltd
Easy St
MANCHESTER M12 7SL

Dear Sir

OVERDUE ACCOUNT: 33521

Further to the statement sent to you on 16 May 20X0 it appears that your account for April 20X0 totalling £1,402.70 remains outstanding. Please find enclosed a copy statement.

The terms of credit extended to your company were agreed as 30 days from receipt of statement.

We should appreciate settlement of the above account at your earliest convenience.

Yours faithfully

N Competant

N Competant
Accounts Department

enc

You check your files. A cheque for the outstanding amount was sent to Britline on 6 June, but no acknowledgement was received. You also wonder if you have forfeited your usual 5% prompt payment discount because of the error.

You need to write an appropriate letter of complaint and query.

3.5 SOLUTION

TRADEWELL OFFICE PRODUCTS & SERVICES LTD
Easy Street, Manchester, M12 7SL

22 June 20X0

Our ref: ML/db
Your ref: NC/nn TO 16

Mr N Competant,
Accounts Department,
Britline Carriers plc.,
Sutton Lane,
LIVERPOOL LW6 9BC

Dear Mr Competant,

ACCOUNT NUMBER 33521

I am concerned by the contents of your letter of 21 June, requesting payment of £1,402.70 outstanding on the above account for April 20X0.

Our files indicate that a cheque payment was made by us on 6 June, within 30 days of the statement dated 16 May. No acknowledgement of payment was received from you.

It would appear there has been an error of some kind, and I would be grateful if you would kindly consult your records.

I am also rather concerned that we may not have been credited with the usual 5% prompt payment discount in these circumstances. Perhaps you can reassure me on this point.

Yours sincerely,

Mai Ling

Mai Ling (Ms)
Senior Accounts Clerk

Notes

1   'Your ref' picks up the reference given on Britline's collection letter.

2   The tone is formal and 'civilised' throughout: the cheque may have been lost in the post - being abusive is of little value.

3   The letter starts by referring to Britline's communication, with relevant details. It then states the nature of your concern, and the actions you expect Britline to take.

3.6   Let us now place ourselves in the situation of an employee of Britline Carriers.

3.7 You are Mr M Barrast, Accounts Manager of Britline Carriers plc. TOPS' complaint has been referred to you and you discover that a cheque was indeed received from them on 7 June. Unfortunately, Britline lost two of its ledger clerks that week due to illness, and it appears that the temporary replacement credited £1,402.70 to another firm's account by mistake.

You need to write an appropriate letter of apology and explanation to Ms Ling at TOPS.

BRITLINE CARRIERS PLC

Sutton Lane, Liverpool LW6 9BC
Telephone: 0151 - 324 7345/6

Directors: Registered office:
D Smith (Managing)   Sutton Lane
P Patel   Liverpool LW6 9BC
C Wilkes   Reg. No 34567
                                                        Reg. in England

Our ref: ML/nn TO 17
Your ref: ML/db   27 June 20X0

Ms M Ling
Senior Accounts Clerk
Tradewell Office Products & Services Ltd
Easy St
MANCHESTER M12 7SL

Dear Ms Ling

PAYMENT OF ACCOUNT: 33521

I was sorry to learn of your complaint of 22 June regarding the statement we sent you indicating that payment of your account was overdue.

Having checked our records, I discovered that we did indeed receive your cheque for £1,402.70 on 7 June. Due to unfortunate circumstances affecting our accounts department at that time, the payment was regrettably credited to another customer account. I am pleased to report that the error has been rectified and that your prompt payment discount has not been affected.

Please accept my sincere apologies for the concern caused to you in this matter. We anticipate no recurrence of our departmental problems, but if I can be of assistance in any other way, do not hesitate to contact me.

Yours sincerely

M Barrast

M Barrast
Accounts Manager

BPP PUBLISHING

Notes

1   The reference picks up Ms Ling's last letter.

2   The tone is apologetic, but positive. Emphasis is on investigation and rectification of the mistake - not shame and guilt.

3   Again, the context is laid out first, followed by an explanation and summary. Note that the details of the clerk's illness etc were irrelevant.

4   Mr Barrast apologises for the 'concern' caused - not the 'inconvenience', which is an over-used cliché.

Activity 5.2   Level: Pre-assessment

It is your first day of work in the purchase ledger at D E Fences Ltd.

Your boss, the Chief Accountant, has given you a pile of correspondence to sort through. He is a busy person, and believes in starting off new employees 'at the deep end'. He requires you to make suggestions about dealing with problems raised.

The first letter is from Reginald Gray, Financial Controller of Jack Use Ltd.

```
                                                    Jack Use Ltd
                                                        Unit 3
                                          Pleading Business Park
                                                       Pleading
                                                          Lincs

To   Purchase Ledger                            2 October 20X7
     DE Fences Ltd
     Chancery Courtyard
     Dock Green
     Putney


To whom it may concern

Dear Sir/Madam

I attach our statement, and must demand immediate payment by return
of post of the overdue balance thereon of £7,424.15. This is the
third time we have written to you. Any further delay will result
in us putting the matter in the hands of our solicitors.

Yours sincerely

Reginald Gray

Reginald Gray
Financial Controller
```

What should you do first of all? Choose one of the options below.

(1)   Pay up without further ado.

(2)   Ignore the letter on principle, as its tone is threatening.

(3)   Phone up and say 'the cheque's in the post', to keep them off your back, and then check the statement.

(4)   Send the letter to the Managing Director of D E Fences Ltd, Roseanne Barrister.

(5)   Look up a firm of solicitors in the 'Yellow Pages' or local business guide, and fax them a copy of the letter with a note from you asking them to help out.

(6)   Interrupt your boss and show him the letter.

(7)   Look in the file for any previous correspondence and tackle it on your own.

Activity 5.3   **Level: Assessment**

You are A Technician, Senior Accounts Assistant of Paywell Services Ltd of 24 Maidstone Road, Taunton TA4 4RP. The date is 24 February 20X7.

Your firm has an account number P942 with Recycle Ltd, a company with which you have traded for many months. Recycle Ltd offers a settlement discount of 2½% for payment within the credit terms. You have recently received a letter from Recycle as shown below.

RECYCLE LIMITED

Jarvis Lane Maidenhead Berkshire SL6 4RS Tel: 01628 722722

Accounts Department
Paywell Services Ltd
24 Maidstone Road   20 February 20X7
Taunton TA4 4RP
Our ref: DW/SB 42

Dear Sir or Madam

OVERDUE ACCOUNT No. P942

I enclose a copy statement of account showing that £2,642.50 remains outstanding on your above account. The original statement was sent to you on 10 January 20X7, and the amount shown on this statement was payable within 30 days of the date of the statement.

We would appreciate immediate settlement of the above account.

Yours faithfully

D Waite

D Waite (Ms)
Accounts Department

On reviewing your files, you find that the outstanding balance was paid by BACS transfer (the usual method of payment to this creditor) on 31 January 20X7. In August and October 20X6, there had been correspondence between Paywell and Recycle Ltd due to Recycle's failure to credit BACS payments to the correct account.

Task

Write an appropriate letter to the creditor.

---

4   MANAGEMENT OF CREDITORS

4.1   It might seem advantageous to pay suppliers (creditors) as *late* as possible. However, you can easily appreciate how such a policy might alienate suppliers. A business will need to take a broader view of its approach to **managing its liabilities to suppliers.**

Objective of creditor management

4.2   The objective of creditor management is **to maximise credit periods taken whilst not jeopardising relationships with suppliers.**

Creditor management policies and procedures

4.3 An awareness of the objective of creditor management will help **members of staff** (whose job includes dealing with suppliers' queries) to do their job well. It will help them to understand why queries should be dealt with in a particular manner. It will also help them to be aware of the organisation's policies, procedures and timescales so that they can observe these in the course of their work.

4.4 A business should **negotiate the terms of credit** with its major suppliers and should set guidelines as to when payments should be made. In reaching this decision on its policies, a business will need to consider various factors.

Factor	Effect
Dependence on supplier	Businesses vary in the extent of their **dependence on particular suppliers.** Some large companies may have small suppliers which are highly dependent on *them*, so that the business can dictate terms to the supplier.
Flexibility of creditors on payment	HM Customs & Excise and the Inland Revenue are extremely **inflexible** with regard to payments of VAT and PAYE respectively. **Late payments incur penalties**.
Long-term importance of the supplier	The supplier may be unique in what it provides or the need for the supplier may increase in future. It will be important to ensure that relationships are kept as positive as possible.

Discounts and early payment

4.5 There may be benefits in paying a supplier early in order to take advantage of **cash discounts** offered. However, it may not be advantageous to take cash discounts if the cost of **financing the early payment is greater than the discount.**

4.6 EXAMPLE: DISCOUNTS

A Ltd owes B Ltd £1,000 at 1 April. B Ltd's credit terms allow A to pay the full amount on 31 May or to take a cash discount of 1% if it pays one month early (ie by 1 May). If A Ltd pays early, it must finance the payment from its bank overdraft, on which it pays monthly interest of 1.5% per annum. Should A Ltd take up the discount?

4.7 SOLUTION

A Ltd has two alternatives.

(a) **Pay on 31 May**

A Ltd will pay £1,000.00.

(b) **Pay on 30 April**

A Ltd will pay £1,000 less 1% = £990.00.

This will increase A Ltd's bank overdraft by £990 for one month, for which A Ltd will *have* to pay interest of £990.00 × 1.5% = £14.85.

The total cost of paying on 30 April is therefore £990.00 + £14.85 = £1,004.85.

The early payment option (b) is more expensive by £4.85 (£1,004.85 − £1,000.00). Therefore, other things being equal, A Ltd should delay payment until 31 May and not take up the cash discount.

Practical tips in creditor management

4.8 A business may negotiate **extended credit terms** with a supplier. Suppliers may accept extended credit terms if they are sure that they will receive payment on particular predecided dates. If payment is late, but the supplier does not know how much later it is going to be, the relationship may suffer. Therefore keep suppliers **informed**.

4.9 **Regular formal and informal meetings** may be arranged with suppliers. These meetings will help to clarify payment terms and dates with the parties involved.

4.10 There may be some advantage in a business **sharing information on suppliers** with other customers of that supplier. A supplier is likely to have negotiated payment terms separately with different customers, particularly with its large customers. Finding out about the terms and discounts given to other customers may provide some useful 'ammunition' in negotiations.

4.11 If a business does run into **cash flow problems,** it may make sense for it to settle its small accounts first. This will enable it to benefit from maintaining a reliable supply from those suppliers at a relatively low cost. The 'credit management' effort can then be concentrated on large creditor balances.

4.12 The **payment method used** may have implications for relationships with suppliers. Although direct transfers by BACS save staff time and costs incurred in handling cheques, **cheque payments do have certain other advantages.**

(a) Payment by cheque has a **cash flow advantage** over bank transfers. There is a time lapse between the creditor receiving the cheque and when it is debited from the payer's bank account. This lapse of time is due partly to delay in banking the cheque and partly to the time taken by the cheque to pass through the banks' clearing system (3 days).

(b) Payment by cheque may have a **psychological advantage** to the paying business in its relationships with its suppliers. Suppliers are more aware of cheques than bank transfers, because they see cheques as they are received.

5   RETAINING FILES

Preparing documents for filing

5.1   When documents have been received, acknowledged, acted upon or have otherwise fulfilled their immediate purpose, they are ready to be added to the storage system.

5.2   The following procedures might be followed when adding new information to the organisation's storage system.

(a)   The document is **indicated as being ready for filing** - perhaps initialled by the recipient or supervisor. This is a signal to the filing clerk that it is OK to go ahead and file it.

(b)   **Paper clips and binders are removed** leaving flat sheets for filing, and holes punched appropriate to the storage method so that documents can be inserted.

(c)   Documents are placed at **random in a filing tray,** or kept in rough order in a **concertina file.**

(d)   If the document is an internally generated one it may have a **file reference** on it already ('Our reference ....' at the head of letters). If not, a **reference number** will have to be determined.

(e)   The **reference number,** or **name** or **subject** of the file into which the document is to be inserted should be shown on the document.

(f)   Batches of documents can then be **sorted** (by each name, subject and so on) and put into the appropriate filing sequence (chronological, numerical or whatever).

(g)   Documents are **inserted in the appropriate place** in appropriate files. This process should be carried out daily to avoid pile-ups and disorganisation.

Opening a new file

5.3   If there is no file existing for a document a **new file** will be opened. This will involve the following.

(a)   In a centralised filing system, a **request** and **authorisation** for a new file to be opened. This is to check for duplication or misnaming of files.

(b)   **Appropriate housing** for the document - a **folder** or **binder,** noting size, colour and so on as necessary. An extra pocket may have to be inserted in sequence for suspended files.

(c)   **Identification.** This will mean writing the number or name on files or suspension pockets or on a suitable tag or label. Colour coding may also be used.

(d)   **Adding** the new file name/number to the index, file list, and cross-referencing system.

5.4   The procedure will be much the same as when a file cannot hold any more documents, and a **continuation file** is needed. Simply mark the cover of the original file 'Volume 1' and add the range of dates its subject matter covers. Then open a new file marked 'Volume 2'.

Activity 5.4   Level: Pre-assessment

What matters should you take account of when you are considering opening a new file for some documents in your possession?

Activity 5.5   Level: Assessment

The following is an extract from your organisation's permanent file on customer number 476/23/3.

Company:	Folworth Ltd
Address:	47 Bracewell Gardens London EC2
Directors:	Robin Folworth Margaret Foster Laurence Oldfield
Purchasing manager:	John Thornhill

You have just had a letter from this company which is shown on the next page.

Your task is to update the permanent file as necessary.

BPP
PUBLISHING

FOLWORTH (Business Services) Ltd

Crichton Buildings
97 Lower Larkin Street   London   EC4A 8QT

D. Ashford
Sales Department
Bosley Products Ltd
Ducannon House
4-6 West Brook Road
LONDON W12 7LY

8 August   20X6

Dear Mr Ashford

Account No. 476/23/3

I should be grateful for a reply to my letter of 30 July regarding the above account.

Yours sincerely

D Simmonds

D. Simmonds
Purchasing Manager

Folworth (Business Services) Ltd, Registered Office:
Crichton Buildings, 97 Lower Larkin Street, London, EC4A 8QT

Registered in England, number 9987654

Directors:
R. Folworth, BA ACA; J. Crichton; M. Foster; L. Oldfield MA; T. Scott; J. Thornhill BSc

Retaining information

5.5   When information contained within files is no longer needed on a daily basis, it is not automatically thrown away. It is generally dealt with in one of the following ways.

(a)   **Microfilmed or microfiched** for long-term storage.

(b)   Retained in its original form and stored elsewhere (**archiving**) for a certain period of time.

(c)   **Securely destroyed.**

5.6 Imagine how distressed you would be if you needed a legal document and you found that it had been destroyed during the latest office spring-clean! (Alternatively, imagine trying to find an urgently needed current file, with *all* the paperwork of the organisation's history still in the active filing system!)

5.7 Information which is no longer current, but which may be needed in future, should be given a revised **status**. Examples include no longer active, but semi-active; no longer semi-active, but non-active - a prime candidate for the **archive**!

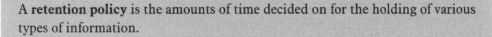

KEY TERM

A **retention policy** is the amounts of time decided on for the holding of various types of information.

5.8 **Retention periods** vary. Documents concerned with the legal establishment of the organisation will have to be kept permanently, as will the annual accounts. Simple legal contracts will have to be kept for six years, and more important sealed ones for twelve. Other documents may be kept at the organisation's discretion but the principle overall is: if you think you might need it - keep it!

Some recommended retention periods include the following.

Document	Years
Agreements	12
Balance sheets	30
Bank statements	6
Cheque counterfoils	1
Correspondence files	6
Credit notes	6
Customs and Excise VAT records	6
Delivery notes	1
Directors' reports	30
Expense claims	1
Insurance claims forms	6
Leases, expired	12
Licences for patents	30
Medical certificates	1
Patents, expired	12
Paying-in books	1
Powers of attorney	30
Prospectuses	30
Purchase orders	6
Quotations, out	6
Royalty ledgers	30
Sales invoices	6
Share applications	12
Specifications, product	6
Tax records	6

5.9 Try to find out what your organisation's policy is for the retention of documentation.

Archiving information

5.10 Even non-active files may need to be kept for future reference. In most organisations, office space is scarce and filing space is limited. Information that needs to be retained is often stored away in boxes in storage spaces such as storehouses, spare cupboards and inaccessible places. Such storage of files is known as **archiving**.

Activity 5.6   Level: Assessment

Dribble Ltd, a very small company, file their correspondence as follows.

(a)   All incoming mail is placed on a 'current' file initially. It is usually actioned within a week after which the correspondence is filed permanently.

(b)   Business customers each have their own separate correspondence file.

(c)   Correspondence with domestic customers is placed on a single file; only one file has been needed per year since the business started in 1944.

(d)   Letters relevant to the latest year's accounts are filed in a file entitled 'Auditors'.

(e)   There is also an extremely thick file entitled 'Miscellaneous 1959 -'.

This is the theory, and Derek Dribble, who founded the business, was an enthusiastic filer. His son, Dominic, however, sees himself as a dynamic entrepreneur and cannot be bothered with it. The current file has not been reviewed for several years and presently includes the following documents.

1   Letter from Miskimin Ltd dated 9.9.04 returning goods.

2   Undated letter from Jacksnares School concerning jumble sale.

3   Letter from London Borough of Greenwich dated 31.12.05 concerning Business Rates.

4   Letter dated 21.7.98 from Dribble Ltd to Mr T N Clipper requesting payment in advance. This has 'Pending - 28.7.98' written across it in red ink.

5   Letter dated 4.3.06 from A J Butterworth Esq requesting '2 × green spats (pair), 1 × red spats (pair)'.

6   Letter from Landlord notifying rent increase as from 1.9.02

7   Letter dated 26.5.96 from Hardman and Free Shoes Ltd ordering '20 pairs spats'.

8   Memo to 'all staff including secretaries' concerning the staff Christmas lunch. This is dated 3.12.03.

9   Letter from Jacksnares School dated 7.5.06 thanking Dribble Ltd for their 'generous donation but unfortunately returning goods unsold'.

10   Letter from Dudley Theatre Company dated 14.4.06 ordering '7 pairs of spats in white'.

11   Letter dated 14.2.06 from Major John Cummings asking for a brochure.

12   Letter dated 14.3.06 from Major John Cummings ordering '1 pair in a conservative colour'.

13   Letter from Miskimin Ltd dated 24.8.04 ordering '2 dozen pairs in white'.

14   Letter from Mr Howard P Wisebacker dated 17.2.00 congratulating Dribble Ltd on 'keeping up a fine old tradition'.

15   Letter dated 17.11.05 from Period Costumiers Ltd ordering '50 pairs, 10 in each colour'.

16   Letter from London Borough of Greenwich notifying dates of refuse collection as from 3.12.05.

17   Letter from Period Costumiers Ltd dated 12.1.06 ordering '50 pairs, 10 in each colour'.

18   Letter dated 15.3.06 from Mrs A J Butterworth returning goods.

19   Letter regarding insurance claim dated 19.4.99.

20   Memo to 'all staff' about summer outing in July 2006.

Task

It is November 2006. Which of these documents would you remove from the current file and where would you place them?

Do you have any suggestions for improving the system?

Deleting or destroying information

5.11   Once information becomes **out-of-date,** it may be **deleted or destroyed**. Be aware that screwing up a piece of paper and throwing it in the bin is not destroying it. Even if information (particularly financial information) is out-of-date it may still be damaging if it falls into the wrong hands. Waste paper bins are the first place that the wrong eyes will look!

5.12   Many organisations have **shredding devices** or a system of disposal which involves **special confidential waste bags**. Find out what your organisation's system is and be sure to use it.

Key learning points

- A business will probably receive a **statement of account** monthly from most or all of its credit suppliers. The date of receipt of suppliers' statements should be noted.

- The supplier's statement of account shows, at the date of the statement, the **supplier's records of the transactions** between the purchasing business and the supplier. This may differ from the records held on the purchase ledger of the purchasing business because of errors or timing differences.

- A **supplier statement reconciliation** shows the items accounting for these differences between the supplier's statement of account and the purchase ledger of the purchasing business.

- Reconciling supplier statements is an **important way of clearing up discrepancies**. If all supplier statements are not reconciled monthly, at least those of major suppliers and a selection of other accounts ought to be.

- **Creditors' queries** should be dealt with promptly and courteously on all occasions.

- **Management of creditors** is not usually given as much emphasis by businesses as the management of debtors through the credit control function. Nevertheless, it is important to ensure that policies and procedures on making payments to creditors are consistent with keeping reasonable levels of stock, maintaining cash flows and keeping good relationships with suppliers.

- **Adding new information** to an information storage system involves the following.

    o   Indicating that the information is ready for filing
    o   Removing any paperclips or binders
    o   Placing information in a filing tray or concertina file
    o   Allocating a reference number if there is not already a file reference
    o   Sorting batches of documents containing information
    o   Inserting the documents into the appropriate place in appropriate files

- Information is usually **destroyed** by using shredding devices or by placing in confidential wastebags.

- In general, when information is no longer needed on a daily basis, it is retained in its original form and stored elsewhere; this is known as **archiving**.

- A **retention policy** is the amount of time decided on by an organisation for the holding of various types of information.

- Material containing information **must be kept in good condition** and stored in an appropriate location.

Quick quiz

1   Why might a business *not* receive a statement of account from a supplier?

2   Why would a supplier statement reconciliation be performed?

3   Give three examples of reconciling items.

4   How often should suppliers' statements (ideally) be reconciled to purchase ledger records?

5   What is the objective of creditor management?

6   When might it *not* be advantageous to take advantage of a cash discount?

7   How is information that is no longer needed on a regular basis dealt with?

Answers to quick quiz

1   A statement might not be sent by a small supplier, or to a business which has only made a 'one off' purchase.

2   A business will want to check that its purchase ledger records are correct.

3   (i)   Payments in transit
    (ii) Omitted invoices and credit notes
    (iii) Errors

4   Monthly.

5   To maximise the credit period taken without jeopardising relationships with suppliers.

6   If the cost of financing the early payment (eg bank overdraft interest) is more than the discount.

7   - Microfilmed or microfiched
    - Archived
    - Destroyed

Part B
Payments

6 Authorising and making payments

This chapter contains

Learning objectives

On completion of this chapter you will be able to:

- Prepare payments according to organisational procedures

- Make authorised payments according to organisational procedures

Performance criteria

2.2.1 Payments are correctly calculated from relevant documentation

2.2.2 Payments are scheduled and authorised by the appropriate person

2.2.3 Queries are referred to the appropriate person

2.2.4 Security and confidentiality are maintained according to organisational requirements

2.3.1 The appropriate payment method is used in accordance with organisational procedures

2.3.2 Payments are made in accordance with organisational processes and timescales

2.3.4 Queries are referred to the appropriate person

2.3.5 Security and confidentiality are maintained according to organisational requirements

Range statement

2.2.1 Payments: creditors

2.2.2 Documentation: suppliers' statements; cheque requisitions

2.2.3 Appropriate person: manager; accountant

2.3.1 Payment methods: cash; cheques; automated payments

2.3.2 Payment: creditors; cheque requisition form

2.3.4 Queries relating to: unauthorised claims for payment; insufficient supporting evidence; claims exceeding prescribed limit.

Knowledge and understanding

- Automated payments: CHAPS, BACS, direct debts, standing orders
- Credit and debit cards
- Documentation for payments
- Legal requirements relating to cheques, including crossing and endorsements
- Credit card procedures
- The nature of the organisation's business transactions
- Organisational procedures for authorisation and coding of purchase invoices and payments

1 INTRODUCTION

1.1 A business needs strict controls over payments. This applies to all payments, from the smallest to the largest. If any business allows some of its employees to pay out its money without permission, the scope for dishonesty becomes very wide.

2 CONTROLS OVER PAYMENTS

2.1 There are three main steps in applying controls over payments.

> *Step 1* Obtain **documentary evidence** of the reason why the payment is being made and the amount of the payment. In the case of payments to suppliers, the documentary evidence will be a supplier's invoice (or statement).

Step 2   **Authorisation** of the payment. This means giving formal 'official' approval to make the payment.

Step 3   **Restricting the authority to actually make the payment** to certain specified individuals.

The difference between Steps 1, 2 and 3 can be illustrated with an example.

2.2   EXAMPLE: CONTROLLING A PAYMENT

A company buys goods costing £5,000.

Step 1   Obtaining **documentary evidence** of the reason why the payment is being made and the amount of the payment.

It will receive an invoice from the supplier. This is the documentary evidence of the reason for and amount of the payment.

Step 2   **Authorisation** of the payment.

The invoice will be approved by the purchasing director. This approval is the authorisation of the payment.

Step 3   **Restricting the authority to actually make the payment** to certain specified individuals.

Later, payment will be made to the supplier by cheque. For a payment of £5,000, perhaps only the finance director and managing director will be permitted to sign the cheque. Therefore the **authority to make the payment** is limited to these two people.

Authorisation

2.3   Every payment must be approved by an **authorised person**. This person will often be a manager or supervisor in the department that initiated the expense. Every organisation has its own system to determine the following.

- **Which individuals** can authorise particular expenses
- The **maximum amount** of expenditure that an individual can authorise

DEVOLVED ASSESSMENT ALERT
You may be asked to state whether an invoice can be passed for payment and if not, why not.

2.4   As just one illustration, the authorisation/approval limits on spending in a company with three departments and a head office might be as follows.

Limit on expenditure	Departments			Head Office
	Purchasing	Production	Sales	
No limit	Chairman or Managing Director	Chairman or Managing Director	Chairman or Managing Director	Chairman or Managing Director
£25,000	Purchasing director Chief accountant	Production director Chief accountant	Sales director Chief accountant	Chief accountant
£5,000	Grade 1 manager	Grade 1 manager	Grade 1 manager	Grade 1 manager
£1,000	Grade 2 manager	Grade 2 manager	Grade 2 manager	Grade 2 manager
£100	Supervisor	Supervisor	Supervisor	Supervisor

2.5 A person authorises a payment by putting a **signature** or **recognisable initials** on the appropriate document and the date. Appropriate documents include the following.

- Supplier's invoice or statement (see Part A)
- Cheque requisition form (see Section 3 below)
- Expenses claim form (see Section 4 below)

2.6 Without authorisation, the accounts department should **refuse to make the payment** and should send the document back to the appropriate department for the approval to be properly given.

2.7 Some companies use a **sticker** or **stamp** which they put on invoices received.

```
┌─────────────────────────────────────────┐
│           INVOICE PAYMENT                │
│            APPROVED BY                    │
│                                          │
│   Name .................................  │
│                                          │
│   Dept .................................  │
│                                          │
│   Date .................................  │
│                                          │
│                    Initials .............  │
└─────────────────────────────────────────┘
```

This makes it easier for the accounts department to check that the invoice has been properly authorised for payment.

3 CHEQUE REQUISITION FORMS

3.1 A **supplier's invoice** usually provides documentary evidence of the reason for a payment, and the amount of that payment. However, a payment may be required in the following circumstances.

- The invoice has **not yet been received,** but payment is required now
- There will be **neither an invoice nor a receipt**

3.2 You may wonder what payments can occur where an invoice or receipt is not obtained eventually. There are few such cases. An example is the filing fee paid to

Companies House to go with the company's annual return. This is a payment required by law, for which no invoice or receipt is provided.

3.3 Documentary evidence of the reason for, and the amount of, the payment is obtained by asking the person requesting payment to complete a **cheque requisition form.**

> **KEY TERM**
>
> A **cheque requisition form** is a request for a cheque to be drawn to make a payment.

3.4 A cheque requisition form is an **internal document** for use within the business and so there is no standard design. The following example shows a typical layout.

3.5 EXAMPLE: CHEQUE REQUISITION FORM

The advertising manager of ABC Ltd wants to put an advertisement into the local weekly newspaper. The newspaper requests payment of £470 (£400 + VAT at 17½%) in advance, by a fax letter. A receipt will be sent later with confirmation that the advertisement has been inserted. The advertising manager needs to complete a **cheque requisition form.**

3.6 SOLUTION

ABC LIMITED
CHEQUE REQUISITION FORM

DATE .... *11 JUNE 20X1* ....

Please draw a cheque on the company's account

PAYABLE TO .... *Popular Newspapers Plc* ....

AMOUNT .... *£470* ....

REASON .... *2 column 5 inch ad in 20 June edition* ....

.... *of Morning Herald newspaper* ....

General ledger code (if known) .... *201/A01101* ....

                                              Please tick as appropriate

Invoice/receipt to follow .... *✓* ....

No invoice or receipt ....

Other evidence attached .... *✓ Fax letter*

Send cheque to *A Davies, Ad Manager, for sending on to Popular Newspapers ASAP*

Signature .... *A Davies* ....

Department .... *15* ....

Telephone extension .... *x326* ....

BPP
PUBLISHING

3.7   This is the routine for preparing a cheque requisition form.

Action	Comment
The form must be **signed** by a person who can **authorise** the payment.	This might be the advertising manager personally or his/her superior.
The **general ledger code** is needed to record the payment in the accounts.	A code will be written on the form either by the advertising manager or by someone in the accounts department.
Supporting documentation should be attached.	In this case the fax letter requesting payment.
The **cheque**, when it has been prepared and signed, will be sent to the person authorising payment.	This will be the advertising manager. In some organisations, the accounts department will only send the cheque to the payee direct.
An **invoice/receipt** may follow.	Some organisations may insist on this.

4   EXPENSES CLAIM FORMS

4.1   In many organisations, employees will make **payments out of their own pocket for items of business expense** and then claim reimbursement. Examples include the following.

- Money spent on **business travel**
- Cost of **newspapers or magazines** that the employee buys for business use
- Part or all of the employee's **domestic telephone bill**
- **Petrol** (for company cars)
- **Car service and repair bills** (for company cars)

> **KEY TERM**
>
> Expenses paid by an employee for which the employee wants reimbursement should be itemised on an **expenses claim form.**

4.2   Proof should be given of the existence and the amount of the expense, and this can be done by attaching **receipts.**

Step 1   The claimant submits the completed and signed form to his or her superior for **approval and authorisation,** before passing it to the accounts department.

Step 2   **Receipts/bills/invoices** should be attached to the form.

Step 3   The **general ledger codes** are entered on the form by the accounts department, although some forms have these codes preprinted.

Step 4   **Payments are separated into the net amount and the VAT element.** This may be done by the individual making the expenses claim, or the accounts department.

4.3   An **example of an expenses claim form** follows.

ABC LIMITED
Expenses claim form

Name: ....*C. PURVIS*...... Month: ....*OCTOBER X7*.......

Department: ....*MARKETING*.......

	Nominal ledger code	NET £	VAT £	TOTAL £
MOTOR CAR EXPENSES				
Petrol		49-20	-	49-20
Repairs and service		100-00	17-50	117-50
Parking		5-00	-	5-00
Car tax				
		154-20	17-50	171-70
OTHER TRAVEL COSTS (Specify) *Taxi*		12.00	-	12.00
TELEPHONE EXPENSES (Attach telephone bill)		24-00	4-20	28-20
NEWSPAPERS AND JOURNALS		12-50	-	12-50
OTHER (Specify) *Stationery*		5-80	-	5-80
TOTAL CLAIMED		208-50	21-70	230-20

Signature of claimant: ....*Claire Purvis*....... Date: ....*3 Nov X7*.......

Authorised by: .... Date: ....

---

5 THE TIMING AND METHODS OF PAYMENTS

When should payments be made and to whom?

5.1 Suppliers submitting invoices will usually grant a **period of credit** to a customer.

- 'Net 30 days' means that payment is due 30 days from the date of the invoice

- Similarly 'net 60 days' and 'net 90 days' allow 60/ 90 days from the invoice date

- Some suppliers specify the latest date for payment eg 'Payment due by 30 November'

- If the invoice is not paid by the specified date, it becomes **overdue** and reminders or telephone calls may be received from the supplier

BPP PUBLISHING

Who decides?

5.2 Decisions about who should be paid and when are made by a **senior person** in the company, perhaps the chief accountant. To help in this, an accounts clerk may be asked to draw up a list of unpaid invoices indicating the following.

- Overdue invoices
- Invoices outstanding for longer than a certain period of time (eg two months)
- Invoices due to be paid soon (eg within the next week)

5.3 EXAMPLE: WHO SHOULD BE PAID AND WHEN?

At the end of May 20X1, the accounts clerk of ABC Ltd is asked to prepare a list of unpaid invoices. She is asked to indicate which are overdue and which unpaid for over two months.

The clerk will begin by preparing a list of unpaid invoices. This might be in invoice date order, or in alphabetical order of supplier name. An example follows.

ABC Ltd's chief accountant will probably pay all the amounts listed in the final column.

Unpaid invoices as at 31 May 20X1

Supplier name	Credit terms	Invoice date	Invoice number	Amount £	Overdue or unpaid for over 2 months £
Archway Ltd	60 days	8.3.X1	32743	535.50	535.50
		15.4.X1	33816	421.80	
B A D Ltd	30 days	11.4.X1	9291	1,100.00	1,100.00
Bray Bros Ltd	60 days	8.4.X1	12534	125.55	
Chalk Ltd	30 days	21.3.X1	0135	245.75	245.75
		31.3.X1	0160	306.35	306.35
		2.5.X1	0297	281.00	
Finsbury Ltd	30 days	16.5.X1	546327	2,427.00	
Jupiter Telephones	-	18.4.X1	83461150	814.39	
Western Water	-	20.3.X1	2778045	650.72	650.72
Willow Ltd	30 days	16.4.X1	W248	173.20	173.20
				7,081.26	3,011.52

5.4 **Miscellaneous (non-trade) payments** will be made at various dates during the month as they fall due. However **trade bills tend to be paid at the end of the month.**

Methods of payment

5.5 The following are the most common methods of **making payments** for goods and services, wages and salaries, rent and rates etc.

- Cheques
- BACS (especially for salaries and wages)

5.6 **Other payment methods**

- Cash
- Banker's draft
- Standing order
- Direct debit

- Company credit card or charge card
- Mail transfer and telegraphic transfer
- CHAPS

5.7 This chapter looks at the procedures for making payments by each of these methods. Small payments by cash are dealt with separately in Chapter 8 on **petty cash**.

> Payments of **wages and salaries** are dealt with in Part C on payroll and are not described here.

6 PAYMENTS BY CASH

6.1 **Cash payments** are used quite often by a business.

- For **small payments** out of petty cash (see Chapter 8)
- For **wages** (see Part C)

6.2 Using cash to pay large amounts of money to suppliers ought to be very rare indeed.

- Cash needs to be kept **secure** as it is easily stolen

- Cash can get **lost in the post**

- Difficulty of keeping **control over cash** used often for making payments

- Unless the supplier issues a **receipt,** there is no evidence that a cash payment has been made (bad for record keeping)

6.3 Not surprisingly, the use of cash to make large payments to suppliers is sometimes associated with shady or dishonest dealers in backstreet or underworld businesses.

7 PAYMENTS BY CHEQUE

7.1 The most common method of payment (excluding wages and salaries) is by **cheque**.

7.2 Cheques are for payments out of a bank **current account**. The accounts department will be provided with cheque books by its bank.

Security

7.3 An individual in the accounts department will be responsible for the **safekeeping** of the cheque book(s). They should be kept under lock and key, perhaps in a **safe** and at the very least in a **locked drawer**. Cheque books, or individual cheques from a book, can be stolen by someone to use fraudulently. To prevent fraud, only an **authorised person** should be able to order new cheque books.

Signatures on business cheques

7.4 A bank will not accept a payment by cheque unless it has been **properly signed**.

(a) For company cheques, only certain **specified individuals** can sign a cheque on behalf of the company. The names and signatures of these individuals must be supplied to the bank on a **bank form or letter**.

(b) Cheques above a certain value must usually contain **two authorised signatures**.

(c) A company's authorised signatories are selected by the company itself, but might consist of the chairman, all directors and the chief accountant or financial controller.

> Revise the legal aspects of cheques, including crossing and endorsements, in your Unit 1 text.

Procedures for preparing cheques

7.5 The starting point for preparing payments to suppliers, or other creditors, is deciding when to write cheques and **which payments to make**.

Step 1	Prepare list of payments	The accounts clerk is instructed to prepare a **list of all the payments due** (see 5.3 above).
Step 2	Payments authorised; sufficient funds available	A business cannot write and send off cheques unless it has enough money in its bank account (or overdraft facility) to cover the payments. So the decision about when and who to pay will normally come from a manager in the accounts department, possibly the chief accountant.
Step 3	Check invoices to be paid	The accounts clerk finds the invoices appearing on the authorised payments list in the unpaid invoices file and checks.
		• The invoice has been properly authorised for payment
		• A general ledger code has been written on the invoice (if not, it should be done now)
		• Any remittance advice is kept with it
Step 4	Prepare the cheques	The accounts clerk uses the information on the invoice to write the cheque. A record should be written on the counterfoil.
		• Name of the payee
		• Amount
		• Date
		• Any other helpful details
		The supplier may specify that the cheque should be marked 'Account payee'. If so, these words should be written between the crossing lines on the cheque (if not already preprinted there).
Step 5	Attach invoice to cheque; sign	The cheque should be attached to the invoice and remittance advice, and submitted to an **authorised person(s)** for signature.

| Step 6 | Mark invoice 'PAID' | The invoice should be detached and stamped PAID, with the date of payment and the cheque number added. |
| Step 7 | Send cheque off to payee with remittance advice | The cheque is sent to the payee, together with the **remittance advice**. If there isn't a remittance advice, some form of covering letter is needed to explain to the payee what the cheque is for. |

7.6 Here is an example of a cheque for £1,520.75 made payable to H V Stern Ltd and crossed 'A/c payee'. It has been prepared on 6 January 20X9 and is a payment of invoice 12345. Cheques over £1,000 need two authorised signatures.

DEVOLVED ASSESSMENT ALERT
You may well be asked to prepare a cheque in the Devolved Assessment.

The **accounting procedures** for recording the payment in the ledgers will be described in the next chapter.

Discounts for early settlement

7.7 If a cash discount is taken, it must be deducted from the payment to be made.

7.8 EXAMPLE: CASH DISCOUNT

The supplier will indicate the availability of a **cash discount** on each invoice, but the method of showing the discount will vary. Here is just one example.

BPP
PUBLISHING

BANGLES LTD

Jewel House
Richmans Road
LONDON SE1N 5AB

Invoice Number: 123456

Tax Point: 01/08/X7

Account Number 3365

INVOICE

CUSTOMER
ABC Ltd
112 Peters Square
Weyford
Kent CR2 2TA

Telephone Number 01427 123 4567
VAT Registration Number 457 4635 19
Northern Bank plc Code 20-25-43
Account Number 957023

Item Code	Description	Quantity	Unit Price	Net Amount
13579A	Deeks	30	250.00	7,500.00
	Delivery	1	100.00	100.00

Terms of payment are 30 days net. A cash discount of 2.5% is available for payment within 7 days.

SALES VALUE:	7,600.00
VAT AT 17.5%:	1,296.75
AMOUNT PAYABLE:	8,896.75

Settlement discount of £190.00 for payments by 8th August 20X7	
Amount payable	8,896.75
Less discount	190.00
Amount payable if payment made by the 8th of August 20X7	8,706.75

7.9 Remember that VAT is calculated on the **sales value net of discount**, regardless of whether the discount is taken.

	£
Sales value	7,600
Less 2.5% discount	(190)
Net sales value	7,410
VAT at 17.5% of £7,410	£1,296.75

7.10 SOLUTION

ABC Ltd's chief accountant decides to take the cash discount. A cheque is written and despatched not later than 8 August. The amount of the cheque will be £8,706.75, as shown at the bottom of the invoice.

The counterfoil of the cheque should include a note to indicate that a 2.5% settlement discount has been taken. The invoice will be stamped PAID with the date and cheque number. An extra note on the invoice that the 2.5% discount has been taken would be useful.

If payment is delayed beyond 8 August, the **full amount** (£8,896.75) is due.

7.11 If a **credit note** is due against the invoice, or has already been received, it should be deducted **before** the cash discount is calculated.

Activity 6.1   Level: Assessment

One of the major suppliers of Pampas Co is Avocado Co. Avocado Co offers the following terms.

30 days net
1% discount for payment within 14 days of invoice date
2% discount for payment within 7 days of invoice date

Pampas makes payments to suppliers on Thursday of each week. Although payment of invoices will sometimes be delayed (for example, if a credit note is awaited), it is the general policy of Pampas to pay within suppliers' terms. At each payment date, all invoices which will become overdue during the period up to and including the next payment date (the next Thursday) are paid. Payment is made by hand delivery of a cheque on Thursdays to Avocado's premises nearby.

Avocado has sent a statement of account to Pampas (with which Pampas agrees) showing the following details (amounts are shown before discount).

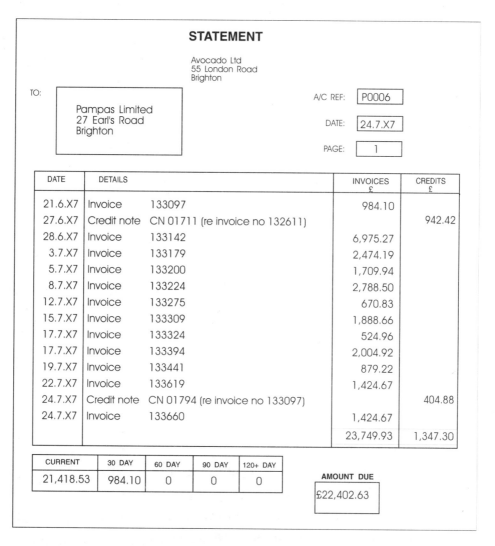

STATEMENT

Avocado Ltd
55 London Road
Brighton

TO:
Pampas Limited
27 Earl's Road
Brighton

A/C REF: P0006

DATE: 24.7.X7

PAGE: 1

DATE	DETAILS		INVOICES £	CREDITS £
21.6.X7	Invoice	133097	984.10	
27.6.X7	Credit note	CN 01711 (re invoice no 132611)		942.42
28.6.X7	Invoice	133142	6,975.27	
3.7.X7	Invoice	133179	2,474.19	
5.7.X7	Invoice	133200	1,709.94	
8.7.X7	Invoice	133224	2,788.50	
12.7.X7	Invoice	133275	670.83	
15.7.X7	Invoice	133309	1,888.66	
17.7.X7	Invoice	133324	524.96	
17.7.X7	Invoice	133394	2,004.92	
19.7.X7	Invoice	133441	879.22	
22.7.X7	Invoice	133619	1,424.67	
24.7.X7	Credit note	CN 01794 (re invoice no 133097)		404.88
24.7.X7	Invoice	133660	1,424.67	
			23,749.93	1,347.30

CURRENT	30 DAY	60 DAY	90 DAY	120+ DAY
21,418.53	984.10	0	0	0

AMOUNT DUE
£22,402.63

Task

Prepare two schedules, following the layouts indicated below, showing the payments to be made to Avocado on 25 July, 1 August, 8 August and 15 August in respect of the items included in the statement of account dated 24 July 20X7, conforming to the following alternative requirements.

(a) Payment is to be made as late as possible within suppliers' payment terms, irrespective of whether or not discounts are given.

107

Ref	Amount £	Due date (invoice date add 30 days)	25.7 £	Payment date 1.8 £	8.8 £	15.8 £

(b) payment is to be made as late as possible such that all available settlement discounts are taken up at the highest possible rate of discount.

Ref	Amount £	Best discount available %	£	25.7 £	Payment date 1.8 £	8.8 £	15.8 £

Any items which are already overdue should be paid on 25 July.

Advantages and disadvantages of paying by cheque

7.12 Cheques are widely used to pay for supplies and other expenses.

Advantages of cheque payments	Disadvantages of cheque payments
Cheques are **convenient to use** for payments of any amount (subject to funds being available).	There are **security problems** with keeping cheques safe from theft and misuse (forged signatures), although cheques are more secure than cash.
The cheque number can provide a useful means of **tracing payments**, in case of queries.	Cheques can be **a slow method of payment,** and a supplier might insist on a more prompt and reliable method, such as standing order.
They are commonly used and **widely accepted.**	Cheques can get **lost in the post.**

Lost cheques

7.13 The loss of the cheque will not become apparent until the supplier contacts you demanding payment.

- **Check on the supplier's account** in the purchase ledger, to see if a cheque payment has been made

- If a payment was made, and the date is not recent (recent cheques might be in the post), the cheque is probably **lost or misdirected**

7.14 The following actions should be taken, when it appears a cheque has been lost.

Step 1	Confirm the cheque has **not gone through the bank account**, by checking the most recent bank statements or by telephoning the bank.
Step 2	Check the details of the **name and address of the supplier** to which the cheque was sent, and the name of any particular person to whom the letter was addressed.

7.15 One of three things will probably have happened.

Circumstances	Action to take
The cheque **has gone through your bank account** and the supplier has been paid.	The error is in the supplier's records. Give the supplier the details of the payment.
The cheque has been sent to the supplier, but to the **wrong person** in the supplier's organisation.	Inform the relevant member of staff at the supplier so that he can retrieve the cheque.
The cheque has either been sent to the **wrong address** or has been **lost in the post**.	If this appears to be the case, you should take measures to *stop* the 'old' cheque and prepare a new one.

Stopping cheques

7.16 Businesses need to stop payments of cheques quite often. Some even have a special form for sending stop instructions to the bank.

7.17 Sometimes the recipient of the cheque has forgotten to bank it until it is out of date. In this case, the bank should not pay the cheque anyway. However the cheque should be returned to you before a new cheque is issued, as a precaution against the bank paying it in error.

7.18 To **stop a cheque from being paid**, you should carry out the following.

Step 1	Telephone **your bank with details of the cheque to be stopped**.
Step 2	Confirm this instruction **in writing**.

An example of a 'stop' form is shown below. The accounts clerk will fill in the form, which will then be signed by an authorised signatory for cheques.

7.19 If the cheque has been stopped because it was **lost**, the supplier still has the right to be paid. A new cheque should be prepared and signed. Bear in mind the following points.

(a) The 'PAID' supplier's invoice should be **altered** to show the old cheque has been stopped, and the date and number of the **replacement cheque** added.

(b) Write 'STOPPED' on the **counterfoil of the old cheque** and the date on which this occurred.

(c) The **counterfoil of the new cheque** should refer to the supplier's invoice and indicate that it is a replacement cheque.

(d) The replacement cheque should be **sent to the supplier**, with a covering letter.

ABC LIMITED

3, The Mews

Barking

The Manager
Bank plc
6 Hill Road
Barking

DATE: _23 July 20X9_

Dear Sir

ABC LIMITED ACCOUNT NO 2467890

We wish to confirm our request by telephone that the payment of the cheque detailed below is stopped.

Cheque No _009372_

Dated _3 July 20X9_

Amount £ _4,276 83_

Payee _A & P Plumb Ltd_

We have inspected our statements up to number _493_ inclusive and the cheque is not listed on them.

We have drawn a replacement cheque no: _00 9406_

Your faithfully

M. P. Jones

FOR ABC LIMITED

Activity 6.2

Level: Assessment

At 7 October 20X7, the unpaid invoices/credit notes file of Keynes & Milton Builders includes the following items in respect of their supplier, Morton Bricks plc, supplier account number C1109.

Date	Details	Amount £
3.8.X7	Invoice 49492	142.91
24.8.X7	Invoice 50140	2,941.17
2.9.X7	Invoice 50311	642.54
4.9.X7	Invoice 50379	1,421.70
7.9.X7	Invoice 50411	6,997.21
9.9.X7	Invoice 50449	354.72
11.9.X7	Invoice 50457	3,428.88
13.9.X7	Credit note 7211 (re invoice 50114)	(864.75)
18.9.X7	Invoice 50601	824.79
25.9.X7	Credit note 7218 (re invoice 50379)	(842.05)
2.10.X7	Invoice 50888	1,752.94

The records of Keynes & Milton show that as at 15 October 20X7, the only payment made to Morton Bricks since 7 October was on 8 October. This payment was for £4,306.27.

The remittance advice shows the following details.

REMITTANCE ADVICE

TO: Morton Bricks plc
London Common
Wallsend
N24 4QP

KEYNES & MILTON
BUILDERS
24 HURLE ROAD
HODLEY
NOTTINGHAM NG4 7SA

Account Ref	C1109		Date	0810X7		Page	1

DATE	DETAILS		INVOICES	CREDIT NOTES	PAYMENT AMOUNT
3.8.X7	Invoice	49492	142.91		142.91
24.8.X7	Invoice	50140	2,941.17		2,941.17
2.9.X7	Invoice	50311	642.54		642.54
4.9.X7	Invoice	50379	1,421.70		1,421.70
25.9.X7	Credit note	7218		842.05	(842.05)
	Total		5,148.32	842.05	4,306.27

Between 7 October and 15 October, the following invoices were received from Morton Bricks.

Date	Details	Amount £
8.10.X7	Invoice 50991	408.00
12.10.X7	Invoice 51042	189.10

Keynes & Milton has received the following statement of account from Morton Bricks.

MORTON BRICKS PLC
London Common
Wallsend
N24 4QP

Telephone: 01794 424710
Fax: 01794 474770

Keynes & Milton Builders
24 Hurle Road
Hodley
Nottingham
NG4 75A

Account number:
0995
Date of statement:
9 October 20X7

STATEMENT OF ACCOUNT

Details			Amount £
3.8.X7	Invoice	49492	-142.91
24.8.X7	Invoice	50140	-2,941.17
2.9.X7	Invoice	50311	-662.54
4.9.X7	Invoice	50379	-1,421.70
7.9.X7	Invoice	50411	-6,997.21
9.9.X7	Invoice	50449	-357.42
11.9.X7	Invoice	50457	-3,428.88
18.9.X7	Invoice	50601	-824.79
25.9.X7	Credit note	7218	+842.05
2.10.X7	Invoice	50888	-1,752.94
8.10.X7	Invoice	50991	-408.00
Total amount due(-)			-18,095.51

Terms: 30 days net
E & OE

You work as an Accounts Assistant with Keynes & Milton Builders. You are asked to establish whether there appear to be any errors and discrepancies on the statement of account supplied by Morton Bricks plc.

Tasks

(a) List the apparent errors and discrepancies which you find in the statement of account.

(b) (i) Calculate the payment which should be made on 15 October 20X7 to clear all unpaid items shown in your firm's records as being over thirty days old.

(ii) Using the blank form provided below, prepare a cheque for signature to make the payment, crossing the cheque 'Not negotiable'.

Portland Bank plc

74-00-88

44 Hazeltine Plaza, West Wharf, Bowthorpe CM47 7PN

_____ 20 ____

Pay

or order

£

KEYNES & MILTON BUILDERS

Cheque Number   Sort code   Account Number   _____

⑊⑊700008⑊⑊   74⑊⑊0088⑊   0099414 2⑊⑊

---

8 BACS

8.1 BACS stands for **Bankers Automated Clearing Services**. It is a company owned by the high street banks which operates the electronic transfer of funds between bank accounts. When a business uses BACS, it sends information to BACS for processing.

8.2 Many different businesses use BACS. Even small businesses can do so because their bank will help to organise the information for BACS. The most important advantage of the BACS system is that it operates with **very reduced amounts of paperwork**. Large amounts of paperwork cause expense, delay and can lack a great deal in the way of security.

8.3 BACS is used for processing of the following.

- Standing orders
- Direct debits
- Salaries (monthly)
- Wages (weekly)
- Some one-off payments

DEVOLVED ASSESSMENT ALERT
You are more likely to be asked what BACS is, rather than how it is used.

Procedures for using BACS

8.4 A company wishes to pay its salaries using BACS. The procedure is as follows.

BPP PUBLISHING

Step 1	The company produces a file with the details of each member of staff.

- Full name
- Amount to be paid
- Bank/branch number
- Bank account number

The file is sent to the BACS processing computer centre. It can be sent on magnetic tape (discouraged by BACS), floppy disk or digitally on an ISDN line.

Step 2	The files are submitted to the computer which sorts the information into that required for certain banks on certain dates. The information can then be read into each bank's computer system direct for processing.
Step 3	On the day specified by the company, the salary due to each member of staff is credited to their bank account and the company's account is debited with the total amount of all payments made.
Step 4	All BACS items are recorded on archive disks so that the user (the company) has a record in case any query arises.
Step 5	The business's records are updated with the same information that was sent to BACS.

9 PAYMENTS BY BANKER'S DRAFT

9.1 A supplier might sometimes ask a customer to pay by **banker's draft**. Unlike normal cheques, a banker's draft **cannot be stopped or cancelled after it has been issued** and so payment is guaranteed. Banker's drafts are only used when a large payment is involved, such as for the purchase of a car.

9.2 EXAMPLE: PAYMENT BY BANKER'S DRAFT

One of your managers wants to buy a car from Fittipaldi Motors, for £33,334.45.

Step 1	Prepare an **application for a banker's draft** to be provided by your bank to pay the car supplier. Although applications for a banker's draft can be made by letter, banks also provide standard forms that can be used instead. A standard form is shown below, filled in by the accounts clerk of the business.
Step 2	**Signatures of (probably two) authorised officials** are required.
Step 3	The signed form is **sent to the bank**.
Step 4	The bank **returns the form to the business with the draft** (see below).
Step 5	The form is signed to **acknowledge receipt of the draft** and returned to the bank.
Step 6	The draft is then sent or taken to the **car supplier**, who will release the car to the business.

Application for Inland Draft

To Swallows Bank Plc

EDGWARE   Date   3.6.X8

Kindly supply a crossed Draft. *Marked ~~`account payee`~~

Payable to   FITTIPALDI MOTORS

£ 33,334.45   amount in words   Thirty three thousand, three hundred and thirty four pounds-45p

*Please debit my/our account no | 8 | 2 | 3 | 7 | 4 | 1 | 1 | 6 |

~~*Herewith cash to cover~~

~~*Herewith cheque to cover~~

Charges (if any) to be   ~~*deducted~~ / charged to me/us   Delete as necessary

Signature(s)   *JP MacHugh*   *B Clive*

Name(s)   J P MACHUGH   B CLIVE

Address
(if not a
customer)

I/We acknowledge receipt of the above mentioned Draft numbered   123455

_____ Signature

(To be signed by an authorised person in the business and returned to the bank)

Swallows Bank

Swallows Bank Plc
Head Office
London EC3V 1AB

15-14-12T

Date *4th June 20X8*

Fittipaldi Motors Limited

the sum of *Thirty Three Thousand Three Hundred and Thirty Four Pounds and Forty Five Pence only*

NOT NEGOTIABLE

£ 33,334 - 45

For Swallows Bank Plc

EDGWARE BRANCH

BR Dowding

SV Pritchard

⑃123455⑃ 15⑃ 1412⑃ 000345⑃

BPP
PUBLISHING

10 PAYMENTS BY STANDING ORDER AND DIRECT DEBIT

Standing orders

10.1 Standing order payments are used by a business to make regular payments of a fixed amount. Examples include the following.

- **Hire purchase** (eg an asset bought under an HP agreement)
- **Rental payments** to the landlord of a building occupied by the business
- **Insurance premiums**

10.2 Although the supplier (the HP company, landlord, or insurance company) may request payment by standing order, **it is up to the paying business to set up a standing order arrangement.**

10.3 The business must specify the following to its bank.

- It wants a standing order arrangement for **regular payments** from its account
- The **fixed amount** of each payment
- The **frequency** of each payment (eg monthly) and the due date
- **Banking details of the supplier** to which the payments should be made

If the business subsequently needs to alter the amount of each payment, or to stop future payments, it must send the relevant instructions to the bank **in writing**.

10.4 A standing order request can be sent in a letter, but banks also supply standard forms called **Standing Order Mandates**. An authorised cheque signatory (eg the chief accountant or a director) will need to sign the request form. It is likely that an accounts clerk will be asked to prepare the mandate form ready for signature.

10.5 EXAMPLE: STANDING ORDER MANDATE

ABC Ltd buys some office furniture on hire purchase, arranging to make monthly payments of £240.25 to the HP company, whose banking details are as follows.

HP company	Smooth Finance Ltd
Bank of HP company	Barminster Bank plc
	Richmond-upon-Thames branch
	Sort code 22-33-44
Bank account number	11742538

ABC Ltd banks at the Weyford branch of Lowlands Bank plc, 5 High Street, Weyford, Kent CR1 1GG, account number 36274859.

The first payment is due on 15 June 20X4 and the final payment on 15 May 20X6.

10.6 SOLUTION

A Standing Order Mandate would be prepared for signature as follows.

Standing Order Mandate

TO   <u>LOWLANDS</u>   BANK

Address   <u>5 HIGH STREET, WEYFORD, KENT</u>

	Bank	Branch Title (not address)	Sorting Code Number
Please pay	BARMINSTER	RICHMOND-UPON-THAMES	22-33-44
	Beneficiary's Name		Account Number
for the credit of	SMOOTH FINANCE LIMITED		11742538

	Regular amount in figures	Regular amount in words
the sum of	£ 240-25	TWO HUNDRED AND FORTY POUNDS & 25 PENCE

	Date and Amount of First Payment		and thereafter every	Due Date and Frequency
commencing	15 JUNE 20X4	£ 240-25		15TH OF EACH MONTH
	Date and Amount of Last Payment		*until you receive further	
*until	15 MAY 20X6	£ 240-25	notice from me/us in writing	
quoting the reference	ABC OFFICE FURNITURE		and debit my/our account accordingly.	

This instruction cancels any previous order in favour of the beneficiary named above, under this reference.

Special instructions:

Account to be debited	Account Number
ABC LIMITED	3 6 2 7 4 8 5 9

Signature(s) _____   Date _____

_____

*Delete if not applicable

10.7 The **reference** (ABC office furniture) will appear on Smooth Finance's bank statements. It will not appear on ABC Ltd's bank statement. A reference for Smooth Finance is not essential and is only supplied at ABC Ltd's choice. An alternative would be a reference **number,** such as the agreement number.

Direct debits

10.8 Direct debits, like standing orders, are used for **regular payments**. They differ from standing orders mainly in the following ways.

- The **person who** *receives* **the payments initiates each payment**, informing the paying bank of the *amount* of each payment

- Payments can be for a **variable amount** each time and at irregular intervals

An example of a completed direct debit instruction follows. This is returned to the **supplier** not the bank. The supplier then makes arrangements with its own bank to collect the payments.

British Gas
South Midlands

British Gas plc (South Midlands)
Gas Payment Plan
Freepost
Coringham CV6 3TT

Gas Payment Plan
Direct Debit Instruction

Instructions to your Bank/Building Society to pay direct debits

Please complete parts 1 to 5 to instruct your Bank/Building Society to make payments directly from your account.

When completed please return the form direct to us.

1. The Manager

| WESTLAKE | Bank/~~Building Society~~ |

(Full Address of your Bank/Building Society)

| 3 Great Way, Dudentry |
| South Midlands |
| DD1 1BC |

2. Name of account holder(s)

| LARKSPUR LIMITED |

3. Bank/Building Society Account Number

| 3 | 5 | 1 | 4 | 9 | 7 | 5 | 5 |

4. Sort-Code

| 6 | 2 | – | 3 | 1 | – | 9 | 5 |

Originator's Identification Number
916258

Instruction Number
Branch use only

Account Reference Number

| 00137200123468 |

Revenue Officer
British Gas plc South Midlands
PO Box 78
Coringham CV6 3TT

After completion the Bank/Building Society branch should detach this part of the form and return it to the address above.

I/We would like to start a Gas Payment Plan and have completed a Direct Debit Mandate

Please send the whole form
to the reply address overleaf

5. Your instructions to the Bank/Building Society and signature

- I/We instruct you to pay direct debits from my/our account at the request of British Gas South Midlands.

- The amounts are variable and may be debited on various dates.

- I/We understand that British Gas South Midlands may change the amounts and dates only after giving prior notice.

British Gas South Midlands
Account Reference Number

| 00137200123468 |

- I/We will inform the Bank/Building Society in writing if I/We wish to cancel this instruction.

- I/We understand that if a debit is paid which breaks the terms of the instruction, the Bank/Building Society will make a refund.

Signature(s)	Date
R. C. Watson	8/9/X3
J. Keats	8/9/X3

- Banks/Building Societies may decline to accept Direct Debits from some types of account.

FOR BANK/BUILDING SOCIETY USE ONLY

Branch Title

Sort Code

A/c no.

A/c name

(maximum 18 characters)

Direct debits in respect of our customer's instruction under the reference number quoted should be made out as above.

Standing Order mandate cancelled.

Last payment made on _____
Standing Order mandate not traced _____

For _____ Bank/Building Society

Manager _____ Date _____

03/09/X3   DIST. 24

LARKSPUR LTD
12 BONNY STREET
DUDENTRY
SOUTH MIDLANDS   DD1 2ER

00137200123468

10.9   Payments by direct debit **might** be for regular bills, such as telephone, gas, electricity and water. The company being paid by direct debit will inform the payer of the amount and date of each payment in a printed statement.

11 PAYMENTS BY OTHER METHODS

11.1 Other methods of payment will be comparatively rare and depend on the type of business involved.

Business credit, debit or charge cards

11.2 Some businesses have credit, debit or charge card schemes (with MasterCard or Visa, Delta and American Express or Diners Club respectively). Under such a scheme, selected individuals within the business are given a card which they use to pay for their business expenses.

- **Limits** can be placed on the amount of spending on an individual card

- Cardholders will normally be **directors**, some senior managers and **sales representatives**

11.3 Individuals using a business credit, debit or charge card to pay for goods and services, should obtain both **a card sales voucher** and **a receipt** from the supplier. These should be given to the accounts department regularly.

- **Receipts** are evidence of payment for Value Added Tax purposes
- **Card sales vouchers** are used to check the card company's statements

11.4 Every month, the card company will send a **statement of account** to the business. It will ask for payment **in full** and the payment will usually be made by **cheque**. The statement will cover the period since the previous monthly statement.

- A summary of the **total amount payable** for all the business cards issued
- A statement of all the **individual items** of spending on each individual card

11.5 An extract from a **monthly statement** for a business card scheme is illustrated below.

(a) *The total amount payable*

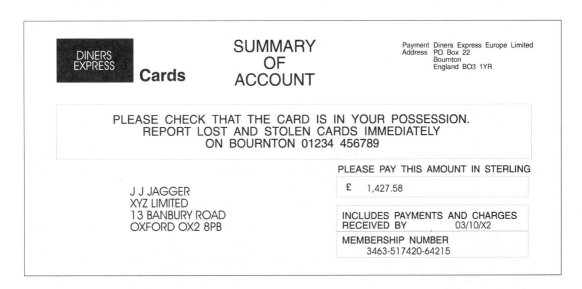

(b) *Extract from listing of charges for each card*

DINERS EXPRESS Cards	**STATEMENT OF ACCOUNT**	Page 1

REFERENCE NUMBER		PREVIOUS BALANCE 2,244.88
1354222	PAYMENT RECEIVED ON 15/09/X2 - THANK YOU	2,244.88CR
	TOTAL FOR CARD 00	
1230652	MULTIPARKS UK LTD, HEATHROW, MIDDX	41.90
1240672	BETTAPETROL UK LTD, OXFORD	24.50
1250672	SWIFT GARAGE, HEADINGTON	325.15
1420672	BISTRO SARTRE, OXFORD	82.00

PREVIOUS BALANCE	NEW CHARGES	NEW CREDITS	NEW BALANCE
2,244.88	473.55	2,244.88	473.55

Please quote your Membership Number 3463-517420-64215   with any query.
You are welcome to telephone us directly on PLEASE SEE OVERLEAF

Cheque No _____ Date Paid _____

PLEASE SEE OVER

11.6 The **itemised listing** for each card should be checked against the matching voucher sent to the accounts department by the cardholder. Any discrepancies or missing vouchers should be queried.

- With the **cardholder** to check whether a voucher does exist and the cardholder did incur the expenditure

- With the **card company** for any discrepancies

Payments by Telegraphic Transfer (TT) or Mail Transfer (MT)

11.7 Occasionally, payments can be arranged by means of an **electronic funds transfer** between the payer's and the payee's bank accounts.

11.8 Electronic funds transfers are made quickly and so are suitable in cases where a supplier wants **immediate payment**. They will only be used for **large** payments and usually at the insistence of the person being paid. Electronic funds transfers can be to a payee in a foreign country, as well as within the UK.

11.9 When a business agrees to make a payment by a funds transfer, it should obtain the following details from the person to be paid (the payee).

- Bank name and branch
- Sort code
- Payee's name and address
- Payee's bank account number and the name in which the account is held

11.10 It must then write to its own bank requesting the payment to be made.

Type of payment	Details
Telegraphic Transfer (TT) or cable payment order	Instructions for the payment are sent from the payer's bank to the payee's bank by cable.
Mail Transfer (MT) or mail payment order	Instructions are sent by mail.

For payments within the UK, TTs are more common.

11.11 The request for a TT payment can be prepared by an accounts clerk, but it must be signed by (usually two) **authorised persons**.

11.12 Here is an example of a request letter.

ABC Ltd

112 Peters Square
Weyford
Kent CR2 2TA

Lowlands Bank plc
Weyford Branch
5 High Street
Weyford
Kent CR1 1GG

16 July 20X5

Dear Sir

Request for a payment by telegraphic transfer

We are writing to ask you to arrange a payment from this company's current account by means of telegraphic transfer. Details are as follows.

This company's account number   36274859

Amount of payment   £11,400.00 (Eleven thousand four hundred pounds only)

Beneficiary   T M Peters Limited
25 Crescent Road
Canterbury CR3 1XX

Beneficiary's bank   Barminster Bank plc
Broad Street Canterbury branch
Sort code 45-67-89

Beneficiary's bank account no   38252849

in the name T M Peters Limited.

Signed on behalf of ABC Ltd

....(R Griffiths)

....(P W Border)

11.13 The bank will subsequently **confirm in writing** that the payment has been made.

Activity 6.3   **Level: Pre-assessment**

Libra Ltd has to make the following payments.

(a)   £6.29 for office cleaning materials bought from a nearby supermarket.

(b)   £231.40 monthly, which represents hire purchase instalments on a new van. The payments are due to Marsh Finance Ltd over a period of 36 months.

(c)   £534.21 to Southern Electric plc for the most recent quarter's electricity and standing charge. A bank giro credit form/payment counterfoil is attached to the bill. There is no direct debiting mandate currently in force.

(d) £161.50 monthly for ten months, representing the business rates payable to Clapperton District Council, which operates a direct debiting system.

(e) £186.60 to Renton Hire Ltd for a week's hire of a car on company business by the Sales Director from Edinburgh Airport. The Sales Director must pay on the spot, and does not wish to use a personal cheque or cash.

(f) £23,425.00 to Selham Motors Ltd for a new car to be used by the Finance Director. Selham Motors will not accept one of the company's cheques in payment, since the Finance Director wishes to collect the vehicle immediately upon delivering the payment in person and Selham Motors is concerned that such a cheque might be dishonoured.

Task

Recommend the method of payment which you think would be most appropriate in each case, stating your reasons.

12 DOCUMENTATION TO GO OUT WITH PAYMENTS

12.1 When a payment is made, it is usual to send a document with the payment to inform the recipient what the payment is for and who it is from. This document might be any of the following.

- A **remittance advice**, either created by the payer or issued by the supplier
- An **order form**, when payments are sent with the order itself
- A **pro-forma invoice**, provided by the supplier for payments with order
- A **bank giro credit form** for telephone, electricity and other similar bills
- A **covering letter** when other forms of documentation do not exist

Remittance advices

12.2 The **remittance advice** should include the following information.

- The name and address of the customer

- The name and address of the supplier

- The customer's account number or code (as specified by the supplier) and/or the supplier code (as specified by the customer)

- The invoice number(s)

- The invoice amount(s)

- The invoice date(s)

- The date of payment

- The total amount of the payment

12.3 Remember that there are **two** types of remittance advices.

- Sent with the **supplier's statement** (eg a separate form, or a tear-off slip)

- Prepared by the **customer's accounts department** and sent to the supplier with the payment (with a copy kept for reference)

12.4 The example below is of a remittance advice **prepared** by ABC Ltd's accounts clerk for the payment of three invoices less a credit note. The total payment is £1,185.50.

ABC Ltd
112 Peters Square
Weyford
Kent CR2 2TA
Telephone: 01329 456272

*REMITTANCE
ADVICE*

Rapid Supplies Ltd
63 Canterbury Road
Weyford
Kent CR3 6UX

Supplier code
603

Date of payment
8/9/X0

Invoice/ credit note date	Details	Invoices £	Credit notes £	Payment amount £
3/8/X7	Invoice 062074	375.80		375.80
10/8/X7	Invoice 063015	405.20		405.20
15/8/X7	Credit note CR2752		120.00	(120.00)
24/8/X7	Invoice 063240	524.50		524.50
	Total payment			1,185.50

Note. The supplier code is the code used by ABC Ltd to identify Rapid Supplies Ltd in its own accounting system.

12.5 This remittance advice is sent to the supplier with a cheque for £1,185.50. A copy of the advice is kept in the accounts department of ABC Ltd. If the supplier sent remittance advices with each invoice and credit note, these should also be sent back with the payment. In this example, the letter posted to the supplier would contain the following.

- A cheque
- ABC Ltd's own remittance advice
- The remittance advice(s) from Rapid Supplies Ltd

Activity 6.4   **Level: Assessment**

Penumbra Ltd is due to pay (or claim credit in the case of credit notes) the following items in respect of two creditors. The date shown is the date of the invoice or credit note.

Feathers Ltd (Ref F011)		Goods £	VAT £	Total £
30.3.X7	Invoice 07114	74.40	13.02	87.42
6.4.X7	Credit note CR084 (re invoice 07101)	142.25	24.89	167.14
7.4.X7	Invoice 07241	248.71	43.52	292.23
9.4.X7	Invoice 07249	724.94	126.86	851.80
14.4.X7	Invoice 07302	141.17	24.70	165.87
22.4.X7	Credit note CR087 (re invoice 07241)	101.24	17.72	118.96
22.4.X7	Invoice 07487	421.00	73.68	494.68
28.4.X7	Credit note CR099 (re invoice 07114)	74.40	13.02	87.42
7.5.X7	Invoice 07714	98.94	17.31	116.25

BPP PUBLISHING

		Goods £	VAT £	Total £
The Furniture People (Ref F017)				
2.4.X7	Invoice 734282	3,742.28	654.90	4,397.18
23.4.X7	Invoice 735110	6,141.04	1,074.68	7,215.72
27.4.X7	Invoice 735192	842.92	147.51	990.43
27.4.X7	Invoice 735204	1,241.70	217.30	1,459.00
4.5.X7	Credit note 274221 (re invoice 732118)	942.41	164.92	1,107.33

The creditors' addresses are as follows.

Feathers Ltd, 247 Marconi Road, Chelmsford, Essex CM1 4PQ
The Furniture People, 4 Kane Street, Northampton NN3 4SR

The procedures manual of Penumbra Ltd specifies the following cheque signatories.

Cheque signatories

C Taylor	Financial Controller
R Hare	Financial Accountant
J Mackie	Finance Director
B Mitchell	General Manager
J Knight	Managing Director
S Lukes	Chairman

Two signatures are required on all cheques.

Cheques up to £1,000	Any two signatories
Cheques up to £10,000	Any two directors
Cheques over £10,000	Chairman or managing director, plus one other director

Tasks

(a) Prepare remittance advices for the payments to be made on 2 June 20X7 to each of the two creditors. You should use the blank forms provided below.

(b) Show the total of the payments to be made.

Penumbra Limited

42 Braintree Road
Bishop's Stortford
Herts CM23 9XY
Telephone: 01279 33942
Fax: 01279 33920

REMITTANCE ADVICE

Supplier account number

Date of payment:

Invoice/ credit note date	Details	Invoices £	Credit notes £	Payment amount £
....	....	....	....	....
....	....	....	....	....
....	....	....	....	....
....	....	....	....	....
....	....	....	....	....
....	....	....	....	....
....	....	....	....	....
....	....	....	....	....
....	....	....	....	....
....	....	....	....	....

Penumbra Limited

42 Braintree Road
Bishop's Stortford
Herts CM23 9XY
Telephone: 01279 33942
Fax: 01279 33920

REMITTANCE ADVICE

Supplier account number

Date of payment:

Invoice/ credit note date	Details	Invoices £	Credit notes £	Payment amount £
. . . .	. . . .	. . . .	. . . .	. . . .
. . . .	. . . .	. . . .	. . . .	. . . .
. . . .	. . . .	. . . .	. . . .	. . . .
. . . .	. . . .	. . . .	. . . .	. . . .
. . . .	. . . .	. . . .	. . . .	. . . .
. . . .	. . . .	. . . .	. . . .	. . . .
. . . .	. . . .	. . . .	. . . .	. . . .
. . . .	. . . .	. . . .	. . . .	. . . .
. . . .	. . . .	. . . .	. . . .	. . . .
. . . .	. . . .	. . . .	. . . .	. . . .

Activity 6.5

Level: Assessment

Carrying on from Activity 6.4, you establish that the following cheque signatories are available in the office today and tomorrow: R Hare, B Mitchell, S Lukes and C Taylor. J Knight is expected back in the office tomorrow.

Tasks

(a) Complete cheques for the payments to be made, using the crossing 'A/c payee'.

(b) State what action you will take to get each of the cheques signed.

(c) State what you would do to the invoices and credit notes now that they have been paid, giving reasons.

Portland Bank plc

74-98-76

7 The Square, Bishop's Stortford, Hertfordshire CM23 1NP

_____ 20 _____

Pay _____ or order

_____

_____

£

FOR AND ON BEHALF OF
PENUMBRA LIMITED

Cheque Number   Sort code   Account Number   _____

⑆720088⑆ 74⑈9876⑉ 64196419⑈

BPP
PUBLISHING

Portland Bank plc

74-98-76

7 The Square, Bishop's Stortford, Hertfordshire CM23 1NP

_____ 20 _____

Pay

or order

£

FOR AND ON BEHALF OF
PENUMBRA LIMITED

Cheque Number   Sort code   Account Number

⑈720089⑈ 74⑈9876⑊ 6619 6619⑈

Key learning points

- It is very important to apply **controls over payments**. Three key features of controls are as follows.

  - Documentation (invoice, statement, cheque request form, expenses claim form)
  - Authorisation of the expenditure item (passing it for payment)
  - Authorised signatures for cheques and payment instructions to banks

- **Cheque requisition forms** are used when primary documentation such as an invoice has not been received. Cheque requisition forms help to ensure authorisation and recording of payments.

- It is important to establish **proper authorisation procedures**, with each person in authority having written limits.

- A business will use a variety of **methods to make payments**. Ignoring payroll (wages and salaries) and petty cash, the most common and convenient methods of payment are by **cheque** and by **BACS**.

- As far as the use of **cheques** is concerned, you should know how to do the following.

  - Prepare a cheque for payment
  - Deal with lost cheques
  - Stop cheques

- **BACS** is a useful method of making and recording payments. It can save a business a lot of time.

- **Other payment methods** are often arranged at the insistence of the supplier.

  - Banker's drafts
  - Standing orders
  - Telegraphic transfers (TT payments)

- **Direct debits** are not often used for payments by businesses, but might occasionally be used for convenience.

- The **timing of payments** may depend on credit terms offered by suppliers, including **discounts** for prompt payment.

- A business should send proper **explanatory documentation** with all payments to avoid confusion. Copies of the relevant documents should be filed in such a way that the documents are easy to retrieve.

- The **accounts department** must carry out the following duties.

- Make all payments and send these to suppliers with associated documentation (remittance advices and so on).

- Have a system for being able to trace each payment in the case of queries. For example by writing the invoice number on the cheque counterfoil and the cheque number on the invoice. Stamping invoices PAID with the date of payment.

- Keep a filing system for paid and unpaid invoices, standing orders, credit card company statements and any other documentation.

- Record payments in the accounts (this aspect of payments is the subject of the next chapter).

Quick quiz

1   What are the three main steps in applying controls over payments?

2   When might documentary evidence not be available for a payment?

3   What is a cheque requisition form?

4   What is an expenses claim form used for and by whom?

5   Which methods of payment are most commonly used by businesses?

6   Should cash be sent by post?

7   What should you do to stop a cheque?

8   What is the main difference between a standing order and a direct debit?

9   When might payment be made by Telegraphic Transfer?

10   What is the document most usually sent with a payment by a business?

11   What does BACS stand for?

Answers to quick quiz

1   The three steps are: obtaining documentary evidence; authorisation of payments; restricting authority to make payments.

2   When an invoice has not yet been received or there will be no invoice or receipt.

3   A cheque requisition form is an internal document requesting that a cheque be drawn for payment.

4   Employees use an expenses claim form to obtain reimbursement for expenses.

5   Cheques and BACS are the most common.

6   No. It might get lost, and there would be no proof of the amount sent and no means of retrieving it.

7   Telephone the bank saying you want the cheque stopped and then confirm the instruction in writing.

8   Standing orders are always for the same amount, whereas direct debits can be for a different amount each time.

9   A TT is most suitable when payment of a large amount is required immediately.

10   A remittance advice is usually sent with a payment.

11   Bankers Automated Clearing Services.

7 Recording payments

This chapter contains

1 Introduction

2 Controls over recording payments

3 The cash book: recording payments

4 Posting cash payments to the main ledger

5 Returned cheques

Learning objectives

On completion of this chapter you will be able to:

- Enter payments into the cash book
- Post payments to the main ledger

Performance criteria

2.3.3 Payments are entered into accounting records according to organisational procedures

2.3.4 Queries are referred to the appropriate person

Range statement

2.3.3 Accounting records: cash book

Knowledge and understanding

- Double-entry bookkeeping
- Operation of manual and computerised accounting systems
- Relationship between accounting system and ledger
- Relevant understanding of the organisation's accounting systems and administrative systems and procedures

BPP
PUBLISHING

1 INTRODUCTION

1.1 If an unauthorised payment is made and not recorded in the cash book, then it will be discovered when a **bank reconciliation** takes place. During the reconciliation, a comparison is made between what is in the cash book and what has passed through the bank account. This is covered in detail in Unit 3. It is the most important control ensuring all payments are recorded.

2 CONTROLS OVER RECORDING PAYMENTS

Fraud

2.1 Someone who makes an **unauthorised payment** (to himself or a third party) will want the payment to be recorded, because of the bank reconciliation, but the **nature of the payment to be hidden**. Therefore the following procedures **must** be in place.

- All payments are **authorised** correctly

- Proper checks are made against supporting documentation

- Whoever writes out the cheques is not the same person who records the payments (**segregation of duties**)

- Each day, a list of the day's payments is checked for **unusual items**, by a senior staff member who investigates anything unusual

- A **minimum number of cheque books** is in use at any time, preferably only one

2.2 It is always possible that someone might organise an unauthorised payment and disappear before the inevitable discovery. However most frauds are carried out over a period of time and involve relatively small individual amounts. Most people could not carry out a one-off fraud large enough to warrant leaving their job (and becoming unemployable).

Completeness

2.3 It is necessary to ensure that **all** payments have been recorded. If a payment has not been recorded by accident, this will become apparent during the bank reconciliation. It will only be discovered, however, when the payment clears through the bank account. Before then it will not appear in the cash book or on the bank statement. To ensure completeness the following controls should be in place.

- Regular **bank reconciliations**

- Cheques should be issued **in sequence** with only one cheque book in use at a time

- A **sequence check** on the cheques entered in the cash book by someone other than the person who normally records them (to ensure no cheques are missing)

- Ensure all payments by **direct debit and standing order** are recorded in the cash book (along with bank interest and charges)

Activity 7.1   **Level: Pre-assessment**

At Alligator Foods plc, among the procedures in operation over the recording of payments are the following.

(a)   Only one company cheque book is to be in use at any one time.

(b)   Numbers of all cheques are to be entered in the cash book even where the cheque is cancelled.

(c)   All cancelled cheques are to be retained.

(d)   The tasks of writing cheques and writing up the cash book are to be carried out by different people.

(e)   Authorised details of all standing orders and direct debits are to be filed and the details of any such payments are to be agreed to the file before being transferred from bank statements in to the cash book.

Task

Comment on the reasons for each of the above procedures.

---

3   THE CASH BOOK: RECORDING PAYMENTS

3.1   To help control the business, the cash book is analysed into different types of payment. Different businesses will do this in different ways depending on several factors.

- **How many categories** of purchases they have
- **How often** they purchase goods in each category
- The way the business is **split up** into separate segments
- How **complicated** the cash book may become

3.2   In the example shown on Pages 132 and 133, there are columns for three different types of purchases and columns for other sundry expense and capital payments.

3.3   There are some important points to note from this example.

Discounts received are recorded in a separate column, a memorandum column which is not part of the cash book balance.

See also the table on page 134.

3.4   In a computerised system, the payments will be automatically analysed by means of the general ledger coding entered on the invoice (see Chapter 6).

Part B: Payments

	Date	Details	Cheque number	Discounts received		Total		VAT		Creditors		Cash purchases - paper etc	
1	1/2/X7	Sharp & Co (creditor)	00349	222	96	4,236	27			4,236	27		
2	1/2/X7	Petty cash	00350			827	35						
3	4/2/X7	H & Co Garage - MD's car	Bnks Dft			22,460	00						
4	4/2/X7	Dye Light (creditor)	00351			327	20			327	20		
5	6/2/X7	Paper Press (trade journal)	00352			550	00						
6	7/2/X7	Sharp & Co (creditor)	00353	277	37	5,270	05			5,270	05		
7	11/2/X7	MRC & Co (creditor)	00354	111	58	4,351	44			4,351	44		
8	12/2/X7	Couinces (cash purchase)	00355			244	00	36	34			207	66
9	12/2/X7	Xerxes Ltd (creditor)	00356			2,372	49			2,372	49		
10	12/2/X7	Telecom	00357			327	40	48	76				
11	14/2/X7	Factory insurance y/e 15/2/95	00358			15,349	50						
12	14/2/X7	Ensa & Co (creditor)	00359			3,297	28			3,297	28		
13	18/2/X7	Oak & Elm Ltd (creditor)	00360			1,005	00			1,005	00		
14	19/2/X7	Post office (franking)	00361			220	00						
15	19/2/X7	Cheque cancelled	00362			-							
16	19/2/X7	ACB's Ltd (cash purchase)	00363			347	20	51	71				
17	19/2/X7	Olivia & Co (cash purchase)	00364			199	90	29	77			170	13
18	21/2/X7	Viola Ltd (creditor)	00365			6,340	00			6,340	00		
19	22/2/X7	London Water plc	00366			4,729	80						
20	26/2/X7	Sharp & Co (creditor)	00367	245	78	4,669	80			4,669	80		
21	26/2/X7	Janus Ltd (creditor)	00368			379	46			379	46		
22	26/2/X7	Ermine & Trude (cash purchase)	00369			127	98	19	06				
23	28/2/X7	February salaries and wages	BACS			33,497	28						
24	4/2/X7	London Electricity plc	S/O			250	00	37	23				
25	7/2/X7	London Gas plc	S/O			300	00	44	68				
26	19/2/X7	Borough of Hackbern	D/D			125	00						
27	27/2/X7	Bank interest	-			273	94						
28	27/2/X7	Bank charges	-			192	76						
		TOTAL		857	69	112,271	10	267	55	32,248	99	377	79

Cash purchases - dye		Cash purchases - sundry		Bank charges interest		Light, heat and phone		Rent, rates and insurance		Motor expenses		Print, post and stationery		Wages and salaries		Fixed assets		Petty cash	
																		827	35
										120	00					22,340	00		
												550	00						
						278	64												
								15,349	50										
												220	00						
295	49																		
								4,729	00										
		108	92																
														33,497	28				
						212	77												
						255	32	125	00										
				273	94														
				192	76			20,204	30			770	00						
295	49	108	92	466	70	746	73			120	00			33,497	28	22,340	00	827	35

BPP
PUBLISHING

Type of payment	Treatment in the cash book
Cash purchases	The columns for cash purchases are **analysed** by type of purchase as this is the first record of the purchases.
Payments to creditors	These are not analysed as the analysis is made in the purchase day book when the credit purchase is made, not when cash is paid. (See Chapter 3)
VAT	Input VAT on credit purchases will be recorded in the purchases day book and so will not appear in the cash book. **VAT on cash purchases** and sundry expenses must be recorded in the cash book as it is **not** recorded elsewhere.
Cancelled cheques	These should be entered in the cash book to allow a complete sequence check, and to make sure the cheque does not pass through the account. **Spoiled cheques** should be retained.
Extent of analysis	This cash book is analysed in quite a lot of detail. This is not always necessary, but it makes it easier to post to the ledger accounts as only the totals need to be posted.
Non-cheque payments	The **standing orders, direct debits**, etc are entered at the end of the page, even though some transactions are dated earlier in the month. This is acceptable and shows that this information is extracted from the bank statements monthly. The validity of all standing orders and direct debit payments must be checked against a **control list** (a complete record of all current standing orders and direct debits, maintained by a responsible person).

Activity 7.2 — Level: Pre-assessment

State whether each of the two statements below is TRUE or FALSE.

(a) Cheque payments are recorded in the cash book only when they have been presented at the bank because it is only then that payment is made from the bank account.

(b) Standing order payments made by the bank should normally be entered in the cash book, but not where they represent payments in advance for goods or services not yet received.

Activity 7.3 — Level: Pre-assessment

You are involved in training some new members of staff at your firm on the recording of payments.

Task

Explain briefly each of the following terms.

(a) Cancelled cheque
(b) Stopped cheque
(c) Paid cheque

Three-column cash book

3.5 An alternative format for a cash book is the **three-column cash book**, which is found in businesses which do not bank all their cash receipts each day. They keep the cash in the till and occasionally bank some of it, the remainder being used to pay expenses. The three columns are for cash payments, bank payments and discounts received. There are analysis columns, which together equal the total of the cash payments and bank payments columns.

Activity 7.4   Level: Pre-assessment

Your employer, Earlsprint Ltd, offers to its credit customers a 2½% discount for payment within 10 days of invoice. The company gives no trade or customer discounts. It operates a three-column cash book, with columns for discount, cash and bank.

At 30 June 20X7, the cash book figures totalled as follows.

Receipts side

Discount allowed	£237.65
Cash	£342.71
Bank	£15,842.65

Payments side

Discount received	£184.29
Cash	£232.40
Bank	£14,221.17

A new trainee has been asked to balance off the book, and has shown balances carried down as shown below.

Receipts   **Payments**

Date	Details	Discount	Cash	Bank	Date	Details	Discount	Cash	Bank
	Totals	237.65	342.71	15,842.65		Totals	184.29	232.40	14,221.17
	Balance carried down	237.65	342.71	1,621.48		Balance carried down	53.36	119.31	
				14,221.17			237.65	342.71	
									14,221.17
July X7	Balance brought down	53.36	119.31		July X7	Balance brought down			1,621.48

Task

Check and identify any errors in the new trainee's work.

Activity 7.5   Level: Assessment

On 4 May 20X7 Marshall's cash book showed a cash balance of £224 and an overdraft of £336. During the week ended 9 May the following transactions took place.

May 4	Withdrew £50 of cash from the bank for business use
May 5	Repaid a debt of £120 owing to R Hill, taking advantage of a 10% cash discount. The payment was by cheque
May 6	Sold £45 of goods for cash
May 7	Paid a telephone bill of £210 by cheque
May 8	Received a cheque from H Larkin for £180. Larkin has taken advantage of a £20 cash discount offered to him
May 8	Purchased £135 of goods from Honour Ltd by cheque
May 9	Received a cheque from D Randle for £482

Marshall is not registered for VAT.

Tasks

Enter the above transactions for Marshall into the cash book, with separate columns for discounts, bank and cash.

The records should be balanced off at the end of the week. Folio numbers are not required.

4 POSTING CASH PAYMENTS TO THE MAIN LEDGER

4.1 It is only when we **post the payments side of the cash book to the cash (or bank) account in the main (general or nominal) ledger that we can be said to have accounted for cash payments.** This is because the posting completes the double entry.

DEVOLVED ASSESSMENT ALERT

It will be a very rare occurrence if you are *not* asked to post cash payments in a Devolved Assessment.

4.2 The following steps apply to posting payments.

Step 1	Add up all the columns.
Step 2	Check that the analysis columns (excluding the discount received memorandum column) add up to the total cash paid column.
Step 3	Identify the main ledger account by marking against the cash book account.
Step 4	Draw up the posting summary and post the main ledger.

4.3 EXAMPLE: POSTING THE MAIN LEDGER

Suppose we wished to post Robin Plenty's cash payments for 1 September 20X7.

ROBIN PLENTY CASH BOOK

PAYMENTS

Date	Narrative	Folio	Total	Input VAT on cash purchases	Payments to creditors	Expenses	Fixed assets
20X7							
01-Sep	(g) Creditor paid: Kew	PL543	120.00		120.00		
	(h) Creditor paid: Hare	PL76	310.00		310.00		
	(i) Telephone expense		400.00			400.00	
	(j) Gas expense		280.00			280.00	
	(k) Plant & machinery purchase		1,500.00				1,500.00
	(l) Cash purchase: stationery		97.00	14.45		82.55	
			2,707.00	14.45	430.00	762.55	1,500.00

The entry for Hare should reflect a discount taken of £10, as only £300 of the debt of £310 was actually paid out. The relevant general ledger accounts are set out below.

	CASH ACCOUNT		CA01
	£		£
1 Sept Balance b/d	2,900.00		

	TOTAL CREDITORS		TC01
	£		£
		1 Sept Balance b/d	42,972.00

	EXPENSES		XP01
	£		£
1 Sept Balance b/d	170,249.00		

	VAT		VAT01
	£		£
		Balance b/d	35,070.00

	FIXED ASSETS		FA01
	£		£

	DISCOUNT RECEIVED		DR01
	£		£

4.4 SOLUTION

Robin Plenty's amended payments side looks like this.

BPP
PUBLISHING

ROBIN PLENTY CASH BOOK

PAYMENTS

Date	Narrative	Folio	Discount received	Total	Input VAT on cash purchases	Payments to creditors	Expenses	Fixed assets
20X7								
01-Sep	(g) Creditor paid: Kew	PL543		120.00		120.00		
	(h) Creditor paid: Hare	PL76	10.00	300.00		300.00		
	(i) Telephone expense			400.00			400.00	
	(j) Gas expense			280.00			280.00	
	(k) Plant & machinery purchase			1,500.00				1,500.00
	(l) Cash purchase: stationery			97.00	14.45		82.55	
			10.00	2,697.00	14.45	420.00	762.55	1,500.00
			DR01	*CA01*	*VAT01*	*TC01*	*XP01*	*FA01*
			CR	CR	DR	DR	DR	DR
			TC01					
			DR					

Step 1	**Add up the columns** (see above)
Step 2	**Check the totals**

	£
Input VAT on cash purchases	14.45
Payments to creditors	420.00
Expenses	762.55
Fixed asset purchases	1,500.00
	2,697.00

Step 3	**Identify the main ledger accounts**. The folio references for the main ledger accounts are marked on the payment page above.
Step 4	Draw up the **posting summary** and post the main ledger.

			£	£
DEBIT	Total creditors (420 + 10)	TC01	430.00	
	VAT	VAT01	14.45	
	Expenses	XP01	762.55	
	Fixed assets	FA01	1,500.00	
CREDIT	Cash	CA01		2,697.00
	Discounts received	DR01		10.00

Cash book payments posting summary on 1 September 20X7

CASH ACCOUNT				CA01
	£			£
1 Sept Balance b/d	2,900.00	1 Sept Cash book		2,697.00

TOTAL CREDITORS — TC01

		£			£
1 Sept	Cash book	430.00	1 Sept	Balance b/d	42,972.00

EXPENSES — XP01

		£			£
1 Sept	Balance b/d	170,249.00			
1 Sept	Cash book	762.55			

VAT — VAT01

		£			£
1 Sept	Cash book	14.45		Balance b/d	35,070.00

FIXED ASSETS — FA01

		£			£
1 Sept	Cash book	1,500.00			

DISCOUNTS RECEIVED — DR01

		£			£
			1 Sept	Cash book	10.00

Activity 7.6   Level: Assessment

The payments side of the cash book for Aria Enterprises is shown on the following page as at 15 February.

The business has a memorandum purchase ledger for suppliers plus a purchase ledger control account in the nominal ledger. Relevant nominal ledger codes and balances are as follows. (Taken *after* the posting of the receipts side)

		Balance at 15.2
Cash	CAB 010	95,609.78 DR
VAT control	VAT 094	11,102.00 CR
Sundry expenses	SUN 490	567.92 DR
Fixed asset cost	FAC 020	272,972.00 DR
Utility costs	UTI 470	1,509.72 DR
Salaries	WAG 510	45,207.69 DR
Purchase discounts	DIS 350	279.48 CR
Purchase ledger control	PLC 110	112,221.80 CR

Tasks

(a) Total the payments side of the cash book and identify the postings to the nominal ledger

(b) Prepare a posting summary. Open up the nominal ledger accounts and post the relevant amounts to them.

Computerisation of payments recording

4.5 In Unit 1, we looked at the implications of a computerised cash book in relation to cash receipts in the general ledger cash account. The implications are the same for recording payments in a computerised cash book.

4.6 Cheques will usually be printed in batches or runs for convenience, on a periodic basis, perhaps weekly. It is usual to obtain a printed list of the cheques issued as a record. The total amount paid will be shown on the printout.

- If a **manual cash book is kept,** then this total is entered in the cash book.

ARIA ENTERPRISES

PAYMENTS

Date	Narrative	Folio	Discount received	Payment total	VAT	Creditors	Salaries	O'heads	Fixed assets	Sundry expenses
01-Feb	Smallsoft Software	PL0054	110.00	2,090.00		2,090.00				
02-Feb	Mailhouse Ltd	PL0467		569.02		569.02				
02-Feb	Champagne (cash)			65.00	9.68					55.32
04-Feb	Stationery Box	PL0503	250.00	4,750.00		4,750.00				
05-Feb	Pacific Computers Ltd			32,894.00					32,894.00	
08-Feb	PR Reps Ltd	PL0004		5,501.40		5,501.40				
09-Feb	Champagne (cash)			19.95	2.97					16.98
09-Feb	Flowers R Us Ltd	PL0962	1.75	33.25		33.25				
10-Feb	BG (for 3 Spring Street)			178.99				178.99		
13-Feb	Window cleaner			25.00	3.72					21.28
14-Feb	Jan/Feb salaries			46,987.65			46,987.65			
14-Feb	CopyRight Ltd	PL0775		36.48		36.48				
15-Feb	Data Warehouse Ltd	PL0087		10,237.95		10,237.95				
	London Electricity (HO)			1,016.00				1,016.00		

Date	Details	Cheque Nos	Total	Purchases
12.7.X2	Purchase ledger cheques	000375-87	£4,276.14	£4,276.14

- A **computerised cash book** will be updated automatically. The print outs of the cheque runs should still be kept in case any query arises as they are probably the only detailed list of the contents of all the cheques.

Activity 7.7   Level: Assessment

Sisyphus Ltd is in the quarrying business. The company uses a computerised accounting system, in which the Bank Account (code 10000) acts as a control account. A manual cash book is operated in parallel. All sales and purchases except for petty cash items are paid for through the bank account. Holdings of cash are dealt with in a separate petty cash book. Receipts and payments are not analysed in the cash book.

On Monday 1 May 20X7, there are four creditor balances on the purchase ledger. All creditors are paid on the Wednesday preceding the week in which the invoice becomes 45 days old.

A schedule has been prepared at 1 May 20X7 of the invoices of each supplier due for payment at different dates in May 20X7. This schedule is set out below.

Creditor	Invoice ref	Invoice amount £	Payment date
ACM Crushers Ltd (A001)	20127	2,012.42	3.05.X7
	20134	7,018.00	10.05.X7
	20182	1,721.29	10.05.X7
	20242	982.00	31.05.X7
Benzade Ltd (B008)	B4241	101.24	3.05.X7
	B4921	94.27	10.05.X7
	B5288	172.19	24.05.X7
	B5298	242.17	24.05.X7
Gadd Ltd (G004)	722421	621.00	17.05.X7
	723724	92.50	17.05.X7
	723890	1,927.91	31.05.X7
Quaygate Ltd (Q001)	31427	205.00	3.05.X7
	31572	700.50	3.05.X7
	31591	401.15	31.05.X7

For payments to creditors, a single entry is made in the cash book for each weekly payment run.

Other payments to be made in the month May 20X7 are as follows.

(a)   On the first of the month, the petty cash imprest is to be made up by drawing a cheque of £127.00 for cash.

(b)   Payments are to be made where applicable under the following standing order instructions.

   (i)   £192.00 on 15 February 20X6 and quarterly thereafter (six payments in total), in favour of Turnmead Ltd.

   (ii)   £342.00 on 30 April 20X7 and monthly thereafter until further notice, in favour of Icarus Ltd.

(c)   The month's salaries, amounting to £5,842.45, are to be paid by BACS transfer on the last Monday of the month.

Cheques are always drawn in numerical sequence. As at Monday 1 May 20X7, the last cheque which had been used was numbered 400601.

BPP PUBLISHING

Tasks

(a) Show the payments to be made *by cheque* during the month of May 20X7, indicating for each payment the cheque number, date, payee and amount. (Deal with each creditor's payment in alphabetical order by creditor name as shown above.)

(b) List *all* of the payments to be made by Sisyphus Ltd in May 20X7 as you might expect to see them in the manual cash book, and calculate a total for the month's payments.

---

5 RETURNED CHEQUES

5.1 **Returned cheques** are cheques which have been drawn by the business, paid, processed by the bank and then returned to the business.

5.2 Banks will return cheques to both individuals and businesses on request, although they charge for the service. The cheque will have been processed and this means that the cheque will have the following additions.

- A 'crossing stamp' on the front identifying which bank and branch it was paid in at
- Encoded along the bottom with the amount of the cheque for bank processing

5.3 **Advantages of receiving returned cheques**

- Extra guard against fraud by **checking the signature, the amounts and the payee on the cheque** (someone might have altered the cheque after signature)

- **Extra guard against bank error**

- **Proof of payment,** if the supplier later queries this

5.4 **Disadvantages of receiving returned cheques**

- Bank charges for this service may become very high and so the **cost will outweigh the benefit**

- **Large numbers of cheques** are difficult and costly to file and store

- **Queries** where holding the returned cheque would be useful are very low; as long as the other controls are in place, then keeping returned cheques should not be necessary

Key learning points

- **Controls** over recording payments are important to avoid fraud and to ensure completeness.

- The **bank reconciliation** is the most important control.

- Analysis of payments in the cash book will help to control the expenditure of the business.

- **Posting** the payments side of the cash book to the **general ledger**.

  - Add up the cash book columns
  - Check that the analysis columns add up to the total
  - Identify relevant general ledger accounts
  - Draw up the posting summary and post to the general ledger

- Receiving **returned cheques** is not necessarily of great value for control purposes, although some businesses may find it useful.

- In a **computer system,** updating the purchase ledger for payments will usually cause the cash book to be automatically updated.

- Remember **BACS** is a useful method of making and **recording** payments; it can save a business quite a lot of time.

Quick quiz

1   What is the best control over cash payments?

2   What other controls will help to prevent fraud involving payments?

3   Discounts received are shown in a memorandum column in the cash book. True or false?

4   What are the advantages of receiving returned cheques?

Answers to quick quiz

1   The bank reconciliation is the best control over payments.

2   Other controls include: authorisation of payments; supporting documentation; segregation of duties; checks for unusual payments; one cheque book in use.

3   True. The column is there so that the total amount owed to creditors can be posted to the purchase ledger, not just the amount paid.

4   Returned cheques are both a check against fraud and a check against mistakes by the bank.

BPP
PUBLISHING

8 Maintaining petty cash records

This chapter contains

1   Introduction

2   The purpose of petty cash

3   Security and control of petty cash

4   The imprest system

5   Petty cash vouchers

6   The petty cash book

7   Recording and analysing petty cash transactions

8   Recording petty cash transactions: VAT

9   Topping up the float, balancing off and posting petty cash

---

Learning objectives

On completion of this chapter you will be able to:

- Make authorised payments out of petty cash
- Reinstate petty cash up to the imprest amount

BPP
PUBLISHING

Performance criteria

2.2.1   Payments are correctly calculated from relevant documentation

2.2.2   Payments are scheduled and authorised by the appropriate person

2.2.3   Queries are referred to the appropriate person

2.2.4   Security and confidentiality are maintained according to organisational requirements

2.3.1   The appropriate payment method is used in accordance with organisational procedures

2.3.2   Payments are made in accordance with organisational processes and timescales

2.3.3   Payments are entered into accounting records according to organisational procedures

2.3.4   Queries are referred to the appropriate person

2.3.5   Security and confidentiality are maintained according to organisational requirements

Range statement

2.2.1   Payments: petty cash

2.2.2   Documentation: petty cash claims

2.2.3   Appropriate person: manager, accountant

2.3.1   Payment methods: cash

2.3.2   Payment: petty cash

2.3.3   Accounting records: cash book

2.3.4   Queries relating to: unauthorised claims for payment, insufficient supporting evidence, claims exceeding prescribed limit

Knowledge and understanding

- Double entry bookkeeping

- Petty cash procedures: imprest and non imprest methods, analysis of items of expenditure including VAT charges

- Methods of handling and storing money from a security aspect

Chapter 8 scenario - Aldgate Plastics Ltd. This scenario applies to all the activities in this chapter.

You are the petty cashier at Aldgate Plastics Ltd. An imprest of £150 is operated for petty cash, with a limit of £25 applying to individual petty cash payments. The imprest float is made up at the end of each week.

The office procedures manual states that you may authorise payments of up to £10, provided they are supported by receipts. Requests for larger sums and for payments which are not supported by receipts must be referred to the Administration Manager.

1 INTRODUCTION

1.1 In every business, there will be a number of small expenses that have to be paid for in notes and coins. Therefore a supply of cash has to be kept on the business premises. This cash is called **petty cash**.

2 THE PURPOSE OF PETTY CASH

DEVOLVED ASSESSMENT ALERT

Being able to state why organisations use petty cash and the procedures employed to control it could well earn you easy marks in your Devolved Assessment.

What items are paid for out of petty cash?

2.1
- **Small** items of expense for which payment in notes and coin is required
- Many businesses **specify what** can be paid for out of petty cash
- **Informal system of judgement** by the petty cash officer or his supervisor

2.2 Here are some typical expenses, limits and recipients for payments out of petty cash.

Typical expense to be paid for	Typical maximum amount	Who directly receives the cash?	Who ultimately receives the cash?
Travel expenses of employee on official business	5.00	Employee	Travel company
Weekly milk bill	10.00	Milkman	Milkman
Items from local shop,			
eg tea, coffee	5.00	Employee	Shop
emergency stationery	5.00	Employee	Shop
stamps	5.00	Employee	Shop
Monthly office window cleaner	20.00	Window cleaner	Window cleaner

BPP
PUBLISHING

Who gets paid out of petty cash?

2.3 From the table in Paragraph 2.2, payments out of petty cash for expenses go:

- To **employees** (to reimburse them for out of pocket expenses)
- To **suppliers,** such as the milkman or window cleaner

2.4 Sometimes employees will ask for petty cash **in advance**. This may occur because they do not have enough cash themselves to pay for the item.

Watch out for casual labour

2.5 If **casual labour** is paid from petty cash (eg the office cleaner), the Inland Revenue will want to know. Your organisation could be liable to pay **National Insurance Contributions** (NICs) and **income tax** for this person, on top of their cash 'wages'.

2.6 Payments out of **petty cash for casual labour** should therefore be **sanctioned by an office manager.** The manager will need to take the necessary measures to satisfy Inland Revenue requirements. This includes a record of the name and address of the person receiving the cash wage.

2.7 It is best if all employees (even casual labour) are paid through the payroll system **not** petty cash.

Activity 8.1   Level: Pre-assessment

Would you say that the items, amount and recipient below are acceptable for petty cash payments at Aldgate Plastics Ltd?

Expense item	Amount	Direct recipient	Acceptable?
Portable air conditioning unit	£75.99	Sam Gardner, office manager	
Coffee filters for office coffee machine	£2.99	Raj Devi, PA	
Bunch of flowers for Valentine's day	£18.00	Orlando Orseo, Sales	
Metro ticket to Plastics Today conference	£2.60	Orlando Orseo, Sales	

3   SECURITY AND CONTROL OF PETTY CASH

DEVOLVED ASSESSMENT ALERT

Many organisations fall at the first hurdle with petty cash - it is physically insecure and so accounting for it accurately is impossible. Being able to explain the basic security and control procedures for petty cash can earn students valuable marks.

The petty cashier

3.1 Looking after petty cash should be the responsibility of one individual, who might be called the **petty cash officer** or **petty cashier**. However a 'deputy' or 'stand-in' will be required when the petty cashier is absent on holiday, through illness etc. The petty cashier has the following responsibilities.

- Ensure the cash is **held in a safe place**
- **Make the actual payments of cash**
- Ensure that all **payments are properly authorised** and are for **valid reasons**

The petty cash box

3.2 Petty cash must be kept **secure**. It is usual to keep it in a lockable box or tin. The box or tin is then kept in a locked drawer or the office safe. The key to the petty cash box (and the key to the desk drawer) will be held by the petty cashier.

3.3 No one should be allowed access to the petty cash box except the petty cashier, the petty cashier's 'deputy' and the office supervisor. In some offices, you will find that more individuals have access to petty cash. This is poor office practice because it encourages a lack of proper control and security for cash.

Why are only small items paid for out of petty cash?

3.4 Petty cash should not be used for large expenses, such as office furniture, large restaurant bills or aeroplane tickets because of **security**.

- A large amount of cash is an obvious target for theft

- A system of payments from petty cash for large items could lend itself to abuse.

Limiting the size of petty cash payments

3.5 There should be a **maximum limit** to the amount of any individual payment. For example, an organisation might have a £40.00 limit. Requests for larger payments should be refused by the petty cashier. Larger payments can be obtained by another method.

- An employee should submit an **expenses claim** or **cheque request form**

- An external supplier (eg the milkman or window cleaner) should submit **invoices** for payment by cheque

Authorisation and authorisation limits

3.6 Payments out of petty cash should be **properly authorised by the appropriate person.**

- The petty cashier can authorise individual payments up to a certain limit, say £20.00, but only if a receipt is provided

- For larger amounts up to the petty cash limit, the authorisation should be by the petty cashier's supervisor

- Exceptionally, a petty cash payment in excess of the maximum limit might be permitted, subject to authorisation by a nominated senior person

Receipts

3.7 A request for payment out of petty cash should be supported by a **receipt**, as proof of purchase. The receipt might simply be a till roll, showing the name of the shop or supplier and the amount of the payment. It is good practice to write down the nature of the item purchased on the receipt, if it does not show this already.

VAT receipts

3.8 If VAT has been paid, which can be reclaimed from Customs & Excise, a **VAT receipt** is needed showing these details.

- The total payment
- The VAT paid (not essential, the petty cashier can calculate the VAT)
- The supplier's name, address and VAT registration number
- The date of the transaction

Customs & Excise do allow VAT to be reclaimed in cases where the total amount (including VAT) is **£25 or less, without** a VAT invoice.

No available receipts

3.9 Sometimes petty cash claims will be submitted without a receipt, eg travelling expenses. Employees are not always required to provide proof of a taxi, bus or train fare. However, the payment should be sanctioned by an authorised person, eg by the supervisor or manager of the individual concerned.

Activity 8.2   Level: Pre-assessment

Orlando Orseo suggests that it would be much more convenient if you could leave an amount, say £30, in a 'kitty box' by Reception. Then employees who are short of cash for parking meters, phones or Metro fares could 'dip in' without all 'that receipt fuss'. Outline for him why this is not such a good idea.

Activity 8.3   Level: Pre-assessment

Raj Devi brings you the following petty cash claims. Which can you pay immediately and which need further action?

(a) £22.00 train travel to a conference, which has not been authorised by the Administration Manager.

(b) £5.20 spent on tea bags, supported by a valid receipt.

(c) £30.00 taxi fare, authorised by the Administration Manager.

(d) £6.25 biscuits for the office, supported by a valid receipt.

(e) £20.00 stationery, with no receipt but authorised by the Administration Manager.

(f) £11.99 spent on office milk, with a valid receipt.

(g) £2.20 spent on postage stamps, with no receipt.

---

4   THE IMPREST SYSTEM

> **KEY TERM**
>
> The **imprest system** is a system in which there is a maximum amount of money in petty cash, the imprest amount. The imprest amount varies from one organisation to another, and might be enough to make petty cash payments for about one month.

4.1   The maximum amount for petty cash in company A is £500.00. At the start of the month, the petty cash box contains this amount. As payments are made out of petty cash, the amount of cash left will diminish. Eventually the petty cashier will decide that petty cash needs to be 'topped up' again to the imprest amount of £500.00.

4.2   **Topping up petty cash** can occur whenever the need arises. However, it is usually done regularly, once each week or once each month. In order to top up petty cash to the imprest amount, cash is drawn from the bank equal to the amount of petty cash payments.

4.3   We will cover the procedure for topping up in Section 9 of this chapter. However an example follows to illustrate the method.

4.4   EXAMPLE: TOPPING UP THE IMPREST

		£
1 May	Imprest amount	1,000.00
1-31 May	Petty cash payments (total of 57 receipts)	(826.40)
31 May	Petty cash in tin at month end	173.60
31 May	Top up drawn from bank	826.40
31 May	Restored imprest amount	1,000.00

4.5   In a non-imprest system the petty cash is topped up to any amount without reference to the petty cash vouchers. The maximum amount of petty cash can vary from month to month depending on likely expenditure; for example £300 January, £150 February, £250 March.

Activity 8.4   **Level: Pre-assessment**

You have the following receipts in the petty cash box at 30 November. By how much should the balance in the box be topped up?

Date	Expense	Amount
		£
3 November	Tea bags	1.99
6 November	Light bulbs	5.99
11 November	Train fare	10.50
17 November	Teapot and cups	24.99
22 November	Desk lamp	19.99
25 November	Stamps book	10.00

---

5   PETTY CASH VOUCHERS

5.1   The initial record of payment is the **petty cash voucher.**

5.2 A voucher must be prepared whenever a payment is requested. The receipt(s) should be firmly attached to the voucher.

5.3 When completed, a voucher should contain the following details.

(a) **Details** of the purpose for which the money was spent

(b) The **amount** paid (and detail if there is more than one item)

(c) The **name of the person receiving the cash** (who should acknowledge receipt by signing the voucher)

(d) The **signature** of the person authorising the payment

(e) The **date** of payment

(f) The **number** of the voucher (see Paragraph 4.7 below)

(g) The relevant **receipt(s)** stapled to it

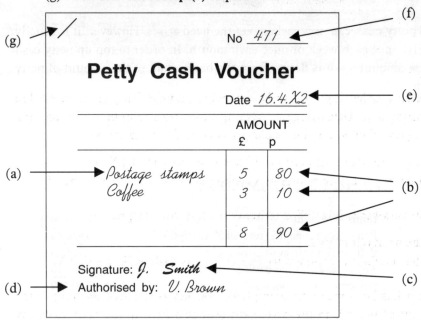

5.4 J Smith should give the petty cashier a receipt for the coffee. There should also be some evidence of purchase of the stamps (a receipt from the shop or Post Office). Otherwise, a note from her manager confirming that the stamps have been obtained. This confirms the stamps were for office, not personal use.

5.5 EXAMPLE: PETTY CASH VOUCHERS

The petty cash system in company B provides for a maximum individual payment of £100.00. The petty cashier can authorise individual payments up to £25.00. Payments between £25.00 and £100.00 must be authorised by the accounts supervisor, R Greene. On 18 December 20X2 a petty cash claim is made for expenses for an office Christmas party. Receipts from a supermarket for food and drink total £82.56. Payment is to be made to the office manager, D Porter.

The petty cashier writes out the voucher. However the supervisor R Greene must sign the voucher to authorise payment.

The petty cash voucher (not yet given its voucher number) would be as follows.

```
                                    No _____

        Petty  Cash  Voucher
                                    Date  18.12.X2

                                        AMOUNT
                                         £      p

        Office party                    82     56


                                        82     56

        Signature:  D.  Porter
        Authorised  by:  R.  Greene
```

Voucher numbers

5.6   Every petty cash voucher is given a **unique voucher number**. They are numbered in sequence, starting at 1. Usually the number sequence restarts from 1 with the first voucher **each year**. Numbering the vouchers allows the following checks.

- Vouchers traced from the petty cash book to where they are **filed**
- **Completeness check** to ensure no vouchers are missing or not recorded

5.7   The voucher's number is inserted at either of the following stages.

- When the payment is made
- When the vouchers are used to write up the petty cash book (Section 6)

5.8   After payment has been made, the completed voucher is attached securely to the relevant receipt(s) and put in the petty cash box. It is kept in the petty cash box until the next 'top up' to the imprest amount.

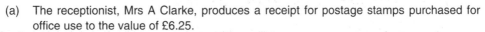

Activity 8.5   **Level: Assessment**

On Monday 14 December 20X7 you receive the following requests for reimbursement. The last voucher used the previous week was numbered 100.

(a)   The receptionist, Mrs A Clarke, produces a receipt for postage stamps purchased for office use to the value of £6.25.

(b)   The sales manager produces a receipt for £7.50 in respect of a return rail ticket, purchased in order to visit a customer.

Task

Using the blank petty cash vouchers provided, complete vouchers for the above two items. Ignore VAT.

No _____
Petty Cash Voucher
Date _____

AMOUNT

£   p

Signature:

Authorised by:

No _____
Petty Cash Voucher
Date _____

AMOUNT

£   p

Signature:

Authorised by:

Petty cash payments for expenses not yet incurred

5.9   There will be occasions when someone needs a petty cash advance.

(a) **Payments in advance** must be authorised by a supervisor or office manager.

(b) The petty cashier writes out a petty cash voucher marked 'cash advance' and gets the recipient's signature.

(c) When the receipt and the change are eventually received, the petty cashier should **alter the voucher** to show the exact amount of the payment.

5.10   EXAMPLE: PETTY CASH ADVANCES

A director of company C needs money to pay for a taxi and asks for £20.00 from petty cash on 5 July 20X0. The payment is sanctioned by the accounts supervisor, T Roberts. The next day, the director returns with a taxi cab receipt for £15.50 and gives back change of £4.50.

The petty cash voucher should be prepared initially as follows.

```
                        No _____

        Petty  Cash  Voucher

                        Date 5.7.X0
        _____
                              AMOUNT
                              £      p
        _____
          Taxi fare          20    00
         (CASH ADVANCE)
        _____
                             20    00
        _____

        Signature: P.  Perkins  (Director)
        Authorised by:  T. Roberts
```

On 6 July the original voucher is altered by the petty cashier.

```
                                No _____

        Petty  Cash  Voucher

                                Date 5.7.X0
        _____
                              AMOUNT
                              £      p
        _____
          Taxi fare          20     00
         (CASH ADVANCE)       15    50
        _____
                             20     00
                             15     50
        _____

        Signature: P.  Perkins  (Director)
        Authorised by:  T. Roberts
```

The change is put into the petty cash box, together with the amended voucher and (attached to the voucher) the receipt. However, if a further amount is required, then either a new voucher is prepared or the old voucher amended to show that the **adjusted figure is authorised**.

Checks on petty cash and vouchers

5.11 Each week, the petty cashier may make a large number of payments. For security and control reasons, there ought to be **regular checks** on the following.

		£
	Notes and coins in petty cash box	X
plus ⟶	Total value of vouchers in the petty cash box	X
equals ⟶	Imprest amount	X

BPP
PUBLISHING

5.12 If the amount of cash plus the value of the vouchers does **not** equal the imprest amount, something has gone wrong. The petty cashier should inform his or her supervisor immediately.

5.13 **Possible reasons for the discrepancy**

- **Mistake** in the cash paid out (eg paid out £10.00 for a voucher of only £9.80)
- **Theft** from the petty cash box

IOUs and petty cash

5.14 In some organisations, individuals may be permitted to borrow money from petty cash. They must, of course, pay it back.

When someone borrows cash, they must put an **IOU** into the petty cash box.

I owe petty cash £10.00

J. Smith
15/10/X5

5.15 When checking the petty cash, **IOUs are equivalent to cash**.

		£
	Notes and coins in petty cash box	X
plus ⟶	Total value of IOUs	X
plus ⟶	Total value of vouchers in the petty cash box	X
equals ⟶	Imprest amount	X

5.16 When the borrowed amount is returned to petty cash, the IOU is given to the borrower marked 'paid'. It is not good practice to allow borrowing from petty cash. However, it does happen and therefore must be properly controlled.

Receiving money into petty cash

5.17 Occasionally, **money is put into petty cash** apart from top ups.

- An employee paying for office stamps used for personal letters
- Employees paying for private calls made from an office phone
- Money from a cash sale may be used to boost petty cash

5.18 When money is paid into petty cash in this way, the petty cashier inserts a **voucher for the money received**. For example, C Trickey pays £1.10 for stamps used for his private mail.

```
                    No _____

          Petty Cash Voucher

                    Date  18.12.X8
          _____
                                    AMOUNT
                                  £        p
          _____
          Cash received for      1      10
          sale of postage
          stamps to
          C Tricky
          _____
                                  1      10
          _____

          Signature:  V. Brown  (Petty cashier)
          Authorised by:
```

5.19 Practice varies, but usually vouchers for cash received are **not** sequentially numbered.

5.20 If a check is made after money has been paid into petty cash in this way, then the following should apply.

		£
	Notes and coins in petty cash box	X
plus ➔	Total value of IOUs	X
plus ➔	Total value of vouchers for payments out of petty cash	X
less ➔	Total value of vouchers for receipts of cash into petty cash	(X)
equals ➔	Imprest amount	X

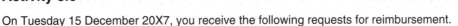

Activity 8.6   **Level: Assessment**

On Tuesday 15 December 20X7, you receive the following requests for reimbursement.

(a) The new office clerk presents bus tickets for amounts totalling £3.60 to support a request for payment for his first week's travel to work.

(b) Ten new typewriter ribbons have been received costing £5.50 each. An invoice has been sent with the goods and a receipt will be issued on payment.

(c) The office caretaker asks for £5 to pay as a gratuity to the refuse collectors, as has been customary in previous years.

(d) A clerk says that the administration manager asked him to purchase coffee, tea and sugar for the office kitchen. The receipt shows a total cost of £15.40.

Task

Using the blank petty cash vouchers provided, complete vouchers for any of the above items which you are able to authorise. Indicate what action you would take in respect of any requests for which you have not completed vouchers.

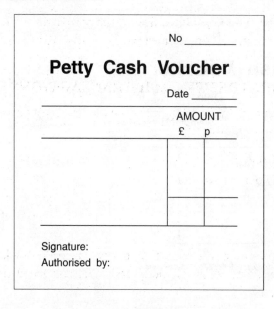

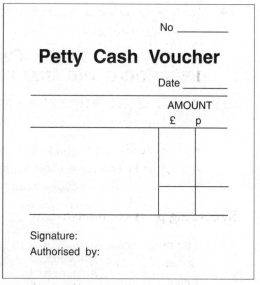

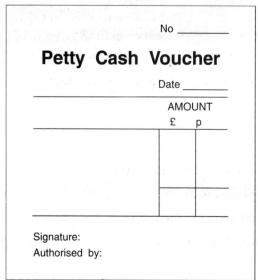

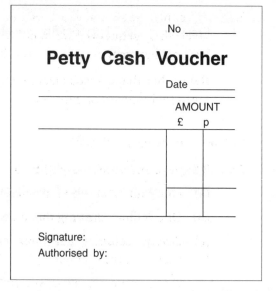

6 THE PETTY CASH BOOK

6.1 The next step to record cash put into the petty cash box and payments out of the petty cash box. This record is the **petty cash book,** which is a book of prime entry.

6.2 **The purposes of the petty cash book**

- To **provide an accounting record** of every petty cash transaction
- To allow for **posting petty cash expenses to the main ledger**

6.3 The petty cash book is a bound book with a large number of columns on each double page.

Left hand side: debit side	Right hand side: credit side
Used to record **cash receipts** into the petty cash box. It consists of about two to four columns.	Used to record and analyse **cash payments**. The number of analysis columns can be quite large.

There is a column in the **middle** for showing the **date of each transaction.**

6.4 Each petty cash transaction is recorded on a **separate line** in the petty cash book. An example of a petty cash book is illustrated on the next page.

7 RECORDING AND ANALYSING PETTY CASH TRANSACTIONS

7.1 **Writing up the petty cash book** should be done fairly regularly, depending on how often petty cash is used in the organisation.

- Typically, every two to four weeks
- **Must** be written up before the float is topped up

Recording petty cash payments

7.2 The petty cashier transfers details of **payments** from the vouchers into the book, on the right side of the double page. Entries in the petty cash book are listed in voucher number order *and* date order.

7.3 There may be several vouchers and, usually, it is at this stage that the vouchers are given their **sequential number**. If there are 20 vouchers and the number of the last voucher written up is 963, the 20 vouchers should be numbered 964-983.

Remember that the vouchers must first be sorted into date order **before** they are given their sequential number.

Columns on the payment side

7.4 The payments side (the **credit** side) will have the following columns.

(a) One column showing the **voucher number**.

(b) One column showing the **total payment** on a voucher.

(c) Several columns **analysing** each payment. Typical column headings are shown on the example.

(d) One column will be for **sundry items**.

(e) One column will be for **value added tax** (VAT).

(f) There should be a 'Details' column. This is used to explain the reason for the payment. **All sundry items** should be explained, to keep a record of why the payment was made.

(j) Details	(i) Net receipt £	(h) VAT £	(g) Total £	Date	(f) Details	(a) Voucher No	(b) Total £	Travel £	Postage £	Enter-tainment £	(c) Office supplies £	(d) Sundry £	(e) VAT £

Receipts — Payments

Analysis of payments

Writing up the payments side

7.5 Entering the details of petty cash expenses in the book should normally be a fairly simple process.

Step 1	*Vouchers in the batch are ordered one at a time, in date order/voucher number order.*

- The date on the voucher (which is the date of the payment)
- The voucher number
- The total amount paid

Step 2	*The petty cashier must then analyse the payment.*

- A payment of £8.75 for rail travel on official business is entered in both the 'total' and the 'travel' columns.

- A payment is made of £9.20 for £8.00 on postage stamps and £1.20 on newspapers for the office. The 'total' entry will be £9.20, with £8.00 in the postage and £1.20 in the sundry column.

7.6 EXAMPLE: WRITING UP PETTY CASH BOOK PAYMENTS

The following four vouchers were taken from the petty cash box and numbered in sequence 1461 to 1464.

		No *1461*
Petty Cash Voucher		
		Date *22.2.X3*
	AMOUNT £	p
Postage stamps	15	20
	15	20
Signature: *B Travis*		
Authorised by: *Admin Manager*		

		No *1462*
Petty Cash Voucher		
		Date *24.2.X3*
	AMOUNT £	p
Coffee	5	50
Biscuits	3	50
	9	00
Signature: *P Sayles*		
Authorised by: *Office Manager*		

No _1463_

Petty Cash Voucher

Date _1.3.X3_

	AMOUNT	
	£	p
Taxi fare	6	40
	6	40

Signature: *R Olney*
Authorised by: *Petty Cashier*

No _1464_

Petty Cash Voucher

Date _5.3.X3_

	AMOUNT	
	£	p
Bus fares	1	35
Payment to charity collectors	10	00
	11	35

Signature: *P Sayles*
Authorised by: *Office Manager*

7.7 SOLUTION

The petty cash book should be written up as follows. (You would normally see a VAT column here, but we deal with this in Section 8.)

Date	Details	Voucher no	Total £	Analysis of payments			
				Travel £	Postage £	Stationery £	Sundry £
20X3							
22.2	Stamps	1461	15.20		15.20		
24.2	Coffee, biscuits	1462	9.00				9.00
1.3	Taxi	1463	6.40	6.40			
5.3	Bus fares, payment to charity	1464	11.35	1.35			10.00

Activity 8.7   Level: Assessment

Assume that items (c) and (d) in Activity 8.6 above have now been duly authorised on vouchers 103 and 104 respectively.

Task

Write up the payments side of the petty cash book below to reflect the authorised petty cash expenditure on 15 December 20X7.

Date	Details	Voucher No	Total £	Analysis of payments		
				Travel £	Postage £	Sundry £
20X7						

Recording receipts of money into petty cash

7.8 If there have been some receipts of money into petty cash, these should be recorded on the left-hand side (**debit** side) of the petty cash book.

Columns on the receipts side

7.9 The receipts side will have the following columns.

(g) A column for the **total receipt** on a voucher
(h) A column for **VAT**
(i) A column for the **net receipt**
(j) A **details** column

7.10 There is a receipt voucher for £4.70 from an employee for a personal telephone call. The £4.70 is a net payment of £4.00 plus 70p for VAT at 17½%.

7.11 The receipt would be recorded in the petty cash book as follows (and the opening balance is also shown).

Details	Net receipt £	VAT £	Total £	Date
				20X9
Balance b/d			400.00	1.8
Telephone	4.00	0.70	4.70	12.8

8 RECORDING PETTY CASH TRANSACTIONS: VAT

8.1 In some petty cash systems, the VAT on payments or receipts is ignored completely. This is on the grounds that the VAT is immaterial and accounting for it is more trouble than it is worth.

8.2 The VAT element in petty cash transactions should be accounted for separately. However, **the transaction must be accompanied by a VAT receipt** (unless the total amount including VAT is less than £25 (3.8)).

8.3 Accounting for VAT payments

- The total payment column shows the payment **inclusive** of VAT
- The amount of VAT paid is entered in the VAT column
- The net amount is entered in the analysis column(s)

8.4 EXAMPLE: PETTY CASH PAYMENTS INCLUDING VAT

Here are two receipts for payments that include a VAT element. A claim from petty cash is made separately for each. How would these be recorded as petty cash vouchers and in the petty cash book?

<table>
<tr><td>

XYZ Ltd
3 High Street, Kingston

VAT Reg No. 228 4135 62
Date 20/4/X4

	£
Electric plugs and fuses	22.00
VAT @ 17.5%	3.85
Total	25.85

</td><td>

ABC Ltd
14 Low Street, Richmond

VAT Reg No. 221 4685 27
Date 22/4/X4

Paid £42.30 for stationery,
inclusive of VAT @ 17.5%

</td></tr>
</table>

8.5 SOLUTION

In the case of receipt from ABC Ltd, the actual amount of VAT is not shown and needs to be worked it out.

$$\text{VAT} = \frac{17.5\%}{117.5\%} \times \text{total payment}$$

$$\text{Payment exclusive of VAT} = \frac{100\%}{117.5\%} \times \text{total payment}$$

(a) $\text{VAT payment} = \frac{17.5}{117.5} \times £42.30$

$= £6.30$

(b) The payment *exclusive* of VAT is (£42.30 − £6.30) = £36.00, or

$$\frac{100}{117.5} \times £42.30 = £36.00$$

Note. For ease of calculations in future you should note that $17^1/_2/117^1/_2$ is equivalent to the fraction 7/47.

No _371_	No _372_
Petty Cash Voucher	**Petty Cash Voucher**

Petty Cash Voucher No 371			Petty Cash Voucher No 372		
Date 20.4.X4			Date 22.4.X4		
	AMOUNT £	p		AMOUNT £	p
Plugs and fuses	22	00	Stationery	36	00
VAT	3	85	VAT	6	30
	25	85		42	30
Signature: J. Smith			Signature: R. Greene		
Authorised by: V. Brown (Petty cashier)			Authorised by: D. Nuttall (Supervisor)		

Here our petty cash book only shows analysis columns for stationery, sundry items, and VAT, in order to keep the illustration as simple as possible.

Date	Details	Voucher no	Total £	Analysis of payments		
				Stationery £	Sundry £	VAT £
20X4						
20.4	Plugs and fuses	371	25.85		22.00	3.85
22.4	Stationery	372	42.30	36.00		6.30

Activity 8.8   Level: Assessment

The following petty cash vouchers were processed during the remainder of the week ending 18 December 20X7.

	No _105_
Petty Cash Voucher	
Date _16.12.X7_	

	AMOUNT £	p
Stationery	10	81
	10	81

Signature: *SM BODY*
Authorised by: *Admin Manager*

	No _106_
Petty Cash Voucher	
Date _17.12.X7_	

	AMOUNT £	p
Sundry expenses	5	17
	5	17

Signature: *A Clarke*
Authorised by: *Petty Cashier*

	No _107_
Petty Cash Voucher	
Date _17.12.X7_	

	AMOUNT £	p
Repairs	22	09
	22	09

Signature: *A Person*
Authorised by: *Administration Manager*

	No _108_
Petty Cash Voucher	
Date _17.12.X7_	

	AMOUNT £	p
Stationary	4	23
	4	23

Signature: *NE Body*
Authorised by: *Petty Cashier*

	No _109_
Petty Cash Voucher	
Date _17.12.X7_	

	AMOUNT £	p
Sundry expenses	2	82
	2	82

Signature: *Anne Onymus*
Authorised by: *Petty Cashier*

	No _110_
Petty Cash Voucher	
Date _18.12.X7_	

	AMOUNT £	p
Sundry expenses	6	58
Stationary	1	41
	7	99

Signature: *C Happe*
Authorised by: *Petty Cashier*

PETTY CASH BOOK

	Receipts							Payments — Analysis of payments					
Details	Net receipt £	VAT £	Total £	Date	Details	Voucher No	Total £	Travel £	Postage £	Stationery £	Repairs £	Sundry £	VAT £
Balance b/d			150.00	20X7									
				14.12	Postage	101	6.25		6.25				
				14.12	Travel	102	7.50	7.50					
				15.12	Sundry	103	5.00					5.00	
				15.12	Sundry	104	15.40					15.40	

BPP PUBLISHING

All of the expenses listed on vouchers 105 to 110 included VAT at 17.5%, and VAT receipts were presented in each case.

Task

Make appropriate entries in the petty cash book (payments side) on page 167, to record petty cash vouchers 105 to 110.

Activity 8.9 Level: Assessment

During the week beginning 14 December 20X7 the following cash sums were received in the office of Aldgate Plastics and banked by you.

15.12.X7	Cash sale: £29.14 (including VAT at 17½%)
16.12.X7	£1.88 received from a member of staff to pay for personal telephone calls
18.12.X7	Cash sale: £13.16 (including VAT at 17½%)

Task

Write up the petty cash book (receipts side) on the previous page for the week beginning 14 December 20X7.

---

9 TOPPING UP THE FLOAT, BALANCING OFF AND POSTING PETTY CASH

DEVOLVED ASSESSMENT ALERT

This is ideal material for a possible processing exercise in the Devolved Assessment. Make sure you can perform all seven steps in the correct sequence.

9.1 Whenever the imprest float is **topped up** by drawing more cash from the bank, the petty cash book must be **balanced off**.

9.2 These steps should be followed.

Step 1 **Add up** the payments in all columns. The analysis columns should **cross-cast** to the total column.

Step 2 Check **amount left** in petty cash box.

		£
	Notes and coins in petty cash box	X
plus	IOUs	X
plus	payment vouchers	X
less	receipt vouchers	(X)
equals	imprest amount	X

All discrepancies, however small, should be investigated and discussed with the petty cashier's supervisor.

Step 3 Prepare cheque requisition for the difference between the imprest amount and the amount of cash left.

		£
	Imprest amount	X
less	Cash in petty cash box	(X)
	Cheque requisition	X

PETTY CASH BOOK

| | ──── Receipts ──── | | | | | ──── Payments ──── | | | | | Analysis of payments | | | |
Details	Net receipt £	VAT £	Total £	Date	Details	Voucher No	Total £	Travel £	Postage £	Enter-tainment £	Office supplies £	Sundry £	VAT £
Balance b/d			250.00	20X0									
				5.3	Light bulbs	635	19.27				16.40		2.87
				8.3	Taxi fares	636	49.50	25.00		24.50			
				12.3	Entertainment	637	56.80			56.80			
				14.3	Window cleaner	638	47.00				40.00		7.00
				20.3									
Sale of postage stamps	1.10	—	1.10	21.3									
				22.3	Stamps	639	6.60		6.60				
				24.3	Magazines	640	12.30					12.30	
				29.3	Bus fares	641	3.65	3.65					

BPP PUBLISHING

Step 4	**Draw cash from bank**, specifying the notes and coins required, and place in box. Enter amount on left-hand (debit) side of petty cash book.
Step 5	**Balance off PCB**. This completes the double page in the book and starts the next one.
Step 6	Ensure that the balancing off is **checked by the accounts supervisor**, who should sign and date the balanced off pages. This shows that the correct amount of cash has been drawn.
Step 7	**Post the totals** to the general ledger.

9.3 EXAMPLE: TOPPING UP, BALANCING OFF AND POSTING

The imprest amount is £250, and at the end of March the petty cashier decides to top up the float in the petty cash box. Using the example on page 169.

Step 1	**Add up the payments** in all columns. The analysis columns should cross-cast to the total columns.

Cross-cast check

	£
Travel	28.65
Postage	6.60
Entertainment	81.30
Office supplies	56.40
Sundry	12.30
VAT	9.87
Total payments	195.12

Step 2	Check **amount** left in petty cash box.

If there are no discrepancies, the cash in the box should amount to £55.98. This is because:

		£
	Imprest amount	250.00
plus	receipts	1.10
		251.10
less	total payments	195.12
equals	cash in box	55.98

Step 3	Prepare a cheque requisition for the difference between the imprest amount and the amount of cash left.

The amount of cash needed to top up the petty cash to the imprest amount can be calculated in either of two ways.

Method 1		£	Method 2		£
Imprest amount		250.00	Total payments		195.12
Cash in the box		(55.98)	Less receipts		(1.10)
Cash needed		194.02	Cash needed		194.02

A **cheque requisition form** should be prepared by the petty cashier. In this example, the cheque requisition should be for £194.02.

An example of a completed form is given below.

Cheque requisition

DATE: *31/3/X0*

PAYABLE TO: *Cash*

AMOUNT: *£194.02*

DETAILS: *Petty cash imprest float*

SIGNED: *Petty cashier*

AUTHORISED BY: *Accounts supervisor*

The cheque should then be prepared, taken to the bank and cashed.

NEWROSE INTERNATIONAL 1 Bower street, The Garden, W4 9EG		22 29 48

NEWROSE INTERNATIONAL

STAG BANK
Forest Lane, The Dell

Date	Pay to the order of			Amount
31/03/X0	Cash			**** 194.02

Hundred Thousands	Ten Thousands	Thousands	Hundreds	Tens	Units
*******	*******	*******	One	Nine	Four

Amount of pounds in words   Pence as in figures

Per Pro NEWROSE INTERNATIONAL

A Rose

⑅10117⑅ 22⑆2948⑈ 50195733⑅

Step 4   Draw cash from bank, specifying the notes and coins required, and place in box.

When the cheque is cashed, the petty cashier should decide the denomination of notes and coins. Since petty cash is for small payments, the petty cashier might decide to ask for the £194.02 to be made up as follows

	Number	*£*
£20 notes	3	60.00
£10 notes	7	70.00
£5 notes	10	50.00
£1 coins	9	9.00
50p coins	6	3.00
20p coins	5	1.00
10p coins	4	0.40
5p coins	7	0.35
2p coins	10	0.20
1p coins	7	0.07
		194.02

The receipt of the money into petty cash must be recorded as follows.

- The cash book (as a cheque payment)
- The petty cash book (as a receipt)

In the petty cash book, the entry should include a reference to the corresponding folio number or entry number in the cash book. CB 324 in this example.

| *Step 5* | Balance off PCB. |

The left-hand (debit) side of the petty cash book is completed as follows.

- Enter the details of the **cash receipt** (Step 4)

- **Total** the columns for receipts

- On the payments side, insert an entry in the total column for the amount of cash in petty cash. This **balance carried down** is the imprest amount. Then total the payments

- The **total for receipts,** including the balance brought forward, **must be equal to the total for payments plus the balance carried down**.

- Show the balance brought down, which should be the **imprest amount**, on the next page of the petty cash book.

These entries are shown on Page 174.

| *Step 6* | Ensure that the balancing off is checked by the accounts supervisor, who should sign and date the balanced off pages. |

The supervisor will probably already have checked the amount of cash in the petty cash box when the cheque requisition form was authorised. The check that is carried out now should be to ensure the following.

- The columns have been properly totalled and cross-cast

- The analysis of payments seems correct

- There are vouchers and receipts for all the payments. The amount on each voucher corresponds with the amount shown in the petty cash book

If the supervisor is satisfied, he or she should sign and date the page.

| *Step 7* | Post the totals to the general ledger. |

This can be done by drawing up a **posting summary** of the totals from the petty cash book. The ledger codes show where in the general ledger the amounts have been posted. In this example, A041 is the petty cash account, the 'E' accounts are expenses and the 'R' account is revenue or income.

	POSTING SUMMARY Day book: Petty cash Date: 31.3.X0			
Step 7 ***(cont.)***		General ledger Account	Dr £	Cr £
	Petty cash	A041	1.10	195.12
	Travel	E151	28.65	
	Postage	E153	6.60	
	Entertainment	E155	81.30	
	Office supplies	E164	56.40	
	Sundry expenses	E180	12.30	
	VAT	E247	9.87	
	Sundry income	R302		1.10
			196.22	196.22

Every item of petty cash expense (or income) should be allocated to an account in the general ledger. There should be a separate account for each of the expenditure items for which there is an analysis column in the petty cash book.

Study the completed petty cash book on the following page and make sure that you can follow through each and every entry. The circled numbers refer to the steps outlined above.

Drawing cash against a crossed cheque

9.4 Did you spot that the cheque in Step 4 above is made out to cash and yet is also a **crossed cheque**? Crossed cheques should **normally** only be paid into another bank account. The bank may ignore the instruction of the crossing, however, under certain circumstances.

9.5 The drawer or some representative well known to the bank (eg the petty cashier) may **present a crossed cheque for payment in cash**. The banks can ignore the crossing on the grounds that there is no risk of the money passing to a person not entitled to it.

9.6 This is an example of practical business and banking needs overriding the rules relating to cheques and banking.

Archive records

9.7 When the recording is complete, all the completed vouchers and receipts in the petty cash box must be **removed.**

9.8 The vouchers must not be thrown away, but kept for **at least seven years**. It must be possible for an auditor to find any voucher for which an entry has been made in the petty cash book. The petty cashier needs a system of **archiving** used vouchers.

PETTY CASH BOOK

Receipts

Details	Net receipt £	VAT £	Total £
Balance b/d			250.00
Sale of postage stamps	1.10	—	1.10
Ledger code A041 (7)	1.10 (5)		194.02 (4)
Cash book folio CB324 (4)			445.12 (5)
Ledger code	£302 (7)		445.12

Payments — Analysis of payments

Date	Details	Voucher No	Total £	Travel £	Postage £	Enter-tainment £	Office supplies £	Sundry £	VAT £
20X0									
5.3	Light bulbs	635	19.27				16.40		2.87
8.3	Taxi fares	636	49.50	25.00		24.50			
12.3	Entertainment	637	56.80			56.80			
14.3	Window cleaner	638	47.00				40.00		7.00
20.3									
21.3									
22.3	Stamps	639	6.60		6.60				
24.3	Magazines	640	12.30					12.30	
29.3	Bus fares	641	3.65	3.65					
			195.12 (1)	28.65 (1)	6.60 (1)	81.30 (1)	56.40 (1)	12.30 (1)	9.87 (1)
31.3	Balance c/d		250.00 (5)						
			445.12 (5)						
	Ledger code A041 (7)			£151 (7)	£153 (7)	£155 (7)	£164 (7)	£180 (7)	£247 (7)

9.9   Practice will vary but the normal system for **holding archive records** follows.

(a)   The vouchers (with attached receipts) should be filed together in number order.

(b)   Until the accounts for that year have been audited, the voucher files are kept available, clearly labelled to show the numbers and dates covered.

(c)   After the annual audit, the vouchers can be archived.

Activity 8.10   **Level: Assessment**

(a)   Total the petty cash book on Page 167 for the week ended 18 December 20X7.

(b)   Complete the cheque requisition form below to top up the imprest float.

(c)   Balance off the petty cash book and bring down the balance at the start of the week beginning 21 December 20X7.

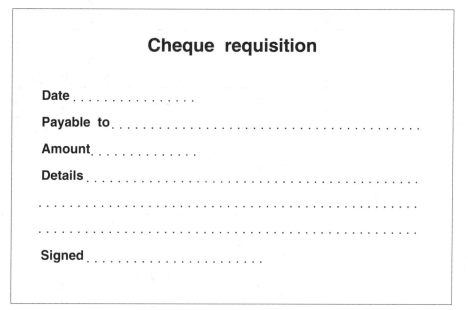

Cheque requisition

Date . . . .

Payable to . . . .

Amount . . . .

Details . . . .

. . . .

. . . .

Signed . . . .

Key learning points

- Petty cash is used to make **small payments** with notes and coins. The cash must be kept **safe**, in a **locked box or tin**, and its **security is the responsibility of a petty cashier**. Payments must be properly **authorised**, and all transactions should be supported by **receipts** and **vouchers**.

- There is usually an **imprest system** for petty cash, whereby a certain amount of cash is held in the box, say £200. At regular intervals or when cash runs low, vouchers are added up and recorded, and the total of the vouchers is used as the amount by which to top up the imprest to £200 again.

	£
	£
Cash in box	X
Total of vouchers = top-up	X
Imprest amount	X

- All **payments** out of petty cash must be **properly authorised**. This is evidenced by a **voucher,** signed by both the person receiving the payment and the person authorising it. Claims for payment must be supported by a **receipt** whenever possible.

- If there is **no receipt** to support a claim for payment, the petty cashier should refer the claim to his or her supervisor.

- At regular intervals, details of payments out of petty cash are recorded from the vouchers into the **petty cash book**. Vouchers should be in date order and **numbered sequentially** and they should be entered into the petty cash book in this order.

- When the **VAT element in petty cash expenditure** is recorded, there must be a VAT receipt as evidence of the payment, and an analysis column for VAT in the petty cash book.

- A **new page** in the petty cash book is started whenever the imprest float is topped up.

- When the **imprest float** is topped up, a sequence of procedures must be followed.

  - The total **expenses and analysis columns** in the book should be added up, and these totals checked to ensure that they cross-cast.

  - The amount of cash in the petty cash tin must be **counted**, and a check made to ensure that the amount needed to top up petty cash to the imprest amount equals the total of voucher payments (minus any receipts).

  - A **cheque requisition form** must be prepared and authorised. When the cheque is written, it should be cashed at the bank. The petty cashier must specify the number of each denomination of notes and coins that he or she wants to make up the total.

  - The cash withdrawal is entered in the **cash book** (payment) and the **petty cash book** (receipts side).

  - The total receipts in the petty cash book must be added up. This should be **equal** to the total expenses (including balance carried down).

  - The page of the petty cash book should be **checked** by the accounts supervisor. The balance brought down, which is the imprest amount, is then **carried forward** to the next page of the petty cash book.

  - A **posting summary** of items on the page of the petty cash book can be prepared, as a preparatory stage in posting the expenses/income details to the general ledger.

  - The petty cashier must remove the completed vouchers from the petty cash box when a page of the petty cash book has been completed, and transfer them to an 'archive' file.

Quick quiz

1   Why do organisations need petty cash?

2   Who is responsible for the safety and security of the petty cash box?

3   What is the nature and purpose of the imprest system?

4   (a)   What details are shown on petty cash vouchers?

    (b)   What information is usually only added to petty cash vouchers when the petty cash book is about to be written up?

    (c)   What should be attached to a petty cash voucher?

5   What items are recorded on the left-hand side of the petty cash book? And what on the right?

6   Why might money be received into petty cash?

7   On what grounds could you ignore the VAT element of petty cash vouchers?

8   State the 7 steps for topping up, balancing off and posting petty cash.

Answers to quick quiz

1   Small items of expense need to be paid for out of notes and coins.

2   The petty cashier; a 'deputy' in his or her absence.

3   The imprest system is designed to keep control of petty cash. The imprest amount is the maximum amount in the petty cash box; payments are made out of this and vouchers created for the payments. The difference between the amount of cash in the petty cash box and the imprest amount is the amount that needs to be paid in to 'top up'. It should also be the sum total of the vouchers.

4   (a)   Purpose of payment; amount paid; name and signature of recipient; name and signature of person authorising payment; date of payment.

       (b)   Voucher number

       (c)   Receipt

5   Receipts of money into petty cash (debit side). Payments of money from petty cash (credit side).

6   Payments from employees for personal use of company property; cash sales (rarely)

7   If it were company policy to do so.

8   (i)   Cast and cross-cast columns in petty cash book

       (ii)   Count cash and vouchers in petty cash box

       (iii)   Calculate amount of, and prepare, cheque requisition and cheque

       (iv)   Specifying notes and coins required, cash cheque at bank and put cash in box, enter in petty cash book

       (v)   Balance off petty cash book

       (vi)   Supervisor checks balancing off

       (vii)   Post totals to general ledger

Part C
Payroll

9 Paying wages and salaries and updating records

This chapter contains

Learning objectives

On completion of this chapter you will be able to:

- Pay wages, salaries and deductions to third parties
- Record the payments in the ledger

1   INTRODUCTION

1.1   Net pay is the amount due to be paid to an employee after deductions (eg company pension, tax, NIC).

1.2   In a **small firm**, with say only ten or fifteen employees, the preparation of the payroll will probably be done every week or month by one of the firm's own clerks. Alternatively, if the expertise is lacking, they might employ an **accountant** or a **bureau** to do the payroll. In either case, the exercise is likely to be fairly simple. The pay is worked out, the necessary documentation is filled in, and arrangements are made for payment.

1.3   Paying people who work for a **large organisation**, on the other hand, can be a **costly** and **time consuming** exercise. No matter how many people an organisation employs, the same requirements for payroll processing apply. It must be

- **accurate** (to the penny)
- **on time** (to the day)
- **secure**, both in terms of the data it contains and the cash

1.4   In this chapter we will deal with actually paying people the money their work has earned them, looking at

- **payslips**
- **methods of payment**

2 THE PAYSLIP

2.1 An employee has a **legal right** to receive a payslip.

KEY TERM

A **payslip** must by law show

- an employee's gross pay
- deductions from gross pay and what they are
- net pay

2.2 It is not always necessary to **itemise** deductions. **Fixed deductions** (ie those which do not change from month to month) can be shown as one deduction provided an employee has been informed of them beforehand. Such a statement must be reissued every 12 months. Broadly speaking, however, a payslip should state the following.

Compulsory disclosures (unless aggregated fixed deductions)	Not compulsory but usually disclosed
The employer's name	The employee's tax code
The employee's name	NICs to date (ie in the current tax year)
Gross pay, showing how made up	The employee's payroll number
Additions to and deductions from pay	The employee's National Insurance number
Employee's pension contributions, if any	The method of payment
Statutory Sick Pay, if any	
Statutory Maternity Pay, if any	
Tax paid to date (ie in the current tax year)	
Tax in the period	
NICs for the period	
Date	
Net pay	
The method of payment for each segment of net pay, if they are paid in different ways	

2.3 There is **no standard format for a payslip,** but you might find that yours looks something like the example below.

BPP PUBLISHING

120 MR A.N. OTHER		EXAMPLE LTD		
NI No: WE123456C Tax Code: 433L Pay By: EFT		Date: 21/02/X0	Tax Period: Mt 11	
DESCRIPTION			AMOUNT	THIS YEAR
01 BASIC SALARY			1,350.00	
02 OVERTIME			10.00	
	TOTAL PAY >>>		1,360.00	14,960.00
INCOME TAX - PAYE			213.29	2,347.11
EMPLOYEE'S NI (EMPLOYER 121.88) TABLE A			107.40	1,181.40
SEASON TICKET LOAN			40.00	
(HOL PAY ACCRUED 0.00)	TOTAL NET PAY >>>		999.31	

2.4 The payslip can be produced

- **Manually**
- By **computer**

DEVOLVED ASSESSMENT ALERT

The AAT have indicated that candidates will need to be able to calculate annual net pay from gross figures, using information given on tax codes, rates and NIC rates. There will be *no* tax tables involved. Therefore it is likely that this will be no more difficult than the following example.

2.5 EXAMPLE: CALCULATING NET PAY

Joe Bloggs has an annual gross salary of £25,000 pa. His tax code for the year 2001/02 is 438L. Calculate his net annual salary given the following information.

(a) The tax-free pay for code 438L is £4,389 for the year.

(b) Any taxable amount over the tax-free pay is taxed at the following rates.

  (i) First £5,000 at 10%

  (ii) Balance at 23%

(c) The NIC rate is 5% for employees.

2.6 SOLUTION

	£	
Annual salary	25,000	
Tax-free pay for year	(4,389)	
Taxable pay	20,611	
Tax due:		
First £5,000 @ 10%		500.00
Next £15,611 @ 23%		3,590.53
£20,611		4,090.53

NIC due:
£25,000 @ 5%   £1,250.00

Therefore net pay for the year is as follows:

	£
Gross pay	25,000.00
Tax	(4,090.53)
NIC	(1,250.00)
Net pay	19,659.47

3 PAYMENT IN CASH

3.1 Employees taken on **since 1 January 1987** do not have the right to demand payment in cash. Employees engaged before that date may require to be paid in cash if this is stipulated in the contract. Cash payment is still quite common in the cases of **part-time employees, temporary staff and casual labour.** Employers are slowly abandoning cash payment for the following reasons.

- **Counting notes and coins is time consuming** and requires more payroll staff

- **Employees have to count their pay** on receipt and **sign for the amount,** causing long queues on pay day

- Cash required for an employee's pay has to be **worked out in detail** and ordered from the bank

- The handling and transport of large amounts of cash pose **security problems.**

Activity 9.1   **Level: Pre-assessment**

Although employers prefer not to pay wages in cash, can you think of any reason why employees might prefer it? List as many as you can.

3.2 However, you might be involved in paying cash wages, so this is described below.

Ordering money

3.3 As stated above, the cash required to pay an employee has to be **worked out in detail** before the bank can be told what to send. To do so, a **coinage analysis** might be prepared for each employee. An example is given below.

NAME	NET WAGE		£50	£20	£10	£5	£2	£1	50p	20p	10p	5p	2p	1p
	£	p												
L Bourbon	178	41	3	1		1	1	1		2				1
C Windsor	99	63	1	2		1	2		1		1		1	1
N Romanov	121	15	2	1				1			1	1		
F Habsberg	156	21	3			1		1		1				1
A Osman	174	51	3	1			2		1					1
R Rajah	180	62	3	1	1				1		1		1	
M Incah	79	90	1	1		1	2		1	2				
VALUE	990	43	£800	£140	£10	£20	£14	£3	£2	£1	30p	5p	4p	4p
NUMBER	——		16	7	1	4	7	3	4	5	3	1	2	4

MONARCH BUILDERS LTD

It should be noted that some employees may not want a note larger than £20.

3.4 Where employees are paid in cash, it is quite common for a breakdown of the notes and coin with which the employee is paid to be added to the documentation. Sometimes it will be **printed on the payslip** next to, or after, the figure for net pay.

3.5 A very simple example, for an employee who received £156.88 net pay for a week, would be.

Notes/Coins		£
£50	× 2	100.00
£20	× 2	40.00
£10	× 1	10.00
£5	× 1	5.00
£1	× 1	1.00
50p	× 1	0.50
20p	× 1	0.20
10p	× 1	0.10
5p	× 1	0.05
2p	× 1	0.02
1p	× 1	0.01
Net pay		156.88

Activity 9.2   **Level: Assessment**

Prepare a note and coin analysis for the following employees.

Name	Net wage due
	£
Bigg	120.12
Little	36.05
Large	129.71
Small	87.04
Stout	276.94
Thynne	110.25
Fatt	89.71
Skinnie	122.43
	972.25

The employees do not want to receive £50 notes, preferring lower denominations.

3.6 Once the analysis has been prepared, a cheque drawing this money from the bank will need to be prepared, the payment **authorised** and the cheque signed.

Handing cash over

3.7 Each employee should be required to **count** the money and then **sign** for it. There are pay packets available which allow this to be done without opening the packet.

(a) If an employee is **unable to collect** his or her wage packet (eg because of illness), the **unclaimed wages packet** would be held in a **safe** until it is collected.

(b) If the employee sends someone else to collect the wages, the employee should send **written authority** naming the person collecting the wages, and that person should provide **proof of identity**.

Payment out of petty cash

3.8 **Part-time** or **casual** workers are sometimes paid out of **petty cash**. This is not good practice because it can lead to problems with the **Inland Revenue**.

3.9 If a person works regularly, then maybe he or she falls into one of the following categories.

- **Self-employed,** in which case his or her tax affairs are nothing to do with the business
- An **employee,** in this case PAYE, NICs and so on are payable

It is the duty of the employer to ensure that PAYE and NICs are paid in such a case. Failure to record all payments to employees can result in **penalties** for the employer, and can mean that the employer is liable to pay the PAYE and NICs which should have been deducted.

3.10 Petty cash is sometimes used to make **informal advances** to employees. If this is the case, the borrower should sign an IOU. Money cannot be deducted from pay unless there is a specific agreement to do so. So, if an IOU is to be repaid in this way, the employee should also sign a form expressly authorising payroll to reclaim the loan from pay. Alternatively, the amount of the IOU should be repaid directly by the employee.

Activity 9.3   **Level: Assessment**

Your company made the following payments out of petty cash this month. What should you, as Petty Cashier, do about each one?

(a) Gina Chatterjee received £50 for looking after the plants in the reception area and meetings room. She receives this sum every month. She works for several other local businesses providing the same service. She does not provide an invoice.

(b) Jo Kent received £100 as an advance of salary. She signed a petty cash voucher. A copy of this has been passed to you.

No. 291		
Petty Cash Voucher		
		Date: 10.3.00
	AMOUNT	
	£	p
Advance of salary for March	100	00
Signature: *Jo Kent*		
Authorised by: *Alison Brown*		

(c) Lewis Taylor received £30 for helping out in the post room on several occasions recently, when a member of staff was off sick. Lewis is a full-time student with various part-time jobs. He signed no receipt.

4   CHEQUE PAYMENTS

4.1 A **cheque** is the simplest form of **cashless pay**. The cheque will display the **name** of the employee, and the **amount** to be paid which will agree exactly to the payslip.

4.2 The payroll should have been **authorised** by the payroll manager before it was passed for payment. Therefore, a copy of the authorised payroll and the payslips, should be passed to the **cheque signatory** so that they can check payment is to genuine employees.

4.3 It is likely that director's pay cheques will be **highly confidential** and so will only be signed by senior personnel. Remember that pay is a highly sensitive issue and details of individual's pay must not be given to anyone without authority.

4.4 The problem with cheque payments is that so much **time** is spent preparing them. Also, while the **security problems** with cheques are less than with cash, there is still the possibility of **theft** or **fraud**. Obviously, any organisation must keep a chequebook, but it can be a problem when it comes to be treated as just another part of the stationery.

4.5 Some of the effort of writing out a cheque can be spared if they are **printed** beforehand, so that only the signature is necessary. Printing the cheque can be the final run of the normal payroll processing. In fact, some organisations have an arrangement whereby the **cheque** is the second half of a perforated sheet of paper which has the **pay slip** on top. The employee receives both, tears off the cheque and takes it to the bank. An example is given on the following page.

4.6 The cheques must be **numbered in sequence**, and must be kept under **strict control**.

4.7 Even though cheques, particularly for monthly paid staff, are used less as **automated payment systems** take over, they will still be used for **exceptional circumstances** such as.

- An **employee leaving** part way through the month
- A **new employee** joining during the month
- **Advances of salary**

EMPLOYEE	NAME	CODE	MONTH	BLOGGS AND CO	
0152	A. WORKER	433L	11	21/2/X0	

Narrative	Amount		Year To Date	
	£	p	£	p
BASIC PAY	1,000	00	11,000	00
GROSS PAY	1,000	00	11,000	00
INCOME TAX	130	49	1,436.31	
NICs	71	40	785.40	
NET PAY	798	11		

Any Bank

449 SOMEWHERE ROAD, LONDON W5 2LF

21 2 20 XO

20-27-48
SOUTHERN BANK PLC

Pay   A. WORKER

or order

SEVEN HUNDRED AND NINETY-EIGHT POUNDS AND ELEVEN PENCE

£ 798-11

Authorised signature   *Any Body*

Authorised signature   *Some Body*

Bloggs and Co

Cheque No.	Branch No.	Account No.
⑈101129⑈	20⑈ 2748⑈	30595713⑈

5 DIRECT CREDIT

5.1 Most companies now use some form of **automated payment system**. This means that instead of filling up pay packets with cash, or signing large numbers of cheques which the employees take to their various banks, the whole operation is done speedily and automatically through the banking system.

KEY TERM

Direct Credit is a system which enables you to make payments by electronic transfer directly into bank or building society accounts. It is operated by **BACS**, the UK's automated payments clearing service, which is owned by the major banks and building societies.

5.2 An organisation can use Direct Credit in one of two ways.

(a) **Indirect access:** the organisation uses a **bureau service** provided by its bank or by a computer bureau. You provide the payroll information by fax, telephone, post or PC input, and in return for a charge, the bureau transmits the data to BACS. The bureau may also provide payslips or a full payroll service.

(b) **Direct access:** the organisation has a direct telecommunications link to BACS, called **BACSTEL**. You need a PC, appropriate modem and the required software. Your transmission is secured using **passwords** and a confirmation receipt comes back from BACS so that you know your transmission was successful. This may be faster and cheaper than indirect access but you incur the initial costs of the software, etc.

5.3 Whichever method you adopt, use the following procedure.

Day 1 Send off a list of payees with the amount of net pay, sort code of their bank or building society and their account numbers

Day 2 Your payment instructions are processed overnight for distribution by the banks and building societies on Day 2.

Day 3 Payment day. Your bank account is debited with a single entry covering the value of all the payments made, and simultaneously the accounts of all individual payees are credited. Your bank reconciliation is therefore simplified as well (compared with paying wages by cheque).

5.4

Benefits to employers	Benefits to employees
Greater security	Having their money in their accounts on pay day as **cleared funds** (guaranteed to be available for withdrawal straight away, unlike cheques)
Reduced costs of cheque stationery or cash handling	**Increased security**
Less administration	**No time wasted** checking pay packet or paying a cheque in

Benefits to employers	Benefits to employees
Increased control of cash flows, as the date of the debit is known exactly and it is on pay day, not before (as with cash payments)	**No difficulty in collecting pay** whilst on holiday or off sick

5.5 The **disadvantage to employees** could be that they have to open a bank or building society account to get paid. However, 80% of the UK population now have a current account at a bank or building society, and over 70% of all salary and wage payments are now made directly to personal accounts. Large organisations pay practically all their employees this way.

5.6 Some **smaller employers** may not consider it worthwhile to use Direct Credit if they only have a small workforce. Others, especially if they have computerised all other aspects of their accounting systems, may see this as a logical next step.

5.7 **Suppliers** can also be paid by Direct Credit, so the initial expense of establishing a BACSTEL link can be spread between Purchase Ledger and Payroll administration.

5.8 The monthly payment of **PAYE** and **NICs** can be made by Direct Credit as well.

Activity 9.4   **Level: Pre-assessment**

You have just started work with a brand new software company which has taken on 20 staff in all. They are all going to be paid monthly. The company's accounting systems will all be computerised (including payroll). What method of payment would you recommend the company adopts for payroll? List the advantages and disadvantages of:

(a) Cash
(b) Cheque
(c) Direct Credit

5.9 EXAMPLE: DIRECT CREDIT

Arnold Bax is an employee. His net pay was £1,380 in June. Arnold Bax banks at Natlays Bank. The sort code of his branch is 17-31-98, and his bank account number is 12345678.

Of the information above, what would you transmit to BACS?

5.10 SOLUTION

Arnold Bax. £1,380. 17 - 31 - 98. 12345678

6 BANK GIRO CREDIT

6.1 **Bank giro credit (BGC)** is being replaced as a form of payment by **BACS**, as it has none of BACS' advantages while still requiring a direct credit to the employee's bank account. From the employee's point of view, it has none of the flexibility of either cash or cheques.

6.2 **Summary of procedure**

- **One cheque is signed** for the total value of the payments to be made.

- A **credit slip** is prepared for each employee, with the employee's name, bank sort code, account number and net pay.

- This paperwork is then processed by the bank.

6.3 In this system the amount of **paperwork** that has to be done is the same as it is for writing cheques. The only difference is that none of the credit transfer slips has to be signed by the authorised signatories.

7 UPDATING THE RECORDS

7.1 Keeping the payroll records is outside the scope of your studies. However you do need to know how to post the payroll payments into the general ledger.

Payroll ledger accounts

7.2 Entering payroll data into the correct **ledger account** is normally quite straightforward.

- Payroll is normally only done **weekly** or **monthly**

- **Same types of entry** take place every period

- The **wages control account** makes it easy to ensure that the entries are being made correctly.

KEY TERM

The **wages control account** is used to complete the double entry which needs to be made for payroll. After all the entries have been made for each pay day in respect of payroll costs, the balance on the account should be NIL.

7.3 EXAMPLE: PAYROLL LEDGER ACCOUNTS

Comecon Ltd pays its workers every month. In Month 1, the payroll details are as follows.

	£
Gross wages	31,200
Employer's NICs	2,000
Net wages paid to workers via Direct Credit (BACS)	25,000
Deductions for PAYE made from workers' wages	4,000
Deductions for employees' National Insurance	1,000
Employees' contributions to the pension fund	1,200
Employer's contributions to the pension fund	1,500

Assume there was £50,000 in the bank at the beginning of Month 1 (an asset of £50,000). Details of these items are beyond the scope of your studies, but you need to know how to post the payments to the general ledger.

7.4 SOLUTION

Let's post the entries to the accounts below, doing one entry at a time. The T accounts are shown later. For convenience here we shall show the entries in **journal** form.

	Step 1	Entry for **gross pay**.

	Debit £	Credit £
Staff costs (gross wages)	31,200	
Wages control		31,200

	Step 2	Wages costs do not only include gross wages, so some more entries are necessary, an entry for other **employer's costs**.

	Debit £	Credit £
Staff costs (employer's NICs)	2,000	
Staff costs (employer's pension contributions)	1,500	
Wages control		3,500

	Step 3	**Net wages** paid to employees out of cash must be entered.

	Debit £	Credit £
Wages control	25,000	
Cash (net paid)		25,000

	Step 4	The **Inland Revenue** must be paid soon after the month end. However, they do not have to be paid at the same time as the workers, so let us enter that into a liability account. This is because we will pay the Inland Revenue at a future date.

	Debit £	Credit £
Wages control	4,000	
PAYE account: Inland Revenue for PAYE		4,000

	Step 5	We also have to set up a creditor for NICs, as we have collected money as **employees' NICs** which must be paid to the Inland Revenue.

	Debit £	Credit £
Wages control	1,000	
PAYE account: Inland Revenue for NICs		1,000

	Step 6	Do the same again for **employer's NIC**

	Debit £	Credit £
Wages control	2,000	
PAYE account: Inland Revenue for NICs		2,000

	Step 7	Then there are **deductions from employees' wages for pension fund contributions**. The amount owed to the pension fund is a liability, as it is owed money. Pension funds are separate legal entities from the companies for whom they operate.

	Debit £	Credit £
Wages control	1,200	
Pension fund		1,200

> **Step 8** Finally there are the **employer's contributions to the pension fund.**

	Debit £	Credit £
Wages control	1,500	
Pension fund		1,500

7.5 By making these entries:

(a) All the amounts owing to **external agencies** have been collected in their own **liability accounts** for them to be dealt with later.

(b) The employees' **gross pay** (ie net pay plus deductions from pay for income tax, NICs and pensions), together with the other payroll related costs of **employer's NICs and pension contributions,** have been collected in a **staff costs expense account.**

7.6 We had better look at the T accounts now to see which accounts have a balance. Don't forget that we had £50,000 cash to start with.

STAFF COSTS ACCOUNT

	£		£
Gross wages	31,200		
Employer's NICs	2,000		
Employer's pension contributions	1,500	Balance c/d	34,700
	34,700		34,700
Balance b/d	34,700		

WAGES CONTROL ACCOUNT

	£		£
Cash - net pay	25,000	Gross wages	31,200
PAYE liability	4,000	Employer's NICs and pension	
NICs liability – employees'	1,000	contributions	3,500
NICs liability – employer's	2,000		
Pension fund liability - employees'	1,200		
Pension fund liability - employer's	1,500		
	34,700		34,700

(Note that both sides have the same total, and so there is no balance to carry forward.)

CASH ACCOUNT

	£		£
Balance b/d	50,000	Wages control - net pay	25,000
		Balance c/d	25,000
	50,000		50,000
Balance b/d	25,000		

PAYE LIABILITY

	£		£
Balance c/d	4,000	Wages control - PAYE	4,000
		Balance b/d	4,000

NICs LIABILITY

	£		£
		Wages control - employees' NICs	1,000
Balance c/d	3,000	Wages control - employer's NICs	2,000
	3,000		3,000
		Balance b/d	3,000

PENSION FUND LIABILITY

	£		£
		Wages control - employees' contributions	1,200
Balance c/d	2,700	Wages control - employer's contributions	1,500
	2,700		2,700
		Balance b/d	2,700

7.7 Study the T accounts carefully and make sure that you can find both entries for each transaction: number them according to the steps in paragraph 7.4.

7.8 In fact, it would have been possible to bypass the wages control account altogether, and simply produce the following **posting summary.**

POSTING SUMMARY: PAYROLL	Month: 1	
Account	*Dr* £	*Cr* £
Staff costs		
- gross wages	31,200	
- employer's NICs	2,000	
- employer's pension contributions	1,500	
Cash - net pay		25,000
Inland Revenue		
- PAYE		4,000
- employees' NICs		1,000
- employer's NICs		2,000
Pension fund		
- employees' contributions		1,200
- employer's contributions		1,500
	34,700	34,700

7.9 This summary helps to show how the total expenses that Comecon incurred in employing staff are settled - most to the employees, but also to the Inland Revenue and the company pension fund.

7.10 The end result is that we have balances of £34,700 on the staff costs account (representing the total staff costs for the month), £25,000 in cash, liabilities of £4,000 and £3,000 to the Inland Revenue for PAYE and NIC respectively, and another liability of £2,700 to the pension fund.

7.11 The liabilities will be settled by payment over the next week or two, clearing the various accounts as if they were any other creditors.

	Debit	Credit
	£	£
PAYE liability	4,000	
NICs liability	3,000	
Pension fund liability	2,700	
Cash account		9,700

The balance on the **staff costs account** stays there - this is the record in the ledger accounts of the payroll expenses for the month. Next month, Month 2's staff costs will be added to it.

Proforma wages control account

7.12 The wages control account contains entries as in the proforma shown below (it is the mirror image of the posting summary at paragraph 7.8).

WAGES CONTROL ACCOUNT

	£		£
Cash - net wages	X	Staff costs	
PAYE liability	X	- gross wages	X
NIC liability - employees'	X	- employer's NICs	X
NIC liability - employer's	X	- employer's pension contributions	X
Pension fund liability - employees'	X	- other staff costs	X
Pension fund liability - employer's	X		
Other deductions liability accounts	X		
	X		X

7.13 The example above is not the only way you could have processed those payroll transactions, though it does have the advantage of being neat and thorough. What never changes, however, is the principle of the **double entry**. There may be a number of different ways to come to a particular result, but that result is always the same. In this case, the result is that the payroll expenses are correctly recorded as expenses in the company's accounting records, and the resulting liabilities are correctly identified as liabilities.

Activity 9.5   Level: Assessment

Popeye plc has the following payroll details in Month 1. Write out the journal entries to post all these transactions and show the wages control account at the end of all the transactions.

		£
Gross wages and salaries:	Administrative staff	102,531
	Sales and marketing staff	226,704
	Production staff	1,067,895
Employer's NICs		104,782
Employees' NICs		83,829
PAYE deductions		351,826
Pension deductions:	Employer's	41,728
	Employees'	37,860
Net wages and salaries		903,893
GAYE donations		10,180
Season ticket loan repayments		9,542

8   PAYMENTS TO THE INLAND REVENUE

Paying the Collector

8.1   Most employers must pay to the Collector **within 14 days of the end of the tax month** the amounts collected as PAYE and NICs for that month.

Tax Month 2, for example, ends on **5 June**. Payment must be made by **19 June**.

8.2   The only exception is for **small employers,** who are allowed to pay **every quarter**.

Quarter ending	*Payment due by*
July 5	July 19
October 5	October 19
January 5	January 19
April 5	April 19

KEY TERM

You are a **small employer** to the Inland Revenue if you estimate that your **average** monthly payment of PAYE tax and NICs for the year is likely to be **under £1,500.** This means of course that for some months you might have paid £1,500 or more, but provided the *average* is less than £1,000 this does not matter.

Activity 9.6   **Level: Assessment**

Bob King has a toyshop. He employs a small staff of full and part-time assistants and therefore has to deduct PAYE and NICs from their wages. He estimates that the total of these deductions each month will be as follows:

	£		£
January	1,500	July	750
February	900	August	700
March	900	September	900
April	900	October	1,200
May	900	November	1,500
June	900	December	2,000

Can Bob pay his PAYE and NICs every quarter instead of every month?

Form P30B

8.3   A **P30B payslip** is a sort of bank giro credit which details how much is paid to the Collector of Taxes at the Accounts Office split between:

- Income tax
- National Insurance

Step 1 Enter in the **Income Tax box** what is due from employees as PAYE, net of any refunds in the month.

Step 2 To find net **National Insurance** first add together the total:

- employees' NICs
- employer's NICs

Then subtract the total of any **SSP** or **SMP** that you are entitled to recover. **You do not need to know the details of this for the purposes of Unit 2.**

8.4 There may be occasions where the total due is a **negative figure**.

Step 1 Write NIL on the P30B and send it in as normal.

Step 2 Deduct the amount from next month's payment.

Activity 9.7   Level: Assessment

The following has been extracted from the Month 1 payroll of Cowry Shells Ltd.

	£
Income tax deducted (gross)	40,000
Income tax refunded	500
Employees' NICs	7,000
Employer's NICs	14,000

What should be paid to the Inland Revenue Accounts Office?

Key learning points

- For the employee the **payslip** is second in importance only to the actual money received. Certain things must be shown on a payslip.

- **Cash payment** is sometimes used for **weekly paid employees,** although payment by **cheque** and **Direct Credit** are most common especially for **monthly paid** employees.

- **Cash payment involves**:
    - ° **security problems**
    - ° **extra time and effort** compared to other payment methods

- **Payment by cheque** requires that a cheque be written or printed for the exact amount of an employee's net pay. This can be time consuming and employees have to wait for the cheques to clear.

- **Payment through BACS (Direct Credit)** requires a list of employee names, bank sort codes, bank account numbers and net pay to be transmitted to BACS (using BACSTEL) either directly or via a bureau or bank.

- Payroll costs must also be recognised in the **ledger accounts** of an enterprise.

    - ° Total wages cost is an **expense** of the business.

    - ° A business deducts tax and NICs from employees' wages on behalf of the government. Until it pays, these amounts are **liabilities** as they are owed by the business.

    - ° The business must also make NI contributions on its own behalf, which also must be paid to the government. This gives rise to an expense **and** a liability.

- One way of ensuring that every payroll expense is properly analysed is to use a **wages control account**, in which every payroll transaction is collected in total.

Quick quiz

1   An employer is legally obliged to provide payslips to all employees. True or false?

2   All deductions from pay must be itemised on the payslip. True or false?

3   List as many disadvantages as you can of paying employees in cash.

4   Prepare a note and coin analysis for an employee who will receive net pay of £187.46 this week and who does not want to receive large denomination notes (over £20).

5   Your office cleaner has been paid £50 per week out of petty cash every week for over a year now. These payments are never put on the payroll. What enquiries should you make about this?

6   List three types of cashless pay.

7   What is the double entry to account for the employer's pension contributions in April, due to be paid into the pension scheme account in May? (Ignore the wages control account here.)

8   When all the entries relating to the payroll have been made, what should be the balance on the wages control account?

Answers to quick quiz

1   True

2   False. If deductions are the same every month (such as Trade Union subscriptions, GAYE donations or SAYE payments) then the employee can be given an annual statement itemising all such fixed deductions and they need not also be itemised on the payslip.

3   Security risks for employer and employees; time consuming to prepare wage packets; expensive in staff time, bank charges and security measures; time consuming distributing them and ensuring employees check them; employees off sick, on holiday or away from site face delays in receiving wages.

4

Denomination	£20	£10	£5	£2	£1	50p	20p	10p	5p	2p	1p
Quantity	9	-	1	1	-	-	2	-	1	-	1
Total value	£180	-	£5	£2	-	-	40p	-	5p	-	1p

5   You or your supervisor should find out from whoever authorises these payments whether the cleaner is self-employed or operating/employed by a limited company. In either case, the cleaner should be submitting invoices showing the full business name. If the cleaner is, in the Inland Revenue's eyes, an employee of your company then he/she should be on the payroll and should have the appropriate deductions made from his/her wages. If the Inland Revenue find out about the cleaner and consider that he/she is an employee, then all the PAYE and NIC that should have been deducted since employment began can be reclaimed. This might also spur the Inland Revenue on to investigate whether there are any other payments missing from the payroll.

6   Payment by cheque; direct credit; bank giro credit.

7   *Debit*   Staff costs (or pension costs, or any other suitably named expense account).

         Credit   Pension scheme account (a creditor – the money is due to the administrator).

8   NIL. The account should balance exactly. If it doesn't, a mistake has been made somewhere.

Answers to activities

Answers to Chapter 1 activities

Activity 1.1

(a)   Liability
(b)   Asset
(c)   Capital (capital introduced)
(d)   Asset
(e)   Asset
(f)   Asset (debtors)
(g)   Liability (creditors)
(h)   Asset

Activity 1.2

$P = I + D - C$

I	= Increase in net assets for the period
	= £36,000 – £0
	= £36,000
D	= Drawings in period
	= £12,000
C	= Capital introduced in period
	= £5,000

Therefore profit   = £36,000 + £12,000 – £5,000
                    = £43,000

Proof:

Net assets = Capital introduced + retained profits – drawings

£36,000   = £5,000 + £43,000 – £12,000

£36,000   = £36,000

Activity 1.3

	£
Total purchases	25,000
Cash paid	10,000
Credit purchases	15,000

Therefore Peter has *creditors* of £15,000.

Activity 1.4

Purchases are an expense of the business, and so the total purchases will have increased the expenses, ie a debit.

The cash paid will have decreased an asset (cash), ie a credit.

The credit purchases will increase a liability (creditors), ie a credit.

In summary:

DEBIT:	Purchases	25,000	
CREDIT:	Cash		10,000
CREDIT:	Creditors		15,000
		25,000	25,000

BPP
PUBLISHING

Activity 1.5 _____

(a)   Revenue expense
(b)   Capital – current liability
(c)   Capital – fixed asset
(d)   Revenue expense
(e)   Revenue income
(f)   Capital – fixed asset
(g)   Revenue expense

Answers to Chapter 2 activities

Activity 2.1

Tutorial note. It is acceptable to show only the unit price and quantity on the purchase order, rather than the total price for each item and for the whole order.

From:	Ordram Quick Ltd Unit 7 Aurora Business Park Lampley LM9 9AS	Purchase order No. 1233
		VAT No 727 0015 54
To:	Lampley Laminates 47 Gorse Road Lampley LM2 9PR	Date: 6 April 20X7

Please supply the following

Your ref.	Description	Quantity	Your list price £ p	Total (exc. VAT) £ p
7050	Trilam 22	180	5 18	932 40
9248	Enlam 20 - polar white	250	5 28	1320 00
9252	Enlam 25 - polar white	200	5 70	1140 00
0048	Onyxel Grade B	300	2 85	855 00

Total	4247 40
Discounts 10%	424 74
Net	3822 66

Notes *Delivery to above address, by 1 May 20X7 at the latest. All quantities in m².*

Activity 2.2

	£
List price	22,000
Less 10% trade discount	2,200
	19,800
Less 2½% cash discount £19,800 × 2½%	495
	19,305

(a) If Ordram Quick pays after 20 days it will receive only the trade discount. The business will therefore pay £19,800.

(b) If payment is made within 20 days, the business will be able to take advantage of the cash discount and pay only £19,305.

Note. The cash discount is calculated as a percentage of the list price **net of trade discount**.

Activity 2.3

(a) VAT for product A = 17.5/117.5 × £705.60 = £105.08936 = £105.08. (So net price is £705.60 – £105.08 = £600.52)

(b) VAT for product B = 0.175 × £480.95 = £84.16625 = £84.16 (So gross price is £480.95 + £84.16 = £565.11)

Activity 2.4

The VAT is calculated as if **all discounts** are taken, so the VAT is the same for both (a) and (b), ie 17½% × £19,305 = £3,378.37.

Activity 2.5

Have all goods ordered been received? Have only those quantities of goods ordered been received? Have only those goods which have been received been invoiced?

Discrepancies and unusual features on the goods received documentation are as follows.

(a) *Onyxel Grade B.* 300m² was ordered on PO no 1233. 200m² was delivered on 14 April, of which 100m² was damaged. A further 200m² was delivered according to GRN H010, completing the delivery of the 300m² ordered. However, 400m² has been charged to us in total.

Action. Stop processing of invoice until credit received as follows.

	£
100m² Onyxel Grade B @ £2.85 per m²	285.00
Less 10% discount	(28.50)
	256.50
Plus VAT at 17.5%	44.88
	301.38

(b) *Enlam 25 - polar white.* 300m² was delivered on 19 April, and invoiced on 30 April, while only 200m² was ordered.

Action. Consult production manager to see if we can use the excess. If so, seek authorisation also from the purchasing manager. If not, organise return of goods and ask for credit.

(c) *Ply-mel 20 and Ply-mel 30.* 150m² of Ply-mel 20 and 150m² of Ply-mel 30 were ordered on PO no 1274. The goods received note specifies 150m² of Ply-mel 30 delivered, but gives the code for Ply-mel 20 (1041). The supplier's invoice no 7264 charges us for 150m² of Ply-mel 20 and 150m² of Ply-mel 30. In addition, the 100m² of Ply-mel 30 ordered on PO 1241 has not been received at all.

Action. Make contact with the goods received section to determine which type was received (for example, by checking against supplier's delivery note or arranging a physical inspection of the goods).

Telephone supplier to inform them of non-deliveries. Stop processing of the invoice until goods are received or credit is given.

(d) *Enlam 20 - polar white*. Two consignments of 250m^2 each of this were ordered (PO nos 1233 and 1274) but only one was received. We have however been invoiced for two consignments.

Action. Telephone supplier to inform them of non-delivery of 250m^2 Enlam 20 - polar white (PO no 1274). Stop processing of the invoice until goods are received or credit is given.

Does the goods received documentation appear otherwise to be in order?

GRN number H010 gives only the month, and not the day of the receipt of the goods. It may be possible to find the date from the supplier's delivery note or from the dates on adjacent GRNs.

The GRNs should be signed by the warehouse staff receiving the goods. Providing a box for a signature on the standard GRNs form would help to ensure that they are signed.

Check the invoices

(a)   Correct coding
(b)   Correct pricing
(c)   Cross-casts and additions
(d)   Correct discount
(e)   VAT

Discrepancies and unusual features on the invoices are as follows.

(a)   On both invoices, Enlam 20 - polar white has been priced at £5.70 instead of £5.28 as shown on the price list.

(b)   A trade discount of only 1% has been given on each invoice, instead of the 10% expected.

Action. The supplier should be informed of these errors, and a credit note requested. The expected amount of credit is as follows. (This is *in addition* to credits due in respect of excess deliveries etc identified above.)

Invoice no 7221		£	£
Net total per invoice			4,051.40
250m^2 Enlam 20 - polar white:	should be £5.28 per m^2	1,320.00	
	charged at £5.70 per m^2	(1,425.00)	
			(105.00)
			3,946.40
Discount @ 10%			(394.64)
			3,551.76
VAT @ 17.5%			621.55
Amount due			4,173.31
Amount due per invoice			4,712.79
Adjustment required: credit note due to Ordram Quick Ltd			539.48

Invoice no 7264	£
Net total per invoice	4,978.50
Overcharge on Enlam 20 - polar white (as above)	(105.00)
	4,873.50
Discount @ 10%	(487.35)
	4,386.15
VAT @ 17.5%	767.57
Amount due	5,153.72
Amount due per invoice	5,791.24
Adjustment required: credit note due to Ordram Quick Ltd	637.52

Activity 2.6

To: A colleague
From: A Technician   Date: 7 April 20X7

SUBJECT: PURCHASE ORDER FORMS

You have suggested dispensing with Copies 3 and 4 of the purchase order form. This may reduce the burden of administration for purchase order/invoice processing, but it would be at the expense of a potentially serious deterioration in internal control.

Copy 3 of the purchase order, which is sent to the goods inwards department, allows goods inwards staff to check that goods received have been ordered on an authorised purchase order. (They may also help goods inwards staff to identify the internal destination of goods if this is not clear from suppliers' delivery notes.)

The purchase ledger section uses Copy 4 in the accounts department to compare and match goods shown on suppliers' invoices with approved order details. This helps to ensure that only goods which were ordered by someone with the correct authority are paid for. Without this check, goods which have never been ordered at all might be invoiced, or goods might be ordered fraudulently by someone for their own personal use.

Due to these considerations, I feel strongly that the use of four-part purchase order forms should continue.

(You could make an alternative suggestion. A 3-part purchase order could be used with copies being sent to the supplier, the purchasing department and the warehouse. Then on receipt of the goods, the warehouse copy, together with a GRN, could be forwarded to the accounts department to be matched against the invoice.)

Activity 2.7

(a) The supplier is acknowledging a reduction in your liability to him. If there are unpaid invoices on your account with him, the account balance will be reduced by the total of the credit note. If you have already settled your account by making full payment, the amount of the credit note will feature as a *debit* balance on your purchase ledger when you process it. It will subsequently be 'cleared' when you purchase further goods or receive a refund from the supplier.

(b) Any three of the following:

   (i)   Wrong goods delivered, rejected by you.
   (ii)   Goods of lower than expected quality, so returned.
   (iii)   Wrong price charged when goods invoiced.
   (iv)   Invoice does not tie in with GRNs.
   (v)   Failure by supplier to give you an agreed discount.
   (vi)   Goods damaged in transit, so rejected by you.

(c) (i)   The credit note may be cancelling or reducing the amount of the original invoice - so you will need to check that the credit note refers to the right purchase.

   (ii)   If the credit note is received for incorrect goods delivered, the GRN will show that the wrong goods were delivered. Checking the GRN lets you know that you are getting the full reimbursement.

   (iii)   You won't need this, as it has nothing to do with a purchase.

   (iv)   You are receiving a credit note for goods returned - this is evidence of the quantities sent back.

   (v)   You are informing the supplier that you expect a credit note and for how much.

   (vi)   This might be useful to trace the transaction back to its origins.

   (vii)   Again this might be used to check the value of the credit note.

   (viii) No marks for guessing why. There is never any harm in checking the arithmetic.

Answers to Chapter 3 activities

Activity 3.1

Answer: (b). The purchase day book records purchases made on credit.

Activity 3.2

Situations (c) and (h) would be reflected in a purchase returns day book. These are situations in which you have returned goods to the supplier. Items (a) and (d) refer to sales you have made, not your purchases. Item (b) is a different sort of dispute. You have received no goods, and you have not entered the invoice in your accounts. Item (g) is similar to item (b), reflecting over-zealous invoicing by a supplier. Item (e) is an error, but refers to a delivery *you* have made. Item (f) is just bad luck! The goods were in perfectly good condition when you received them, and you are ordering more.

Activity 3.3

This is a significant digit code. The digits are part of the description of the item being coded. '1' in 100000 represents fixed assets, the '2' in 100200 represents plant and machinery etc.

Activity 3.4

(a) DEBIT   Purchases (Profit and Loss Account)
     CREDIT   Creditors control account (Balance Sheet)

   (The creditors control account might be referred to as the purchase ledger control account.)

(b) A *debit note* is issued to someone when you wish them to reduce your liability. A debit note has the effect of telling the supplier that you think you owe him less. (You have *debited* his credit balance in your books.) It is an indication that you expect him to make a corresponding credit entry in respect of your account in his *sales* ledger. It is an alternative, therefore, to your supplier sending you a **credit note.**

BPP PUBLISHING

Activity 3.5

(a)

	A	B	C	D	E	F	G	H	I	J	K	L	M
1	Bodgett		Purchase day book analysis						Page 41				
2	Date	Ref	Supplier	Supplier account	Total	VAT	Purchase cost	Tools	Painting & decorating	Bathroom items			
3													
4	23/11/X7	712	Pitiso Tools	1550	1,858.02	276.72	1,581.30	1,581.30					
5		713	Macin	1310	13,336.25	1,986.25	11,350.00		11,350.00				
6		714	Throne Bathware	2010	2,542.46	378.66	2,163.80			2,163.80			
7		715	Payper, Overr, Crackes	1510	1,134.63	168.98	965.65		948.75	16.90			
8													
9													
10	Total for	23/11/X7			18,871.36	2,810.61	16,060.75	1,581.30	12,298.75	2,180.70			
11													
12													
13													
14													

(b)

ACCOUNT POSTINGS			DR	CR
Account code	Ref		£ p	£ p
4000	PDB41	Tools purchases	1,581.30	
5000	PDB41	Painting & decorating purchases	12,298.75	
6000	PDB41	Bathroom	2,180.70	
0694	PDB41	VAT	2,810.61	
0730	PDB41	Creditors (PLCA)		18,871.36
		TOTAL	18,871.36	18,871.36

DATE   23/11/X7

Posted by ....

Helping hand. If you decided that the curtain rails purchased from Paper, Overr, Crackes were for shower curtains and therefore came under the Bathroom category, the relevant totals would be:

Painting and decorating	£11,678.75
Bathroom	£2,800.70

Activity 3.6

(a)

Page 5

Bodgett Purchase returns day book

Date	Debit note ref	Supplier	Supplier account	Total	VAT	Purchase return total	Tools	Painting& decorating	Bathroom items	Purchase ref
23/11/97	64	DotheLot	8523	176.25	26.25	150.00			150.00	613
	65	C and R	7211	259.67	38.67	221.00		221.00		612
	66	House Foundation	6644	1,127.51	167.92	959.59			959.59	627
Total for 23/11/97				1,563.43	232.84	1,330.59		221.00	1,109.59	

(b)

ACCOUNT POSTINGS			DR	CR
Account code	Ref		£ p	£ p
0730	PRDB5	Creditors (PLCA)	1,563.43	
6050	PRDB5	Purchase returns (bathware)		1,109.59
5050	PRDB5	Purchase returns (painting & decorating)		221.00
0694	PRDB5	VAT		232.84
		TOTAL	1,563.43	1,563.43

DATE   23/11/X7

Posted by ....

Activity 3.7

The main advantage of computerised accounting systems is that a large amount of data can be processed very quickly. A further advantage is that computerised systems are more accurate than manual systems.

Ivan's comment that 'you never know what is going on in that funny box' might be better expressed as 'lack of audit trail'. If a mistake occurs somewhere in the system it is not always possible to identify where and how it happened.

Answers to Chapter 4 activities

Activity 4.1

(a) A creditor is a *liability* of a business. A creditor is owed money by a business.

(b) *Trade creditors* are those with whom you deal to carry on your own trade. They supply you with materials, goods and services to enable you to carry out your own business and they offer you a credit period. Items (i), (iv) and (vii) are trade creditors by this definition.

The other creditors mentioned, although creditors, are not *trade* creditors. Taxation paid to the Inland Revenue and Customs & Excise is a legal obligation, based on the profits of a business, not payment for a service.

A bank overdraft is not a trade creditor. A bank supplies funds which are used to run a business on a day to day basis. A bank can also provide a long-term loan, say to finance the purchase of a fixed asset.

Drawings are appropriations of profit and reduce the proprietor's capital account. Although the amount outstanding on the proprietor's capital account is a liability, it is really long-term funding not a trade creditor.

Activity 4.2

(a) The *Account name and address update* is used to set up some of the basic details of a supplier account on the computer system.

Updating can include both adding and deleting accounts. To tidy up the ledger, you can rid yourself of old 'dead' accounts.

(b) Many transactions are posted to the purchase ledger accounts, for example:

(i) invoices received from suppliers

(ii) credit notes from suppliers

(iii) payments to suppliers

(iv) refunds of cash from suppliers (ie *Debit* Cash, *Credit* Creditors)

(v) discounts received

(vi) correction of mispostings

(vii) allocation (in open item systems where monies paid are set against individual invoices, rather than simply used to reduce the balance)

Activity 4.3

You may feel that delaying payment of creditors for as long as possible is the most astute commercial option. Disadvantages of this policy include:

(a) losing discounts
(b) loss of supplier goodwill
(c) losing the facility to buy on credit

A creditors age analysis may indicate that you cannot pay your debts, or that you are delaying payment longer than is necessary.

Activity 4.4

The list will probably include:

(a) purchase and purchase returns day books
(b) supplier account statement of transactions and current balance
(c) remittance advices
(d) VAT analysis
(e) purchases analysis
(f) list of supplier accounts
(g) mailing list of suppliers' names and addresses

Activity 4.5

(a) By the open item method, cash paid is matched exactly to invoices.

So, the invoices for which no cash has been paid are:

		£
2/9/X7	P901	453.10
7/9/X7	P904	25.50
30/9/X7	P909	92.70
		571.30

(b) By the balance forward method, cash paid is matched to the oldest invoices, so the outstanding balance is made up as follows.

		£
25/9/X7	P908	478.60
30/9/X7	P909	92.70
		571.30

Activity 4.6

Journal 28 August 20X7

		Debit £	Credit £
(a)	*Memorandum account adjustment (JNL 1)*		
	Purchase ledger - MPV Ltd	97.40	
	Purchase ledger - Kernels Ltd		97.40
	Being correction of misposting of invoice (Kernels' ref 21201)		
(b)	*Memorandum account adjustment (JNL 2)*		
	Purchase ledger - ASR Ltd	400.00	
	Purchase ledger - Kernels Ltd		400.00
	Being correction of misposting of 21/8 cash payment to ASR Ltd		
(c)	*Nominal account journal (JNL 3)*		
	Purchase ledger control account (£42.84 × 2)	85.68	
	Purchases		85.68
	Being correction of misposting of Kernels Ltd credit note C91004		
(d)	*Nominal account adjustment (JNL 4)*		
	Purchase ledger control account	64.17	
	Purchases		64.17
	Being correction of double posting of invoice 20642		
	Memorandum account adjustment (JNL 5)		
	Purchase ledger - Kernels Ltd	85.68	
		64.17	
	Being adjustment to reflect JNL 3 and JNL 4		

(*Note.* As the memorandum account does not form part of the double entry, it does not necessarily have to balance.)

		Debit £	Credit £
(e)	*Nominal account adjustment (JNL 6)*		
	Purchase ledger control account	37.50	
	Sales ledger control account		37.50

Being double entry to reflect contra between Kernels Ltd's sales ledger and purchase ledger accounts.

		Debit £	Credit £
	Memorandum account adjustment (JNL 7)		
	Purchase ledger – Kernels Ltd	37.50	
	Sales ledger – Kernels Ltd		37.50

Being adjustment to reflect JNL 6

KERNELS LIMITED

20X7			£	20X7			£
28/08	Misposted credit note	JNL5	85.68	27/08	Balance b/d		644.26
28/08	Misposted invoice	JNL5	64.17	28/08	Misposted invoice	JNL1	97.40
28/08	Contra	JNL7	37.50	28/08	Misposted cash	JNL2	400.00
28/08	Balance c/d		954.31				
			1,141.66				1,141.66
				28/08	Balance b/d		954.31

Answers to Chapter 5 activities

Activity 5.1

(a)   There are a number of reasons why suppliers' statements are useful.

A supplier's statement can be used to check the following.

(i)   That you have *received* everything the supplier says you have
(ii)   That you have *recorded* everything the supplier says you have received
(iii) That the supplier has *received* payments you have sent
(iv)   That the supplier has *recorded* payments that you have sent
(v)   That both you and the supplier agree on the amount that you owe

In summary, obtaining and checking a supplier statement is a way of checking that both your records are correct. This is why both internal and external auditors, when checking creditor balances, use supplier statements to verify the liability.

(b)   Checking a *sample* of 10% might indicate that the system for processing transactions is working and, by implication, that the balances on the other accounts are correct.

Activity 5.2

There are three issues to be considered here.

(a)   You are new to the company and, although your boss likes to delegate, you have no prior information about your employer's relationship with Jack Use Ltd.

(b)   Being threatened with legal action is quite serious. Your boss should be told about it, even if he does not take the threat seriously.

(c)   Jack Use Ltd may themselves be making a terrible mistake - this claim may not be valid.

So, Option 6 is your best choice. It would not hurt to look up the file first to see if there is any relevant information. However it is unlikely that you could tackle this query on your own, which is why option 7 is not the best choice.

Activity 5.3

PAYWELL SERVICES LIMITED
24 Maidstone Road, Taunton TA4 4RP

Ms D Waite
Accounts Department
Recycle Limited
Jarvis Lane
Maidenhead
SL6 4RS

Your ref: DW/SB 42

24 February 20X7

Dear Ms Waite,

Account number - P942

I am concerned at having received your letter of 20 February 20X7 stating that £2,642.50 remains outstanding on the above account for December 20X6.

Our records show that payment of this amount was made by BACS under the usual reference on 31 January. We have not received any acknowledgement of the payment from you.

It would seem that some error has been made, and I would be grateful if you would check whether you have a record of the payment. I note that on previous occasions there have been some problems in matching BACS payments to our account.

I am also concerned that we may not have been credited with the usual 2½% discount for prompt payment. Can you reassure me on this point?

Yours faithfully

A Technician

Senior Accounts Assistant

Activity 5.4

A good deal of thought needs to go into the opening of new files.

(a)   Is there already a file for this purpose?

(b)   What other files are related to this purpose? In other words, what cross-referencing needs to be done?

(c)   Are the documents to be filed of an unusual size or material, requiring special storage facilities?

(d)   Are the documents confidential?

(e)   Will the documents be needed by you frequently, so that a personal or departmental file would be more appropriate than a central one?

(f)   What title should be given to the file to make it clear to all potential users what it contains?

(g)   How should documents be arranged within the file?

You may have thought of other points in addition to the above. Point (a) is the most important.

Activity 5.5

The updated file should show the following information.

Company:	Folworth (Business Services) Ltd
Address:	Crichton Buildings 97 Lower Larkin Street London EC4A 8QT
Directors:	Robin Folworth BA ACA J..................... Crichton Margaret Foster Laurence Oldfield MA T........................ Scott John Thornhill BSc
Purchasing manager:	D Simmonds

Note that space has been left to fill in the new directors' first names.

Activity 5.6

Business customers' files	Domestic customers' files	Auditors' file	Miscellaneous file
13, 1	5, 18	3	2, 9
7	11, 12		14
10			
15, 17			

(a)   Given its date, document 3 is likely to be relevant to the current year, 2006.

(b)   Document 4 may as well be thrown away.

(c)   Document 6 should be placed on the auditors' file for 2002.

(d)   Documents 8 and 20 can be thrown away, or kept with personnel records, perhaps in a file for 'staff entertainment'.

(e)   Document 16 could most appropriately be given to whoever is responsible for cleaning or pinned up on a noticeboard.

(f)   Document 19 could be thrown away, or else put in the auditors' file for 1999.

It would be sensible to close the old 'miscellaneous' file and either start a new one or else have a file for 'unusual orders'.

Maintaining a single file for domestic orders seems sensible as these are likely to be 'one-off' purchases. However, it would be helpful if this were arranged alphabetically so that related documents (for example 5 and 18) could be quickly matched.

Answers to Chapter 6 activities

Activity 6.1

(a)

Ref	Amount	Due date (30 days)	25.7	1.8	8.8	15.8
	£		£	£	£	£
133097	984.10	21.7	984.10			
CN 01711	(942.42)	-	(942.42)			
133142	6,975.27	28.7	6,975.27			
133179	2,474.19	2.8		2,474.19		
133200	1,709.94	4.8		1,709.94		
133224	2,788.50	7.8		2,788.50		
133275	670.83	11.8			670.83	
133309	1,888.66	14.8			1,888.66	
133324	524.96	16.8				524.96
133394	2,004.92	16.8				2,004.92
133441	879.22	18.8				879.22
133619	1,424.67	21.8				1,424.67
CN 01794	(404.88)		(404.88)			
	20,977.96		6,612.07	6,972.63	2,559.49	4,833.77

Note. Invoice 133660 for £1,424.67 will be paid on 22 August. Credit notes are taken as early as possible. No settlement discounts are due.

(b)

Ref	£	(%)	£	Best discount available 25.7 £	1.8 £	8.8 £	15.8 £
133097	984.10		-	984.10			
CN 01711	(942.42)		-	(942.42)			
133142	6,975.27		-	6,975.27			
133179	2,474.19		-		2,474.19		
133200	1,709.94		-		1,709.94		
133224	2,788.50		-		2,788.50		
133275	670.83	(1)	6.71	664.12			
133309	1,888.66	(1)	18.89	1,869.77			
133324	524.96	(1)	5.25	519.71			
133394	2,004.92	(1)	20.05	1,984.87			
133441	879.22	(2)	17.58	861.64			
133619	1,424.67	(2)	28.49	1,396.18			
CN 01794	(404.88)		-	(404.88)			
133660	1,424.67	(2)	28.49	1,396.18			
	22,402.63		125.46	15,304.54	6,972.63	-	-

Note. Credit notes are taken as early as possible.

Activity 6.2

(a) The following errors or discrepancies are apparent.

   (i) The payment made on 8 October is not reflected in the statement. This is probably because the payment was in transit when the statement was prepared.

   (ii) Invoice 50311 (2.9.X7) is shown on the statement as £662.54 instead of £642.54.

   (iii) Invoice 50449 (9.9.X7) is shown on the statement as £357.42 instead of £354.72.

   (iv) Credit note 7211 (13.9.X7) for £864.75 is not shown on the statement.

(b) (i) The items over thirty days old and remaining unpaid as at 15 October 20X7 are as follows.

Date	Details	Amount £
7.9.X7	Invoice 50411	6,997.21
9.9.X7	Invoice 50449	354.72
11.9.X7	Invoice 50457	3,428.88
13.9.X7	Credit note 7211	(864.75)
Total payment to be made		9,916.06

(ii)

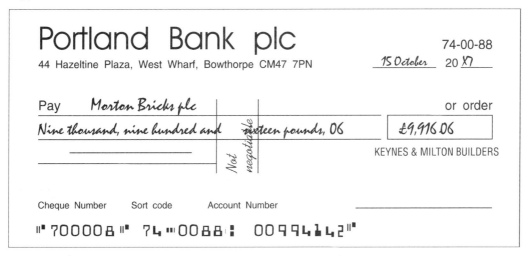

Activity 6.3

(a) **Recommended method: cash**

This is a small business payment which should be paid out of petty cash for the sake of convenience.

(b) **Recommended method: standing order**

A standing order is convenient for regular fixed payments. Once the standing order instruction is made, the bank will ensure that all payments are made on the due dates and will stop making payments at the date specified in the instruction. Some finance companies may insist on a standing order being set up, as it is convenient for them to receive instalments regularly without having to issue payment requests or reminders.

(c) **Recommended method: by cheque at the bank**, accompanied by the bill and completed bank giro credit form. The bank clerk will stamp the bill as evidence that the payment was made.

Paying by cheque is safer than paying by cash and is more usual for such a large payment. Handing the cheque over at the bank will be convenient and evidence of payment will be obtained. If the payment is made at a bank other than that at which Libra holds an account, the bank receiving the payment will probably make a small charge for processing it.

An alternative method is to send a crossed cheque by post, enclosing the payment counterfoil.

(d) **Recommended method: direct debit mandate**

The direct debit mandate will allow the Council to debit the amounts due direct from Libra's bank account on the due dates. The mandate will be effective until it is cancelled. The Council must inform Libra in advance of the amounts it will be debiting.

(e) **Recommended method: credit card or charge card**

Payment by credit card or charge card avoids the need to pay immediately by cash or cheque. If the Sales Director's personal card is used, he will claim payment later from the company, which may pay him by cheque or with his monthly salary payment. If a company credit or charge card is used, the company will be responsible for paying the amounts shown on the monthly statement.

(f) **Recommended method: banker's draft**

A banker's draft cannot be stopped or cancelled once it is issued. Being effectively like a cheque drawn on the bank itself, it is generally accepted as being as good as cash. It is therefore most likely to be accepted by Selham Motors.

Activity 6.4

(a)

Penumbra Limited			REMITTANCE ADVICE	
42 Braintree Road **Bishops Stortford** **Herts CM3 9XY** Telephone 01279 33942 Fax: 01279 33920			Supplier account number	
Feathers Limited *247 Marconi Road* *Chelmsford, Essex CM1 4P2*			FO 11 Date of payment: 2 June 20X7	
Invoice/ Credit Note	*Details*	*Invoices* £	*Credit Notes* £	*Payment Advice* £
30 3 X7	Invoice 07114	87 42		87 42
6 4 X7	Credit note CR084		167 14	(167 14)
7 4 X7	Invoice 07241	292 23		292 23
9 4 X7	Invoice 07249	851 80		851 80
14 4 X7	Invoice 07302	165 87		165 87
22 4 X7	Credit note CR087		118 96	(118 96)
22 4 X7	Invoice 07487	494 68		494 68
28 4 X7	Credit note CR099		87 42	(87 42)
7 5 X7	Invoice 07714	116 25		116 25
	Total payment			1,634 73

Penumbra Limited			REMITTANCE ADVICE	
42 Braintree Road **Bishops Stortford** **Herts CM 3 9XY** Telephone: 01279 33942 Fax: 01279 33920			Supplier account number	
The Furniture People *4 Kane Street* *Northampton NN3 4SR*			FO 17 Date of payment: 2 June 20X7	
Invoice/ Credit Note	*Details*	*Invoices* £	*Credit Notes* £	*Payment Advice* £
2 4 X7	Invoice 734282	4,397 18		4,397 18
23 4 X7	Invoice 735110	7,215 72		7,215 72
27 4 X7	Invoice 735192	990 43		990 43
27 4 X7	Invoice 735204	1,459 00	1,107 33	1,459 00
4 5 X7	Credit note 274221			(1,107 33)
	Total payment			12,955 00

(b) The total payments to be made are as follows.

	£
Feathers Ltd	1,634.73
The Furniture People	12,955.00
Total	14,589.73

Activity 6.5

(a)

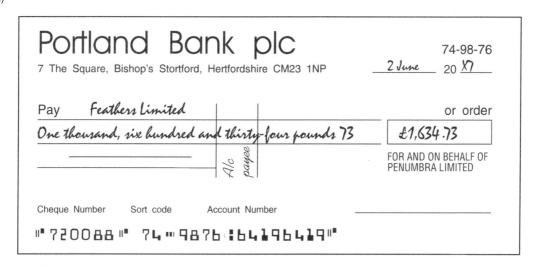

(b) The cheque to Feathers Ltd requires the signatures of two directors; the cheque to The Furniture People requires the signature of the Chairman or the Managing Director and that of one other director. I would take the cheques for signature (together with invoices and any other supporting documentation) to S Lukes (Chairman). Neither of the other two directors (J Knight and J Mackie) are in today, but I would ask J Knight, who is in tomorrow, to sign the cheques as early as possible.

(c) I would stamp the invoices to indicate that payment of the invoice has been approved and made, and on what date. In some firms, a sticker may be used for this purpose. This procedure provides a record of the approval of the payment for later reference and may help to prevent an invoice being paid twice in error.

Answers to Chapter 7 activities _____

Activity 7.1

(a)   As a matter of physical security, using only **one cheque book** at a time minimises the risk that a cheque book will fall into the wrong hands. Cheque books which have not yet been started should be locked securely in a safe, as should the current cheque book when it is not in use.

Using only one cheque book at a time also makes it simpler to keep a check on the sequence of cheques being issued. Cheques will be issued and entered in the cash book consecutively.

(b)   Entering the number of all cheques in the cash book even if **cancelled** makes it easier to check that all payments by cheque have been entered. It also means that the cash book will provide a record of all cheques in case of later queries or when checking the bank statement with the cash book.

(c)   If cancelled cheques are not retained, anyone carrying out checks (for example, an internal or external auditor) cannot be sure what has happened to cheques which are recorded as having been cancelled. There is a risk that someone has taken the cheque with the intention of misusing it even though it has been recorded as cancelled. **Retaining cancelled cheques** provides conclusive evidence that the cheque has not fallen into the wrong hands.

(d)   This is an example of **segregation of duties**. It will be less tempting for an employee to act dishonestly if he knows that related aspects of transactions which he deals with are handled by somebody else.

(e)   Payments by **standing order or direct debit** will probably appear on the bank statement before they are entered into the cash book. It is not acceptable simply to transfer the details of payments made from the bank statement to the cash book, since the wrong payments may have been made by the bank as the result of some error. The bank may have made a payment even though the standing order or direct debit mandate has been cancelled, or the company may have failed to cancel a mandate which should have been cancelled. It is therefore a good idea to check that any standing order or direct debit payments which *have* been made *should* have been made before the details are entered in the cash book.

Activity 7.2 _____

Both (a) and (b) are FALSE.

The cash book records

*   money received by the business
*   money paid by the business

The name 'cash book' is still used even though money may be in the form of cheques or other media.

We record cheque payments in the cash book as soon as possible after we issue the cheques: (a) is therefore false. Payments could be very difficult to keep track of if we waited until the cheque was presented before recording the payment.

A standing order is a payment like any other, and needs to be recorded in the cash book regardless of whether we have yet received the benefit: (b) is therefore also false.

Activity 7.3 _____

(a)   When a cheque is being written by hand, the writer may make an error. A computer-printer cheque might similarly have been printed incorrectly. Rather than making an alteration (which must be signed by the cheque signatories), it is generally better to **cancel** the cheque. The writer may do this by writing a line through the whole cheque and writing the word 'CANCELLED' across it.

There may be a good reason for cancelling a cheque even if it has been completed correctly. For example, it may be decided before the cheque is sent that a different amount should be paid to the supplier.

(b) Payment of a cheque may be **stopped** after it has been sent out by issuing an instruction to the bank. This instruction tells the bank not to pay the cheque, and when a collecting bank attempts to clear the cheque our bank will decline to honour it. A reversing entry will need to be made in the cash book.

It will not often be necessary to stop a cheque. If it is discovered that a cheque has been lost in the post, then stopping payment is a sensible precaution against the possibility that someone will attempt to present the cheque fraudulently. Most banks will accept a stop instruction by telephone, although this should be confirmed in writing to the bank. The bank will generally make a charge for stopping a cheque.

(c) A **paid cheque** is one which has been cleared through the bank account. The paid cheque will either be retained by the drawer's bank or sent to the drawer.

Activity 7.4

The new trainee has made three errors.

(a) It is incorrect to try to balance the two discount columns. The discounts allowed shown on the receipts side of the cash book are an expense of the business, representing the cost of allowing discounts for early settlement. Discounts received, from the payments side of the cash book, represent a benefit to the business, gained from making early payment to suppliers. Therefore, discounts received and discounts allowed need to be treated separately and not 'netted off' against each other.

(b) The cash balance carried down should be £110.31 and not £119.31 (£342.71 – £232.40).

(c) The bank balance carried down should be £1,621.48 DR and not £1,621.48 CR, ie it is on the wrong side of the cash book. The added up totals of each side of the bank column would then be £15,842.65.

Activity 7.5

CASH BOOK

20X7		Bank £	Cash £	Discount £	20X7		Bank £	Cash £	Discount £
4.5	Balance b/d		224		4.5	Balance b/d	336		
4.5	Cash withdrawal		50		4.5	Cash withdrawal	50		
6.5	Cash sales		45		5.5	R Hill (W1)	108		12
8.5	H Larkin	180		20	7.5	Telephone bill	210		
9.5	D Randle	482			8.5	Honour Ltd	135		
9.5	Balance c/d	177			9.5	Balance c/d		319	
		839	319	20			839	319	12
9.5	Balance b/d		319		9.5	Balance b/d	177		

Workings

$$1 \quad £120 \times \frac{100 - 10}{100} \% = £108$$

BPP
PUBLISHING

Activity 7.6

(a)

ARIA ENTERPRISES

PAYMENTS

Date	Narrative	Folio	Discount received	Payment total	VAT	Creditors	Salaries	O'heads	Fixed assets	Sundry expenses
1-Feb	Smallsoft Software	PL0054	110.00	2,090.00		2,090.00				
2-Feb	Mailhouse Ltd	PL0467		569.02		569.02				
2-Feb	Champagne (cash)			65.00	9.68					55.32
4-Feb	Stationery Box	PL0503	250.00	4,750.00		4,750.00				
5-Feb	Pacific Computers Ltd			32,894.00					32,894.00	
8-Feb	PR Reps Ltd	PL0004		5,501.40		5,501.40				
9-Feb	Champagne (cash)			19.95	2.97					16.98
9-Feb	Flowers R Us Ltd	PL0962	1.75	33.25		33.25				
10-Feb	BG (for 3 Spring Street)			178.99				178.99		
13-Feb	Window cleaner (cash)			25.00	3.72					21.28
14-Feb	Jan/Feb salaries			46,987.65			46,987.65			
14-Feb	CopyRight Ltd	PL0775		36.48		36.48				
15-Feb	Data Warehouse Ltd	PL0087		10,237.95		10,237.95				
	London Electricity (HO)			1,016.00				1,016.00		
			361.75	104,404.69	16.38	23,218.10	46,987.65	1,194.99	32,894.00	93.57
			PLC110 DR	CAB010 CR	VAT094 DR	PLC110 DR	WAG510 DR	UTI470 DR	FAC020 DR	SUN490 DR
			DIS350 CR							

(b)

ARIA ENTERPRISES

CASH BOOK PAYMENTS POSTING SUMMARY 15 FEBRUARY

Narrative	Nominal ledger account	DR	CR
		£	£
Cash	**CAB010**		104,404.69
Purchase discounts	**DIS350**		361.75
VAT control	**VAT094**	16.38	
Purchase ledger control	**PLC110**	361.75	
	PLC110	23,218.10	
Salaries	**WAG510**	46,987.65	
Utility costs	**UTI470**	1,194.99	
Fixed asset cost	**FAC020**	32,894.00	
Sundry expenses	**SUN490**	93.57	
		104,766.44	104,766.44

	CASH		CAB 010
	£		£
15 Feb Bal b/d	95,609.78	15 Feb Cash book	104,404.69

	VAT CONTROL		VAT 094
	£		£
15 Feb Cash book	16.38	15 Feb Bal b/d	11,102.00

	SUNDRY EXPENSES		SUN 490
	£		£
15 Feb Bal b/d	567.92		
Cash book	93.57		

	FIXED ASSET COST		FAC 020
	£		£
15 Feb Bal b/d	272,972.00		
Cash book	32,894.00		

	UTILITY COSTS		UTI 470
	£		£
15 Feb Bal b/d	1,509.72		
Cash book	1,194.99		

	SALARIES		WAG 510
	£		£
15 Feb Bal b/d	45,207.69		
Cash book	46,987.65		

	PURCHASE DISCOUNTS		DIS 350
	£		£
		15 Feb Bal b/d	279.48
		Cash book	361.75

	PURCHASE LEDGER CONTROL		PLC 110
	£		£
15 Feb Cash book	23,218.10	15 Feb Bal b/d	112,221.80
Cash book discount	361.75		

Activity 7.7

(a)

Cheque number	Date 20X7	Payee	Amount £	
400602	1 May	Cash	127.00	
400603	3 May	ACM Crushers Ltd	2,012.42	
400604	3 May	Benzade Ltd	101.24	
400605	3 May	Quaygate Ltd	905.50	(£205.00 + £700.50)
400606	10 May	ACM Crushers Ltd	8,739.29	(£7,018.00 + £1,721.29)
400607	10 May	Benzade Ltd	94.27	
400608	17 May	Gadd Ltd	713.50	(£621.00 + £92.50)
400609	24 May	Benzade Ltd	414.36	(£172.19 + £242.17)
400610	31 May	ACM Crushers Ltd	982.00	
400611	31 May	Gadd Ltd	1,927.91	
400612	31 May	Quaygate Ltd	401.15	

(b) Payments

Date 20X7	Details	Cheque nos/ref	Amount £	
1 May	Petty cash	400602	127.00	
3 May	Purchase ledger	400603-605	3,019.16	(W1)
10 May	Purchase ledger	400606-607	8,833.56	(W2)
15 May	Turnmead Ltd	Standing order	192.00	
17 May	Purchase ledger	400608	713.50	
24 May	Purchase ledger	400609	414.36	
29 May	May salaries	BACS	5,842.45	
30 May	Icarus Ltd	Standing order	342.00	
31 May	Purchase ledger	400610-612	3,311.06	(W3)
			22,795.09	

Workings

1   £2,012.42 + £101.24 + £905.50 = £3,019.16

2   £8,739.29 + £94.27 = £8,833.56

3   £982.00 + £1,927.91 + £401.15 = £3,311.06

Answers to Chapter 8 activities

Activity 8.1

Expense item	Amount	Direct recipient	Acceptable?
Portable air conditioning unit	£75.99	Sam Gardner, office manager	No – exceeds £25 limit
Coffee filters for office coffee machine	£2.99	Raj Devi, PA	Yes
Bunch of flowers for Valentine's day	£18.00	Orlando Orseo, Sales	No – not an **office** expense
Metro ticket to Plastics Today conference	£2.60	Orlando Orseo, Sales	Yes

Activity 8.2

Reasons for not adopting the 'kitty box' suggestion

1   An open box is not a safe place physically for cash - it could easily get lost or stolen.

2   'Dipping in' means that there are no checks that the expenditure is authorised and for a valid reason.

3   A float of £30 in the kitty box means that, in theory, £30 can be spent on one item of expenditure. This breaches the £25 limit on individual items of petty cash expense.

4   Usually petty cash can only be paid out against a receipt. The 'kitty box' suggests that payment can be made without a receipt. This is only permissible with the authority of the Administration Manager.

Activity 8.3

(a)   There is no receipt and no authorisation, therefore you cannot yet pay this claim. Raj should be asked to obtain authorisation from the Administration Manager.

(b)   This is less than £10.00 and supported by a valid receipt. Therefore you can authorise this payment yourself, provided the tea bags were for office use.

(c)   Even though this payment has been authorised, it is over the individual payment limit of £25. Therefore it cannot be paid out of petty cash. Alternative methods of payment can be offered, eg cheque.

(d)   This is an office expense, supported by a valid receipt and below your £10 limit. Therefore you can authorise the payment yourself.

(e)   This is below the £25 limit and has been authorised by the Administration Manager, therefore you can pay this claim.

(f)   Although this has a valid receipt, it is over your £10 authorisation limit. Therefore Raj will need to obtain authorisation from the Administration Manager before payment can be made.

(g)   There is no receipt and so the claim will need to be authorised by the Administration manager before you can pay it.

Activity 8.4

The receipts total £73.46, which means that there is £76.54 (£150 – £73.46) left in the box. To bring it back to £150, a top up of £73.46 is needed.

Activity 8.5

No 101		

Petty Cash Voucher

Date 14.12.X7

Postage	6	25
	6	25

Signature: A Clarke
Authorised by: Petty Cashier

No 102		

Petty Cash Voucher

Date 14.12.X7

Rail ticket	7	50
	7	50

Signature: Sales Manager
Authorised by: Petty Cashier

Activity 8.6

You are not able to complete vouchers for any of the items in this exercise.

(a) The cost of an employee's daily travel to work is not an expense of the business.

(b) This request exceeds the £25.00 limit applying to petty cash disbursements. The bill should be paid from the main bank account.

(c) No receipt will be available and the request should therefore be referred to the Administration Manager.

(d) The sum exceeds your £10.00 authorisation limit and should be referred to the Administration Manager.

Activity 8.7

				Analysis of payments		
Date	Details	Voucher No	Total £	Travel £	Postage £	Sundry £
20X7						
15.12	Gratuity	103	5.00			5.00
15.12	Coffee, tea & sugar	104	15.40			15.40

Activity 8.8 and 8.9

See Page 232.

Activity 8.10

(a) and (c) See Page 232.

(b) The amount of the cheque requisition is payments (£87.26) less receipts (£44.18).

Cheque requisition

Date ...*18.12.X7*...........

Payable to ...*Cash*.....................................

Amount ...*£43.08*..................................

Details ...*Petty cash imprest float*.....................

....

....

Signed ...*Petty Cashier*.............................

BPP
PUBLISHING

PETTY CASH BOOK

Receipts

Details	Net receipt £	VAT £	Total £
Balance b/d			150.00
Cash sale	24.80	4.34	29.14
Telephone	1.60	0.28	1.88
Cash sale	11.20	1.96	13.16
Cash book			43.08
	37.60	6.58	237.26
Balance b/d			150.00

Payments

Date	Details	Voucher No	Total £	Travel £	Postage £	Stationery £	Repairs £	Sundry £	VAT £
20X7									
14.12	Postage	101	6.25		6.25				
14.12	Travel	102	7.50	7.50					
15.12	Sundry	103	5.00					5.00	
15.12	Sundry	104	15.40					15.40	
16.12	Stationery	105	10.81			9.20			1.61
17.12	Sundry	106	5.17					4.40	0.77
17.12	Repairs	107	22.09				18.80		3.29
17.12	Stationery	108	4.23			3.60			0.63
17.12	Sundry	109	2.82					2.40	0.42
18.12	Sundry	110	7.99			1.20		5.60	1.19
21.12	Balance c/d	-	150.00						
			237.26	7.50	6.25	14.00	18.80	32.80	7.91

Answers to Chapter 9 activities

Activity 9.1

Employees may prefer to be paid in cash because

- it's what they're used to

- they don't need to have a bank or building society account

- they can spend some of their money straight away without waiting for a cheque to clear

- they know how much they have been paid with absolute certainty

- they can immediately give part of their wages to whoever does the housekeeping, even if that person does not have a bank or building society account

- they may not trust banks or building societies, and/or perceive them as expensive

- they get paid weekly (whereas cashless pay is more often monthly) and they find it easier to budget for a week at a time than a longer period

Activity 9.2

NAME	NET WAGE		£20	£10	£5	£2	£1	50p	20p	10p	5p	2p	1p
	£	p											
Bigg	120	12	6								1		1	
Little	36	05	1	1	1		1				1		
Large	129	71	6		1	2		1	1				1
Small	87	04	4		1	1						2	
Stout	276	94	13	1	1		1	1	2			2	
Thynne	110	25	5	1					1		1		
Fatt	89	71	4		1	2		1	1				1
Skinnie	122	43	6			1			2			1	1
VALUE	972	25	£900	£30	£25	£12	£2	£1.50	£1.40	10p	10p	12p	3p
NUMBER	———		45	3	5	6	2	3	7	1	2	6	3

Note. As well as calculating each employee's note and coin requirements, you must **check** your calculations by making sure that the totals for each denomination add up to the total of net wages.

Activity 9.3

(a) Gina seems likely to be **self-employed** as she works for several businesses. She should, therefore, be responsible for her own income tax and NICs. However it would be **good business practice** for her to provide an **invoice** with her **business name** and **address** on it. The Inland Revenue would certainly want these details if they ever **investigated** your company's affairs, so that they could ensure that Gina is declaring her income and paying tax. You should recommend this to the accounts department manager who authorises these payments.

(b) Jo should be asked to sign a **form** expressly authorising the payroll department to deduct the £100 advance from her net pay at the end of the month. It is always best to make arrangements like this crystal clear to avoid disputes.

(c) Lewis Taylor is a **casual worker**. As he is a full-time student, it is possible that he has no taxable income, but his part-time work may provide him with high enough earnings to be subject to tax and NICs. He should certainly sign a receipt for his earnings, giving his name and address, as this will be needed by the Inland Revenue. If he knows his NI number, he should also provide that.

Activity 9.4

This is a small workforce and as the company is new it will want to save as much money as possible on overheads. It will also be looking for a method of payment which will be acceptable to the employees and secure. A software company's employees are likely to be comfortable with new technology; the majority probably already have current accounts with banks or building societies.

Bearing all this in mind:

Payment by	Advantages	Disadvantages
Cash	• Employees get immediate access to pay	• Old fashioned
		• Time consuming
		• Expensive
		• Security risk to company and employees
Cheque	• More secure than cash	• Risk of fraud and theft for company
	• Simple system to set up and operate	• Cheques can get lost
	• Not too time consuming to operate in a small company, especially if cheques are printed automatically	• Delay for employees in getting cleared funds
		• More payments to check on bank statement
		• Not as modern as direct credit
		• Could mean high bank charges
Direct Credit	• Up to date, projects right image for a software company	• Direct access could be expensive because of the cost of the BACSTEL link (a software company would probably have all the hardware needed) and the low number of payments
	• Quick	
	• Secure	
	• Hardware probably already in use in company	• Indirect access might still be expensive compared with cheques
	• Integrates well with the rest of the accounting system	
	• Helps cashflow management for company	
	• Cleared funds on pay day for employees, even when off sick or on holiday	

Assuming that a cost comparison shows that direct credit would be cheaper than cheque payment (or very little more expensive), this seems the best choice for this company. If it would be too expensive, then cheque payment would be much more satisfactory than cash payment.

Activity 9.5

	Dr £	Cr £
Gross wages expense, administrative staff	102,531	
Gross wages expense, sales & marketing staff	226,704	
Gross wages expense, production staff	1,067,895	
Wages control		1,397,130
Employer's NIC expense	104,782	
Wages control		104,782
Employer's pension contributions expense	41,728	
Wages control		41,728
Wages control	79,588	
Pension fund creditor (£41,728 + £37,860)		79,588
Wages control	540,437	
PAYE & NIC creditor (£351,826 + £104,782 + £83,829)		540,437
Wages control	10,180	
GAYE creditor		10,180
Wages control	903,893	
Bank (asset)		903,893
Wages control	9,542	
Season ticket loans (asset)		9,542

WAGES CONTROL

	£		£
PAYE & NIC creditor	540,437	Gross wages expense	1,397,130
Pension fund creditor	79,588	Employer's NIC expense	104,782
GAYE creditor	10,180	Employer's pension contributions	
Bank	903,893	Expense	41,728
Season ticket loans	9,542		
	1,543,640		1,543,640

Activity 9.6

The average payment is found by adding all the monthly totals together (which gives £13,050) and dividing this by 12.

> £13,050 ÷ 12 = £1,087.50 monthly

So Bob can pay quarterly, as he is a small employer.

Activity 9.7

	£	£
Income Tax		40,000
less refund		(500)
		39,500
Employees' NICs	7,000	
Employer's NICs	14,000	
		21,000
Total payable		60,500

In the payslip P30B an amount of £39,500 would be allocated to Income Tax, and £21,000 to net NICs.

List of Key Terms and Index

238

These are the terms which we have identified throughout the text as being KEY TERMS. You should make sure that you can define what these terms mean; go back to the pages highlighted here if you need to check.

BPP PUBLISHING

REVIEW FORM & FREE PRIZE DRAW

All original review forms from the entire BPP range, completed with genuine comments, will be entered into one of two draws on 31 January 2002 and 31 July 2002. The names on the first four forms picked out on each occasion will be sent a cheque for £50.

Name: _____   Address: _____

_____

_____

How have you used this Interactive Text?
(Tick one box only)

☐ Home study (book only)

☐ On a course: college _____

☐ With 'correspondence' package

☐ Other _____

Why did you decide to purchase this Interactive Text? *(Tick one box only)*

☐ Have used BPP Texts in the past

☐ Recommendation by friend/colleague

☐ Recommendation by a lecturer at college

☐ Saw advertising

☐ Other _____

During the past six months do you recall seeing/receiving any of the following?
(Tick as many boxes as are relevant)

☐ Our advertisement in *Accounting Technician* magazine

☐ Our advertisement in *Pass*

☐ Our brochure with a letter through the post

Which (if any) aspects of our advertising do you find useful?
(Tick as many boxes as are relevant)

☐ Prices and publication dates of new editions

☐ Information on Interactive Text content

☐ Facility to order books off-the-page

☐ None of the above

Have you used the companion Assessment Kit for this subject? ☐ Yes ☐ No

Your ratings, comments and suggestions would be appreciated on the following areas

	Very useful	Useful	Not useful
Introductory section (How to use this Interactive Text etc)	☐	☐	☐
Chapter topic lists	☐	☐	☐
Chapter learning objectives	☐	☐	☐
Key terms	☐	☐	☐
Assessment alerts	☐	☐	☐
Examples	☐	☐	☐
Activities and answers	☐	☐	☐
Key learning points	☐	☐	☐
Quick quizzes and answers	☐	☐	☐
List of key terms and index	☐	☐	☐
Icons	☐	☐	☐

	Excellent	Good	Adequate	Poor
Overall opinion of this Text	☐	☐	☐	☐

Do you intend to continue using BPP Interactive Texts/Assessment Kits? ☐ Yes ☐ No

Please note any further comments and suggestions/errors on the reverse of this page.

Please return to: Nick Weller, BPP Publishing Ltd, FREEPOST, London, W12 8BR

REVIEW FORM & FREE PRIZE DRAW (continued)

Please note any further comments and suggestions/errors below

FREE PRIZE DRAW RULES

1   Closing date for 31 January 2002 draw is 31 December 2001. Closing date for 31 July 2002 draw is 30 June 2002.

2   Restricted to entries with UK and Eire addresses only. BPP employees, their families and business associates are excluded.

3   No purchase necessary. Entry forms are available upon request from BPP Publishing. No more than one entry per title, per person. Draw restricted to persons aged 16 and over.

4   Winners will be notified by post and receive their cheques not later than 6 weeks after the relevant draw date.

5   The decision of the promoter in all matters is final and binding. No correspondence will be entered into.

See overleaf for information on other
BPP products and how to order

AAT Order

To BPP Publishing Ltd, Aldine Place, London W12 8AW
Tel: 020 8740 2211. Fax: 020 8740 1184
E-mail: Publishing@bpp.com Web:www.bpp.com

TOTAL FOR PRODUCTS £ [ ]

POSTAGE & PACKING

Texts/Kits

	First	Each extra	
UK (max £10)	£2.00	£2.00	£
Europe*	£4.00	£2.00	£
Rest of world	£20.00	£10.00	£

Passcards/Tapes

	First	Each extra	
UK	£2.00	£1.00	£
Europe*	£2.50	£1.00	£
Rest of world	£15.00	£8.00	£

Grand Total (Cheques to *BPP Publishing*) I enclose a cheque for (incl. Postage) £ [ ]
Or charge to Access/Visa/Switch
Card Number [ ][ ][ ][ ][ ][ ][ ][ ][ ][ ][ ][ ][ ][ ][ ][ ]
Expiry date _____ Start Date _____
Issue Number (Switch Only) _____
Signature _____

Mr/Mrs/Ms (Full name) _____
Daytime delivery address _____
Postcode _____
Daytime Tel _____
E-mail _____

Product	5/01 Texts	6/01 Kits / 8/01 Kits	Special offer	5/01 Passcards	Tapes
FOUNDATION (ALL £9.95)					
Unit 1 Recording Income and Receipts	☐	☐			
Unit 2 Making and Recording Payments	☐	☐	All Foundation Texts and Kits (£80) ☐		
Unit 3 Ledger Balances and Initial Trial Balance	☐	☐		£4.95 ☐	£10.00 ☐
Unit 4 Supplying Information for Mgmt Control	☐	☐			
Unit 20 Working with Information Technology	☐	☐			
Unit 22/23 Healthy Workplace & Personal Effectiveness	☐				
INTERMEDIATE (ALL £9.95)					
Unit 5 Financial Records and Accounts	☐	☐	All Inter'te Texts and Kits (£65) ☐	£4.95 ☐	£10.00 ☐
Unit 6 Cost Information	☐	☐		£4.95 ☐	£10.00 ☐
Unit 7 Reports and Returns	☐	☐			
Unit 21 Using Information Technology	☐	☐			
TECHNICIAN (ALL £9.95)					
Unit 8/9 Core Managing Costs and Allocating Resources	☐	☐	Set of 12 Technician Texts/Kits (Please specify titles required) (£100) ☐	£4.95 ☐	£10.00 ☐
Unit 10 Core Managing Accounting Systems	☐	☐		£4.95 ☐	£10.00 ☐
Unit 11 Option Financial Statements (A/c Practice)	☐	☐			
Unit 12 Option Financial Statements (Central Govnmt)	☐	☐			
Unit 15 Option Cash Management and Credit Control	☐	☐			
Unit 16 Option Evaluating Activities	☐	☐			
Unit 17 Option Implementing Auditing Procedures	☐	☐			
Unit 18 Option Business Tax (FA01)(8/01 Text)	☐	☐			
Unit 19 Option Personal Tax (FA 01)(8/01 Text)	☐	☐			
TECHNICIAN 2000 (ALL £9.95)					
Unit 18 Option Business Tax FA00 (8/00 Text & Kit)	☐	☐			
Unit 19 Option Personal Tax FA00 (8/00 Text & Kit)	☐	☐			
SUBTOTAL	£	£	£	£	£

We aim to deliver to all UK addresses inside 5 working days; a signature will be required. Orders to all EU addresses should be delivered within 6 working days. All other orders to overseas addresses should be delivered within 8 working days. * Europe includes the Republic of Ireland and the Channel Islands.